AF539713

AMERICAN INDIAN RHETORICS OF SURVIVANCE

PITTSBURGH SERIES IN COMPOSITION, LITERACY, AND CULTURE

DAVE BARTHOLOMAE AND JEAN FERGUSON CARR, EDITORS

AMERICAN INDIAN RHETORICS OF SURVIVANCE

WORD MEDICINE, WORD MAGIC

EDITED BY

Ernest Stromberg

UNIVERSITY OF PITTSBURGH PRESS

Published by the University of Pittsburgh Press, Pittsburgh, Pa., 15260
Copyright © 2006, University of Pittsburgh Press
All rights reserved
Manufactured in the United States of America
Printed on acid-free paper
10 9 8 7 6 5 4 3 2 1

Library of Congress Cataloging-in-Publication Data

American Indian rhetorics of survivance : word medicine, word magic / Edited by Ernest Stromberg.
p. cm. — (Pittsburgh series in composition, literacy, and culture)
Includes bibliographical references and index.
ISBN 0-8229-4286-0 (cloth : alk. paper) — ISBN 0-8229-5925-9 (pbk. : alk. paper)
1. Indians of North America—Ethnic identity. 2. Indians of North America—Government relations. 3. Rhetoric—United States. 4. Oral traditions—United States. 5. United States—Ethnic relations. I. Stromberg, Ernest. II. Series.
E98.E85A48 2006
808.0089'97—dc22
2006008972

For Sherry, steadfast throughout

CONTENTS

Part 3: Writing, Rhetoric, and Pedagogy

Part 4. A Theory of Rhetoric, a Rhetoric of Theory

ACKNOWLEDGMENTS

I would like to acknowledge Anne Laskaya for her original encouragement and inspiration for this project; Suzanne Clark for being both a mentor and a role model; Sidner Larson for his insights and humor; and my colleagues at the University of Oregon, James Madison University, and California State University Monterey Bay for their friendship and support. I am grateful to the outside reviewers who read this collection with care and offered encouraging and critical suggestions. Thanks to Kendra Boileau Stokes for supporting this project and seeing it through the process. A tremendous thank you to all of the contributors, both for their fine work and their indefatigable patience. A deep note of acknowledgement to all of the Native rhetors, past, present, and future—may your words attain their aims. And finally, my unending gratitude to Sherry Smith-Stromberg, who was always there.

RHETORIC AND AMERICAN INDIANS

AN INTRODUCTION

✦

Ernest Stromberg

The Indian is an ascribed name, and the name is not native; the ascriptive simulations are the creases of inconceivable discoveries, ethnographic surveillance, and fugitive poses in the pageantry and portraiture of dominance.

Gerald Vizenor, *Fugitive Poses*

Gorgias: I call it the ability to persuade with speeches either judges in the law courts or statesmen in the council chamber or the commons in the assembly or an audience at any other meeting that may be held on public affairs

Plato, *Gorgias*

What

TO collect a series of essays beneath the terms "American Indian," "rhetoric," and "survivance" raises significant and potentially vexing questions. The terms of the subject matter are themselves contested. To begin with, why "survivance" rather than "survival"? While "survival" conjures images of a stark minimalist clinging at the edge of existence, survivance goes beyond mere survival to acknowledge the dynamic and creative nature of Indigenous rhetoric. But "survivance" is the easiest of the three terms to explain. For what is meant by "rhetoric?" Are there multiple rhetorics? Is rhetoric merely ornamentation: "the embellishment of speech first in tropes and figures, second in dignified delivery," as Peter Ramus would have it (684)? Or worse, is it the art of deception, making the weaker case seem the stronger? To swing about to the eulogistic side, we might consider the claim that rhetoric is epistemic, a means of actually determining or even creating knowledge. Both condemned and praised since at least the time of Plato, rhetoric defies easy definition. Yet in an age of post-structuralist uncertainty and renewed attention to the symbolic nature of the reality we inhabit, the importance of rhetoric cannot be ignored.

However, even as we grapple with various definitions of rhetoric, additional questions arise regarding the appropriateness or limitations of applying theories of Western rhetorical traditions to analyze the communication practices of North America's indigenous peoples. As George Kennedy observes, "Some might argue that 'rhetoric' is a peculiarly Western phenomenon, a structured system of teaching public speaking and written composition developed in classical Greece" (2–3). However, if in answer to this position we consider Kenneth Burke's universal definition of human beings as "the 'symbol-using, symbol-making, and symbol-misusing animal'" (*Language as Symbolic Action* 6), then rhetoric as a distinctly human practice, whether it be the art of persuasion or the art of eloquence, surely transcends cultural boundaries.

Nevertheless, engaging the definition of rhetoric only addresses half of our lexical equation. For the term "American Indian" raises equally challenging questions. As Louis Owens indicates, "[W]e are confronted with difficult questions of authority and ethnicity: What is an Indian? . . . Must one be raised in a traditional 'Indian' culture or speak a native language or be on a tribal roll?" (3). Examined from another angle, we might consider the extent to which the "Indian" is simply "a white invention and . . . a white image" having little to do with actual indigenous peoples (Berkhofer 3). Questions of authenticity and assimilation further complicate the meaning of "American Indian." All of these questions raise the larger question of the degree to which the idea of the Indian is itself a rhetorical trope designed to perform specific functions within various discourses. As Gerald Vizenor asserts, "The word *Indian* . . . is a colonial enactment . . . an occidental invention that became a bankable simulation" (*Manifest Manners* 11). In Vizenor's argument, there are no "real Indians," only more simulations that "undermine the simulations of the unreal in the literature of dominance" (*Manifest Manners* 12).

To further explore and complicate the definitions of both rhetoric and American Indians, consider the cross-cultural encounter at play in the juxtaposition of the terms "rhetoric" and "American Indian." Again, if we limit the definition of rhetoric to a system of techniques for achieving eloquence and effective argumentation, then those who assert that it makes little sense to talk of American Indian rhetoric are correct. For there is little evidence of an effort among North America's indigenous peoples to develop theories of communication as a distinct and isolated field of knowledge or activity, and certainly not in a manner parallel to the professional rhetoricians of the Sophistic tradition or the systematic studies of rhetoric developed by theorists such as Aristotle, I. A. Richards, or George Campbell.

Yet this is a very limited definition of rhetoric, one to which few contemporary rhetoricians would grant their assent. Indeed, to confine our understanding and definition of rhetoric to the systematic theories of the Western rhetorical tradition is a problem that the essays in this collection implicitly and explicitly address. The very exclusion of voices and practices from outside the Western tradition may be seen as a process of what Stephen Riggins terms "the rhetoric of othering." This division of self and other, us and them, however, brings forth one definition of the universal rhetorical situation; as Burke asserts, "If men were not apart from one another, there would be no need for the rhetorician to proclaim their unity" (*A Rhetoric of Motives* 22).

Even as Burke defines rhetoric as a process of establishing "identification" between self and other(s), the call for unity remains troubling for many American Indians haunted by an official United States rhetoric of assimilation that proclaimed a unity just so long as it was "our" unity. In other words, the transformation to consubstantiality, a shared sense of identity, was to be only one way: the white way. As a number of the essays in this collection show, the complex negotiation for many American Indian rhetoricians has been to bridge communication divisions while maintaining an insistence of difference.

It would thus seem, like grasping at water, that a workable definition of rhetoric splashes out even as we close our fist upon it. In *Rhetoric: Concepts, Definitions, Boundaries,* William Covino and David Jolliffe define rhetoric as a linguistic knowledge-making/knowledge-conveying art that "gives rise to potentially active texts" (5). Covino and Jolliffe use Burke's famous parlor metaphor to define a text "as the momentary entry into an unending conversation" (6).

> Imagine that you enter a parlor. You come late. When you arrive, others have long preceded you, and they are engaged in a heated discussion, a discussion too heated for them to pause and tell you exactly what it is about. In fact, the discussion had already begun long before any of them got there, so that no one present is qualified to retrace for you all the steps that had gone before. You listen for a while, until you decide you have caught the tenor of the argument; then you put in your oar. Someone answers; you answer him; another comes to your defense; another aligns himself against you, to either the embarrassment or gratification of

> your opponent, depending on the quality of your ally's assistance. However, the discussion is interminable. The hour grows late, you must depart. And you do depart with the discussion still vigorously in progress. (*The Philosophy of Literary Form* 110–11)

While Burke's metaphor of the parlor is an inviting representation of the rhetorical situation, it implies equal access to the parlor and the equal opportunity to "put in your oar." As Catherine Lamb notes in the context of women's rhetoric, the producer of the parlor text "takes it for granted that he is invited and can enter the parlor; he also seems to have no doubts about being able to speak, using the proper forms, and being listened to once he speaks" (154). Just as women have historically not been able to take these assumptions for granted, American Indians, burdened by a rhetoric and discourse of othering and often forced to participate in languages and forms not their own, cannot take these assumptions for granted either. The Indian in the parlor, indeed.

Despite these obstacles, many American Indians have, of necessity and by force of will, entered the rhetorical parlor. In studying these indigenous rhetoricians, it is vital to (re)consider Aristotle's assertion that "Rhetoric may be defined as the faculty of observing in any given case the available means of persuasion" (Bizzell and Herzberg 153) with an understanding of the limits created by social hierarchy, racist assumptions, cultural differences, language, and education. As most of the essays in this collection indicate, a primary rhetorical task for American Indian speakers and writers since the coming of Columbus has been the process of discovering and applying another's "available means of persuasion." Beginning with Columbus's first step upon the Caribbean shores and continuing through the present moment, the indigenous people of the Americas have been engaged in a serious study of the available means of persuading the newcomers. One can only imagine the persuasive efforts attempted by the five young men, seven women, and three children Columbus "ordered to be detained" and taken to Spain (80). What futile elocutionary gestures did they make to an obdurate audience that could not or would not hear them?

In the light of this history, this collection takes as its foundation, if not its limit, a definition of rhetoric as the use of language or other forms of symbolic action to produce texts (in the broadest possible sense) that affect changes in the attitudes, beliefs, or actions of an audience. In this sense, rhetoric is both an art of persuasion and epistemic—epistemic inasmuch as Native Americans use language to alter our understanding of the world we inhabit. With this rather open definition in mind, the five-hundred-year relationship between America's indigenous people and Europeans and their descendants may easily be described as an unending chain of rhetorical situations, replete with "exigence, audience, [and often overwhelming] constraints" (Bitzer 306).

Indeed, for much of this period, one of the most pressing exigencies has been the need for native people to establish their equal humanity with Europeans. Roger Williams's publication of 1643, *A Key into the Language of America,* hints at the constraints imposed by Europeans on this claim: "First by what *Names* they are distinguished. . . . [T]hose of the *English* giving: as *Natives, Salvages, Indians, Wild-men . . . Abergeny men, Pagans, Barbarians, Heathen*" (235). Williams's litany of English appellations displays the overarching trend of Europeans to see New World Natives as the savage antithesis to European civilization. As late as 1893, historian Frederick Jackson Turner's "Frontier Hypothesis" would define the United States' frontier as the "meeting point of civilization and savagery." The suasive effects of such "terministic screens" (Burke, *Language as Symbolic Action*) can be identified in numerous policies continued well into the twentieth century, including assimilation-oriented pedagogies and relocation programs. For many Native rhetoricians, the task has been to revise, replace, or tear down these screens.

The tendency of Europeans and Euro-Americans to define Native Americans as the embodiment of barbarism and to enact policies designed to transform them places an immense burden on Native rhetoricians. In the aftermath of white military conquests and subjugation, Indians who would speak or write on behalf of Native rights and cultures were and often still are addressing an audience that generally assumes its own superiority. It is not a rhetorical situation conducive to mutual dialogue. For many American Indian speakers and writers, establishing a measure of identification with their white audience has been a primary demand. As Burke asserts, "You persuade a man *[sic]* only insofar as you can talk his language by speech, gesture, tonality, order, image, attitude, idea, *identifying* your ways with his" (*A Rhetoric of Motives* 55).

While individual American Indian communities each have their own rich and complex rhetorical traditions developed for numerous ceremonial and decision-making purposes, the majority of the contributors to this collection have focused their attention on the post-contact rhetoric of American Indian orators and speakers who have bridged the communication gap between their own traditions and cultural traditions of the European and American colonizers. While tribally specific rhetorical traditions call for attention in their own right, this project seeks to enrich our understanding of what might be considered Pan-Indian rhetorical traditions developed over five hundred years of ongoing struggle.

For this reason, a number of the authors in this collection examine the ways in which Native rhetoricians appropriate the language, styles, and beliefs of their white audiences in order to establish a degree of consubstantiality. Across divides of language, beliefs, and traditions, Native rhetoricians have had to find ways to make their voices heard and respected by a too frequently uninterested and even hostile audience. Thus, in the post-contact rhetoric of Native North Americans, one finds an acute awareness of audience. Many of the Native rhetoricians examined in this study confirm the truism that in situations of extreme oppression, the oppressed of necessity know more of the oppressors' ways than the oppressors understand the ways of those whom they oppress. This collection may serve as a small corrective to this intellectual imbalance.

Why

The conceptual field of rhetorical studies has, in recent years, been expanded, enriched, and complicated by important scholarship in such areas as women's rhetoric and African American rhetoric. Nevertheless, despite the publication of a number of essays in various journals and an increasing number of panels at academic conferences devoted to the subject of American Indian rhetoric, this topic has yet to receive the sustained attention of a book-length project. As the scope of rhetorical studies expands, any attempt to comprehend the rhetorical traditions of the United States that neglects the practices of American Indians remains significantly incomplete.

Although he does not discuss rhetoric explicitly, in *Tribal Secrets: Recovering American Indian Intellectual Traditions,* Robert Allen Warrior pursues a related course as he argues for "the possibility of understanding contemporary [Native] intellectual production in the context of over two centuries of a written, Native intellectual tradition. In this way American Indian intellectual discourse can now ground itself in its own history the way that African American, feminist, and other oppositional discourses have" (2). In line with Warrior's goal of understanding the American Indian intellectual tradition, the authors in this collection aim at illuminating our understanding of this intellectual tradition as a powerful rhetorical tradition. The rhetoricians and rhetorical practices examined here, from the eloquence of the Seneca orator Red Jacket to Gerald Vizenor's postmodern trickster discourse, demonstrate not only a mastery of the available Western means of persuasion, they also enlarge conceptions of rhetoric itself. That is, by bringing an *other,* in some ways incommensurably different, understanding of the world into the rhetorical parlor, these rhetoricians expand the terministic reality we all inhabit.

At the same time, Warrior's text illustrates the degree to which recent academic interest in American Indians has been for the most part dominated by studies of literary texts. Not that this is inherently a problem. Indeed, as Wayne Booth demonstrates in *The Rhetoric of Fiction,* the line between poetics and rhetoric is often hard to sustain. Nevertheless, in terms of Native American textual studies, there has been a conspicuous absence of attention to American Indians as rhetoricians. To some extent, a recent trend initiated by scholars such as Elizabeth Cook-Lynn, Craig Womack, and Jace Weaver has at least implicitly taken the rhetorical turn. Cook-Lynn and Womack both ask how Native literature might function rhetorically to aid Native communities in their defense of sovereignty (Womack 192–93). Weaver has coined the term "communitist" to define the rhetorical function of Native literature: "Literature is communitist to the extent that it has a proactive commitment to Native community" (xiii). Yet in the work of these three scholars, the emphasis remains on Native literature as literature.

In "Rhetorical Sovereignty: What Do American Indians Want from Writing?" Scott Lyons argues that "we begin by prioritizing the study of American Indian rhetoric—and the rhetoric of the Indian" (464). In this same article, Lyons notes that there have been some forays into the analysis of American Indian rhetoric. For instance, George Kennedy devotes a chapter of his *Comparative Rhetoric* to "North American Indian Rhetoric." Yet this chapter and its list of references treat American Indians and Indian rhetoric as a thing of the past, something practiced by so-called traditional cultures. Kennedy concludes his chapter with the following statement: "Rhetoric among the Indians, as in other traditional societies, was largely a conservative, defensive force in transmitting and preserving the independence, way of life, and values of the culture" (108). Regardless of whether his assessment of "traditional" rhetoric is correct, his use of the past tense—"was"—relegates American Indians to the dustbin of history. Kennedy's study reflects an unfortunate reinscription of the "vanishing Indian" narrative. This narrative, rehearsed in numerous representational texts from government policies to cinematic Westerns, has produced in the American social imagination an image of Indians as elements of our past—tragic, noble even, but no longer around.

This collection springs from a desire to alter that perception. American Indians continue to exist, and they continue to develop and apply sophisticated rhetorical practices. From debates over casinos, controversies over mascots, through the insistence of treaty rights and the return of Native lands, North America's indigenous people have been and are insisting upon access to the parlor. As rhetoricians, Indian writers, activists, lawyers, teachers, and political leaders are carrying on rhetorical traditions developed by their elders. For scholars of rhetoric and composition, speech communication, literature, history, and Native American studies, among other disciplines, the essays in this collection are an invitation and an introduction to these traditions.

Who

In organizing the essays in this collection, I have used thematic guidelines. Clearly there are other valid ways in which these essays could be arranged, yet I believe the groupings illustrate shared concerns that weave together the essays in each section. My hope is that the arrangements will make these concerns explicit and illustrate some of the patterns that the scholars have pursued or discovered in their explorations of the American Indian rhetorical tradition as it has developed over the last three hundred years.

The essays in part 1 examine the appropriations of elements of Christian discourse, sentimentalism, democratic discourse, and an emerging nationalism in the service of sophisticated arguments made on behalf of Native rights and identity. This section illuminates both the burden imposed on Native rhetoricians of communicating in a language and tradition not their own and their success in assuming that burden. Matthew Dennis reveals how the Seneca leader Red Jacket merged Seneca oral rhetorical traditions with white American concepts of "sensibility," nationalism, and Christian ethics. According to Dennis, Red Jacket developed a mediating or "middle ground" rhetoric to successfully argue for the legitimacy of Seneca political status within an expanding United States. As a work of revisionary history, this essay undermines the belief that the autonomy and land Indians still possess are the result of sympathetic and enlightened white leaders who persuaded other whites to allow Indians to retain some rights. What we see instead is an example of the powerful role that Indian rhetors played in successfully arguing on their own behalf.

Patricia Bizzell examines how Pequot author and Methodist minister

William Apess successfully appealed to Christian beliefs, specifically the Jeremiad, to indict whites for their treatment of Indians and to argue for the humanity of Native Americans. Apess's rhetoric is multicultural *avant la lettre* as he applies logic to argue that God must love people of color—he made more of them than white people. Like Red Jacket's syncretic rhetoric, Bizzell describes Apess's rhetoric as "mixed" in that he moves fluidly between allusions to Indian figures, beliefs, and narratives and the figures, beliefs, and narratives of the dominant white culture.

While most students of American history have some knowledge of Cherokee Removal and the Trail of Tears, fewer are aware of the sophisticated written arguments employed by the Cherokee to prevent their removal. Angela Pulley Hudson looks at the rhetorical work of the *Cherokee Phoenix*, the first Native American newspaper in North America, and its editor Elias Boudinot. Boudinot's anti-removal rhetoric appealed to Enlightenment ideals of rationality, justice, and liberty to counter the removal policy. Pulley argues that removal resulted because of a refusal to grant the Cherokee official subjectivity—no matter how well they spoke or wrote, their voices would not be heard. As a work of rhetorical recovery, this essay shows how the rhetoric of the victor is what we usually remember, despite the frequently superior logic and eloquence of the vanquished.

Borrowing the title "Rhetorical Self-Fashioning" from James Clifford's concept of ethnographic self-fashioning, part 2 brings together essays joined in a shared examination of the rhetorical work performed by a selection of Native American autobiographies. These essays explore how the lives narrated are powerfully responsive to the rhetorical conditions of purpose and audience. Malea Powell's essay situates a reading of Sarah Winnemucca Hopkins's autobiography in a period dominated by anti-tribal legislation. Powell argues that Winnemucca's text is a performance of "Indianness" aimed at the expectations of a white audience. Her essay shows how gender stereotypes and the iconic symbolism of Indian women continue to influence how Winnemucca's text is read. Against scholars who read this text as a simple life story, Powell shows it to be a rhetorically sophisticated construction of a self designed to obtain assistance for her people.

In a chapter on Indian boarding school narratives by Francis La Flesche and Zitkala-Sa, I explore how these two Native writers employ irony in order to critique assimilation educational policies. For both authors, irony provides a means to level serious criticisms of white policies and even white culture without thoroughly offending and alienating a mainly white audience. This essay examines assimilation rhetoric and pedagogies and the ambivalent responses that assimilation education engendered in two of its most successful "products."

Jana Knittel examines the prison memoir of American Indian activist and political prisoner Leonard Peltier. Knittel argues that Peltier draws upon specific Native oral traditions in order to successfully construct an image of himself as a symbol of the historical injustices committed by the US government against Indian people. Knittel shows how Peltier calls on American ideals of justice, elements of his personal history, and the history of American Indian policy to argue that he is a symbol of America's ongoing Indian wars.

In part 3, Holly L. Baumgartner analyzes Native American autobiographies as a genre. Examining a range of works through theorist Mikhail Bakhtin's concept of heteroglossia, she illuminates common threads that link writers across time periods and tribal affiliations. Baumgartner shows how, via techniques of cultural appropriation and code switching, American Indian autobiographers mediate a non-Native form, the individual autobiography, in order to perform a collective Native rhetorical purpose.

Karen A. Redfield examines the rhetoric of storytelling in order to challenge commonly held distinctions between written and oral texts. Drawing on her own experiences teaching at the Lac Courte Oreilles Ojibwe Community College, Redfield examines the function of Native newspapers and journalism to create an Indian discourse directed at an Indian audience. Redfield shows how Native newspapers perform a rhetorical function that is similar to the function of the oral storyteller. She argues that Native newspapers provide an important mechanism for including Native rhetoric in our classes.

An interest in theory as a Western construct and the theorizing of American Indians unite the essays in part 4. First, Robin DeRosa looks at the theoretical work performed by Zitkala-Sa's *Old Indian Legends*. DeRosa provides an overview of various positions on the relationship between critical theory and cultural specificity in order to consider the extent to which a theory can be translated and/or transformed into a culturally specific idiom. She then reads the trickster stories in *Old Indian Legends* as a model of engaging such concepts as history, culture, author, and reading context.

Anthony G. Murphy's essay is a study of postmodern historiography and postcolonial rhetoric in James Welch's *Killing Custer*. Murphy illuminates the rhetorical essence at the heart of writing history. In his argument, Welch's study of the Battle of the Little Bighorn amounts to a transvaluation of history, a reorientation of the meaning of this symbolic event. Against those who would dismiss Welch's work as not being "history," Murphy shows how the writing of history is always a process of determining which symbols count and whose voices are heard.

Ellen L. Arnold examines Leslie Marmon Silko's novel *Almanac of the Dead* as a work of recuperative and prophetic rhetoric. Silko uses the novel form to retell oral narratives from a variety of traditions. Like the Ghost Dance tradition, Silko's novel argues that the European mind-set will fade from this continent as indigenous values regain their proper standing. Exploring Silko's melding of oral and written forms of expression, Arnold's essay is especially helpful in distinguishing between an indigenous epistemology and a Cartesian understanding of the world.

The power of language is at the center of Peter D'Errico's "American Indian Sovereignty: Now You See It, Now You Don't." D'Errico examines the meaning of the word "sovereignty" as part of his analysis of the rhetoric of dominion and conquest used to legitimize dispossessing indigenous people of their lands and rights. In tracing the ghost of Christian rhetoric that continues to haunt contemporary Indian legal policies, D'Errico notes the power of subtle semantic shadings to determine the fate of entire peoples. D'Errico concludes that as the meaning of sovereignty erodes as an international concept, it behooves Indian people to find new, indigenous, terms for self-determination.

Fittingly, the last piece in the collection is a performance of Native American rhetoric. Richard Clark Eckert provides a postmodern tale of the traditional Anishinaabe trickster hero Wennebojo. In this written instantiation of an oral performance, Eckert illustrates the complicated nature of contemporary American Indian identity and the limitations of language in defining it. Eckert's comic narrative ironizes much of the conventional discourse of Indianness and clears a space for more discourse. In a similar fashion, the purpose of this text is not aimed at achieving the closure of a conclusion; rather, it suggests future directions for the study of American Indian rhetoric.

Works Cited

Berkhofer, Robert F., Jr. *The White Man's Indian: Images of the American Indian from Columbus to the Present.* New York: Vintage, 1978.

Bitzer, Lloyd F. "The Rhetorical Situation." *Rhetoric: Concepts, Definitions, Boundaries.* Ed. William A. Covino and David A. Jolliffe. Boston: Allyn and Bacon, 1995. 300–310.

Bizzell, Patricia, and Bruce Herzberg, eds. *The Rhetorical Tradition: Readings from Classical Times to the Present.* 2nd ed. Boston: Bedford/St. Martins, 2001.

Burke, Kenneth. *Language as Symbolic Action: Essays on Life, Literature, and Method.* Berkeley: U of California P, 1966.

———. *The Philosophy of Literary Form*. 1941. 3rd ed. Berkeley: U of California P, 1973.

———. *A Rhetoric of Motives*. Berkeley: U of California P, 1950.

Clifford, James. *The Predicament of Culture: Twentieth-Century Ethnography, Literature, and Art*. Cambridge: Harvard UP, 1988.

Columbus, Christopher. "From *Journal of the First Voyage to America*." *The Heath Anthology of American Literature*. General editor Paul Lauter. Lexington, MA: DC Heath, 1990. 67–80.

Cook-Lynn, Elizabeth. *Why I Can't Read Wallace Stegner and Other Essays: A Tribal Voice*. Madison: U of Wisconsin P., 1996.

Covino, William A., and David A. Jolliffe, eds. *Rhetoric: Concepts, Definitions, Boundaries*. Boston: Allyn and Bacon, 1995.

Kennedy, George A. *Comparative Rhetoric: An Historical and Cross-Cultural Introduction*. New York: Oxford UP, 1998.

Lamb, Catherine E. "Other Voices, Different Parties: Feminist Responses to Argument." *Teaching Argument in the Composition Course*. Ed. Timothy Barnett. Boston: Bedford/St. Martins, 2002. 154–65.

Lyons, Scott Richard. "Rhetorical Sovereignty: What Do American Indians Want from Writing?" *College Composition and Communication* 51 (2000): 447–68.

Owens, Louis. *Other Destinies: Understanding the American Indian Novel*. Norman: U of Oklahoma P, 1992.

Plato. "Gorgias." *The Rhetorical Tradition: Readings from Classical Times to the Present*. 2nd ed. Ed. Patricia Bizzell and Bruce Herzberg. Boston: Bedford/St. Martins, 2001. 87–138.

Ramus, Peter. "From *Arguments in Rhetoric Against Quintilian*." *The Rhetorical Tradition: Readings from Classical Times to the Present*. 2nd ed. Ed. Patricia Bizzell and Bruce Herzberg. Boston: Bedford/St. Martins, 2001. 681–97.

Riggins, Stephen Harold, ed. *The Language and Politics of Exclusion: Others in Discourse*. Thousand Oaks, CA: Sage, 1997.

Vizenor, Gerald. *Fugitive Poses: Native American Indian Scenes of Absence and Presence*. Lincoln: U of Nebraska P, 1998.

———. *Manifest Manners: Postindian Warriors of Survivance*. Hanover, NH: Wesleyan UP, 1994.

Warrior, Robert Allen. *Tribal Secrets: Recovering American Indian Intellectual Traditions*. Minneapolis: U of Minnesota P, 1995.

Weaver, Jace. *That the People Might Live: Native American Literatures and Native American Community*. New York: Oxford UP, 1997.

Williams, Roger. "From *A Key into the Language of America*." *The Heath Anthology of American Literature*. General editor Paul Lauter. Lexington, MA: DC Heath, 1990. 234–54.

Womack, Craig. *Red on Red: Native American Literary Separatism*. Minneapolis: U of Minnesota P, 1999.

1

APPROPRIATION AND RESISTANCE

RED JACKET'S RHETORIC

POSTCOLONIAL PERSUASIONS ON THE NATIVE FRONTIERS OF THE EARLY AMERICAN REPUBLIC

✦

Matthew Dennis

RHETORIC proved critical in protecting Seneca homelands and buying time for Seneca communities to negotiate new ways to be Seneca within a postcolonial United States. At critical moments Seneca people affirmed and deployed the power of rhetoric; that is, in their postcolonial predicament, to paraphrase Aristotle, they discovered and utilized well the available means of persuasion. Seneca diplomat Red Jacket employed a hybrid discourse, in print as well as oratory, designed to engage and persuade white missionaries, government officials, and the public of the Seneca right to autonomy. While such speech was understood as "Indian" by whites, and as "white" by many Senecas, in fact it represented the innovative attempt by Native speakers to find an authentic voice that whites would nonetheless understand and find compelling. Not "mere" rhetoric, such ways of speaking and thinking would ultimately reshape Seneca "traditions," in the end helping to promote new traditions, support Native revitalization, and invent new ways to be Seneca, while contesting white conquest.

Before proceeding, we must confront a difficult question: Did Red Jacket and other Indian orators actually say that which was attributed to them? Perhaps not, or not exactly. The lack of letters, memoirs, or other writings directly from the pen of Indian authors, the absence of sound recording technologies, and the mediation of white translators, scribes, reporters, and publishers all challenge our confidence that our archives preserve the true words of Red Jacket or other Seneca leaders. But what if they actually did say the lines (or essentially similar ones) that have frequently been credited to them? Or what if their rhetorical attempts to use the available means of persuasion were actually aided (not undermined) by white mediators, who polished translations into effective white rhetoric and saw to their wide publication, allowing white readers, reading in culturally prescribed ways, to finish the task of giving the texts meanings that supported Seneca political objectives? Evidence suggests that Red Jacket at least said words to the effect of those reported—there are eyewitness accounts of public speeches, for example, that were widely published in contemporary newspapers, like the words of other, white statesmen—and there is no reason to believe that the Seneca orator was not adept at speaking in ways that would captivate white audiences' feeling and reason. In short, we know some of what Red Jacket actually said, and it is reasonable to expect that he spoke self-consciously and with a purpose. If Red Jacket was to a certain extent a captive of white print culture, like more recent media figures he could affect, even manipulate, those who wrote or read him into the historical record. While recognizing that we know Red Jacket's persona much better than the man himself, I nonetheless take the recorded speeches of Red Jacket seriously and consider them critically for what they tell us both about the public positions he was understood to advocate and (at least indirectly) about his intentions in employing the available means of persuasion within the context of his people's difficult circumstances.

By the early nineteenth century, Seneca (and Iroquois) rhetorical hybridity was not new. Since the beginnings of sustained contact with European colonists, Iroquois people had adapted their traditional discourses of diplomacy to the unique situations they encountered. After a century of frustration in which Iroquois leaders sought to incorporate European outsiders into their world on their own terms, in the first years of the eighteenth century the Five (and later Six) Nations of the Iroquois formed a "covenant chain" alliance with the English, while maintaining neutrality with New France. The greatest expression of this neutrality and alliance was a diplomatic ritual of condolence, derived from Iroquois tradition but remade into an intercultural discourse of peace. It served colonial as well as Native interests, making it a classic expression of the "Middle Ground," in Richard White's formulation, a place of Native-colonial interdependence in which neither side was able to dominate or to disengage (Dennis, *Cultivating a Landscape of Peace*; White 50–53).

But following the American Revolution, the conditions of Indian-white interdependence that made Iroquoia a middle ground had eroded. Senecas and their Iroquois kinspeople found themselves in a world of crisis and increasing dependency after the Treaty of Paris in 1783. With their confederacy divided (many Iroquois loyalists took refuge in British Canada), their homeland destroyed and substantially expropriated, and their population reduced by half, the Senecas and other Iroquois huddled in a few small reservations in western New York, the residual properties they managed to hold, in a state of disorganization and demoralization (Wallace; Abler and Tooker; Tooker).

The humiliating Treaty of Fort Stanwix (1784), while requiring substantial land cessions in the Erie triangle and Ohio country, had confirmed the Iroquois' "peaceful possession" of this New York and northwestern Pennsylvania territory, but the new citizens and speculators of the American republic considered such title transitory. Immediately, the states of Pennsylvania, New York, and Massachusetts or their agents initiated efforts to acquire Indian lands by questionable or downright fraudulent sale or lease. The confusion of interstate competition for Seneca lands was compounded by the efforts of private land companies, which procured "preemptive rights" to buy land (technically, when and if Indians chose to sell), or which sought to circumvent state prohibitions on the private purchase of Indian land by fashioning clever leasing arrangements (Densmore 23–24). Meanwhile, the national government asserted its role in Indian affairs, through diplomatic missions and the new War Department (which assumed control of Indian affairs when it was established in 1789), as well as in trade and intercourse legislation designed to pacify the volatile frontier. In 1790, Congress declared in "an Act to regulate trade and intercourse with the Indians tribes," that "no sale of lands made by any . . . shall be valid to any person or persons, or to any states, whether having the right of pre-emption to such lands or not, unless the same shall be made and duly executed at some public treaty, held under the authority of the United States" (Prucha 14–15). It was only in 1823, with Chief Justice John Marshall's opinion in *Johnson v. McIntosh,* that the principal was established that tribes held an ownership interest in their aboriginal lands superior to all but that of the United States itself, and that as a result tribes could sell their lands, not to individuals or even to states, but to the federal government exclusively. The Six Nations, and the Senecas specifically, despite the statements of President Washington and congressional legislation, faced a confusing mix of private, state, and federal jurisdictional claims and competing propositions (Washington 1790, 772–76; Wilkinson 120–21).

Simultaneously, they found themselves objects of the various missionary programs that proliferated following the American Revolution with the Second Great Awakening, which began in the 1790s. Already on the scene was the New Light minister Samuel Kirkland, who failed as a missionary to the Senecas in the 1760s. He succeeded among another of the Six Nations—the Oneidas—and continued to guide them during the war, serving Congress as a chaplain and political agent as well as missionary. After the war, Kirkland remained among the Oneidas, supported by the Boston-based Society for Propagating the Gospel among the Indians and Others in North America (founded 1787), as well as by the Scots Society for Propagating Christian Knowledge. Kirkland was joined in Iroquoia by other Congregational, Presbyterian, and Baptist missionaries to the Senecas and Tuscaroras, supported by the New York Missionary Society (founded in 1796), the Massachusetts Missionary Society (founded 1799), and the Shaftsbury Baptist Association (constituted in 1780). Most successful were the missionaries sent by the Indian Committee of the Philadelphia Society of Friends (Quakers) beginning in 1795. This proselytizing built on the Christianizing attempts of generations of missionaries who first entered Iroquoia in the seventeenth century. Zealous Jesuit priests and the occasional dominie of the Dutch Reformed Church, followed by waves of Congregational, Presbyterian, Moravian, Baptist, Methodist, and other evangelists, worked hard over a period of more than a hundred years to impart Christian ideas, undermine Native beliefs, and transform Native social and cultural life, remaking Senecas and other Iroquois people into Christians (Severence; Berkhofer, *Salvation and the Savage*). At the end of the eighteenth century, at a time when they were most vulnerable, Senecas endured a new wave of proselytizing and cultural colonialism. But Seneca people, while continuing their practices of selective adaptation and embracing some aspects of the religious and social programs promoted by missionaries, were not without their own cultural and diplomatic resources, which enabled them to resist ethnic annihilation.

What were these resources? They included a long tradition of diplomatic and oratorical skill, knowledge of their white interlocutors and of the changing world of the early American white republic, and their own diminished but hardly negligible military capabilities. They also retained some influence among the western tribes, who contested United States power militarily in the Old Northwest in the 1790s through the War of 1812. Senecas and other Iroquois people understood their declining circumstances and the limits of their own power to live autonomously in a traditional way, uninfluenced by the pressures of encroaching white society and culture. Yet their leaders—men like Red Jacket—proved to be perceptive observers of the white world that was enveloping them, and they sensed opportunities to use white American ideals, assumptions, expectations, and the rhetoric that expressed them for their own purposes. In their interactions with white outsiders, they fashioned their arguments accordingly. The available means of persuasion for Senecas, then, were mostly not of their own making, but to an astonishing degree they made them into an idiom of their own.

Seneca orators such as Red Jacket became beneficiaries of the new American republic's culture of sensibility. As the United States invented itself, its citizens sought to discover and define themselves as a moral community. As historian Andrew Burstein has demonstrated, "the most distinctive emotional force of those years was sentiment and sympathy" (3). America's self-image privileged charitable concern and active self-restraint; Americans voiced their sense of moral superiority over Europeans (uncomfortably acknowledged as their cultural and economic betters), based on their virtuous simplicity and their sensibility, in contrast to Great Britain's unfeeling, authoritarian king and Parliament. The Declaration of Independence, and the American Revolution itself, made literal, physiological "sense" to the nation's citizens; that is, the Declaration and the Glorious Cause had a kind of sensory power, evoking noble feelings that coursed through the patriotic body as well as the body politic. The Revolution released Americans from the throes of artificial and arbitrary bonds to the British king, liberating them to create a rational yet passionate republic governed by "moderated sensibility," to borrow Adam Smith's term. In an independent America, authenticity, natural feeling, social obligation, and disinterested virtue would reign. Such virtue depended on public-spiritedness and fellow feeling, which could be easily read on the faces of one's countrymen at public events, or shared as sensitive fellow readers within the republic of letters. Against base self-interest, faction, and calculation, Americans sought to cultivate a law of the heart and a nation of benevolence, balancing reason, principle, and conscience (Burstein 3–21; Waldstreicher).

We know that despite its romantic self-image and its aspirations to form a sentimental democracy, the United States was riddled with bitter political antagonisms in the 1790s, which laid the groundwork for the contentious party politics that would continue in the nineteenth century and beyond. More to the point, we might ask where American Indians fit into America's sentimental vision. Certainly, many whites showed little regard for Indians as fellows, and they often sought to deceive Indians, not to disclose to them their self-interested, hostile motives and plans. Yet Indians often embodied, at least for men like Thomas Jefferson, a natural nobility and eloquence. And, indeed, by the early nineteenth century, Indian oratory—or at least white representation of Indian speech and oral performance—had won a place within the American literary canon.

But if the noble savage was the embodiment of primitive simplicity and virtue, who faded into oblivion, white Americans still faced real Indians with whom they had to interact, and such relations had to be conducted in ways congruent with the new nation's benign perception of itself. If "sympathy and sentiment—and the culture of sensibility in general—were used to sustain the enterprise of nation building" (6), as Andrew Burstein writes, this national construction was physical and territorial, not merely ideological. America's culture of sensibility would therefore influence postcolonial expansion as a "counterpoint to plain masculine assertiveness and national aggressiveness" (Burstein 6). Native people victimized by United States expansionism would still suffer great harm, but ironically the colonialism they endured bore the face of America's culture of sensibility, as did Native attempts to resist it. Let me stress that I am *not* arguing that United States Indian policy actually was benevolent or less devastating to Native people than recent scholars have demonstrated; my focus here is how that policy was constructed, perceived, and justified by white officials. By now it has become clear that "good intentions" are culturally specific, not universal, and that they often produce destructive outcomes.

Secretary of War Henry Knox, in his report of June 15, 1789, on the Northwestern Indians—that is, the Native people of the Old Northwest—clearly articulated this "sensible" policy designed to redound to the credit of the United States. In it, Knox rejected a policy of conquest in favor of one based on benevolence: "It is presumable, that a nation solicitous of establishing its character on the broad basis of justice, would not only hesitate at, but reject every proposition to benefit itself, by the injury of any neighboring community, however contemptible and weak it might be, either with respect to its manners or power." Entertaining for a moment a calculating, "abstract view of the question," which might accept a "just war" argument, Knox tallied the costs in men and money required to conquer the Indians of the Wabash, and he found that price too high. But with a moderated sensibility, Knox rejected such a policy not primarily because of its expense but because, he argued, it defied justice and humanity. Conceding Indians' right to the lands they possess, he wrote, "the dignity and interest of the nation will be advanced by making it the basis of the future administration of justice toward the Indian tribes" (Prucha 12–13).

In a report that followed in July, Knox more clearly expressed the humanitarian policy he envisioned, reflecting America's culture of sensibility and its sense of human perfectibility through the cultivation of good taste. Contemplating the demise of the Indian and white complicity in the extinction of a fellow part of humanity, Knox pondered, "How different would be the sensation of a philosophic mind to reflect, that, instead of exterminating a part of the human race by our modes of population, we had persevered, through all difficulties, and at last had imparted our knowledge of cultivation and the arts to the aboriginals of the country, by which the source of future life and happiness had been preserved and extended." While this assimilationist task would be difficult, to dismiss it as impossible was, for Knox, "more convenient than just." Embracing an idea of progress that served the United States' benevolent self-image, the secretary of war refused to accept the possibility of failure: "[T]o deny that, under a course of favorable circumstances, it could not be accomplished, is to suppose the human character under the influence of such stubborn habits as to be incapable of melioration or change—a supposition entirely contradicted by the progress of society, from the barbarous ages to its present degree of perfection" (*American State Papers: Indian Affairs,* 1: 53). Washington echoed such sentiments in his third annual address of October 25, 1791, concluding, "A System corresponding with the mild principles of Religion and Philanthropy toward an unenlightened race of Men, whose happiness materially depends on the conduct of the United States, would be as honorable to the national character as conformable to the dictates of sound policy" (Washington 1791, 788).

By the advent of Jefferson's administration, such a "sensible" Indian policy had become conventional. Writing confidentially to William Henry Harrison, governor of Indiana Territory, in 1803 Jefferson expressed his sincere hope that Indians might be assimilated into the republic of feeling: "Our system is to live in perpetual peace with the Indians, to cultivate an affectionate attachment from them, by everything just and liberal which we can do for them within the bounds of reason. . . . It is essential to cultivate their love." For Jefferson, "our strength and their weakness is now so visible that they must see we have only to shut our hand to crush them"; ironically, for Jefferson this power—and implicit threat—validated United States' claims "that all our liberalities to them proceed from motives of pure humanity only" (Jefferson 1118). Thus American leaders balanced reason and feeling, calculation and disinterested friendship. Native people might have hoped that they would not be loved to death, or that Jefferson's velvet glove would not close so tightly on them so frequently—this would prove to be a tough love indeed.

In the midst of a tangle of diplomatic connections, the United States government asserted its claim of jurisdiction over relations with the Senecas, when President Washington appointed Timothy Pickering (1745–1829) to intercede in negotiations with the Senecas in 1790. At a council in November, Pickering first encountered Red Jacket and another prominent Seneca chief and orator, Farmer's Brother. Pickering, showing himself to be a man of feeling, was impressed; he wrote to Washington, "I was an utter stranger to the manner of the Indians, and to the proper mode of treating with them. But, Sir, I have found that they are not difficult to please. A man must be destitute of humanity, of honesty, or common sense, who should send them away disgusted. He must want sensibility, if he did not sympathize with them, in their recital of the injuries they have experienced from white men" (Densmore 33).

As this passage suggests, Pickering, like those educated men discussed above, felt "an openness of heart and an elevation of mind" typical of America's culture of sensibility. Being "more sensible of the dignity of human nature," such men believed themselves uniquely attuned "to the voice of justice & of consanguinity" (Fliegelman 62). Pickering was thus moved by Red Jacket's rhetoric—the words of someone whom he could imagine as his fellow man—and Red Jacket no doubt spoke in a way that appealed to his white interlocutor's heart as well as head.

Red Jacket's prominence, at least among white observers and readers, dated from the time of this encounter with Pickering at Tioga Point in 1790 and continued for forty years. During this period, his recorded speeches frequently appealed to the sense and sensibility of white audiences. Red Jacket, speaking at treaty negotiations leading up to the 1794 Treaty of Canandaigua, for example, declared, "You white people have increased very fast on this island which was given to us Indians by the Great Spirit; we are now become a small people, and you are cutting off our lands piece after piece—you are a hard-hearted people, seeking your own advantage" (Densmore 43). These were words that would sting men of feeling, tarring them as ungenerous and uncaring, who took advantage of a vulnerable people, and calculatingly served their own base self-interest. Worst of all was charge of hard-heartedness, particularly to one's "children," as the Senecas and other Indian people were often regarded in relation to their Great Father, George Washington, and subsequent presidents. This was the claim of filial neglect or cold disregard made against George III by American patriots so recently; now Red Jacket applied the charge to those same Americans.[1] Though it is difficult to measure the effects of such rhetoric, the Treaty of Canandaigua represented an immediate success for the Iroquois, as it recognized existing reservations, insured real peace, and restored land taken from Six Nations a decade earlier (Densmore 41–45; Campisi and Starna 467–90).

Red Jacket was even capable of deploying to good effect the conventions of the Vanishing Indian, a white discourse that imagined various individual Indians as "the last of their race." In 1797 in Hartford, Connecticut, the Seneca orator said: "We stand on a small island in the bosom of the great waters. We are encircled—we are encompassed. The evil spirit rides upon the blast, and the waters are disturbed. They rise, they press upon us, and the waves once settled over us, we disappear forever. *Who then lives to mourn us? None.* What marks our extinction? Nothing. We are mingled with the common elements" (Densmore 47).[2]

Such apocalyptic language, and the pathos of the evocation of death, seem well designed to appeal to a sentimental Protestant audience and move it, perhaps to tears. Red Jacket may well have spoken from his heart, but it seems unlikely that he accepted the fate he prophesied, that his people would in fact vanish; instead, one might speculate, his encouragement of mourning itself—and indulgence of feelings of pity, sympathy, tender sorrow, and guilt—might prod sensible whites to reverse the course of Indian envelopment and annihilation.

Red Jacket is best remembered for three speeches, first printed in 1809 and 1816 (and later anthologized), attributed to remarks spoken earlier, in 1805 and 1811. In his alleged reply to the Reverend Jacob Cram at Buffalo Creek in 1805, Red Jacket began with a romantic history of Native life, "at a time when our forefathers owned this great island," which "the Great Spirit had made . . . for the use of the Indians." But an "evil day" had dawned when "your forefathers crossed the great water," he told Cram, "and landed on this island." Though these immigrants "found friends and not enemies," and though the Indians "took pity on them," granted their request for "a small seat" in the land, and "gave them corn and meat," in return the newcomers gave the Indians "poison." Here the orator claims for Indians the mantle of civility and generosity for their sensitive aid to the pathetic colonists. As the balance of power between Natives and newcomers reversed, however, unfeeling, selfish whites refused to reciprocate; indeed their "gift" to Indians was poison (alcohol is the likely referent here) and worse. Red Jacket followed the story as white population swelled, colonial settlements expanded, wars erupted, and Indian land was stolen. "Brother," Red Jacket intoned, "Our seats were once large and yours were small. You have now become a great people, and we have scarcely a place left to spread our blankets." If the culture of sensibility valued benign treatment of the weak by the strong and judged men accordingly, then the powerful new citizens of the republic paled by comparison to Red Jacket's people. Men like the Reverend Cram now added insult to injury. The Seneca orator charged, "You have got our country, but are not satisfied; you want to force your religion upon us" (Red Jacket 1809, 221–24).

What followed in Red Jacket's speech was a thorough indictment of Cram's evangelical message, based both on assertions of Indians' essential difference—perhaps suggesting a new Seneca nationalism, or at least an ethnic fundamentalism—and on charges of white, Christian hypocrisy. "The Great Spirit has made us all, but he has made a great difference between his white and red children. He has given us different complexions and different customs," Red Jacket observed; he asked, "may we not conclude that He has given us a different religion according to our understanding?" Red Jacket questioned white authority, which claimed "you are right and we [that is, Indians] are lost," or that sacred knowledge resided in a holy book. "How do we know this to be true . . . ?" he asked. "We only know what you tell us about it. How shall we know when to believe, being so often deceived by the white people?" Whites were insincere, deceiving hypocrites as well in the way that they claimed "but one way to worship and serve the Great Spirit," for as a people who had endured generations of missionary incursions knew, whites themselves were divided on religion. "If there is but one religion; why do the white people differ so much about it?" Red Jacket asked pointedly. Moreover, he wondered, why had Christianity had such limited impact on the Senecas' difficult white neighbors? "We will wait . . . and see what effect your preaching has upon them. If we find it does them good, makes them honest, and less disposed to cheat Indians; we will then consider what you have said," Red Jacket told the Reverend Cram (Red Jacket 1809, 223–24).

Today such words are frequently reprinted, and we read them with a feeling of superiority over our white predecessors and in solidarity with Native people who resisted (and continue to resist) colonialism. But why would Red Jacket's apparently anti-Christian message resonate with white, Christian Americans of his day? How did such words become successful rhetoric? Perhaps because they could be interpreted by various Christians as constituting less an anti-Christian diatribe than a critique of factional struggles within the larger Protestant Benevolent Empire. In a broadside (published almost immediately and frequently republished) of an "Indian Speech" delivered in May of 1811, Red Jacket told the Reverend John Alexander of the New York Missionary Society that "the forms of worship are indifferent to the Great Spirit; it is the homage of a sincere heart that pleases him." If Red Jacket's intention was to insist that Senecas "do not"—and need not—"worship the Great Spirit as the white people do," Christian readers of his published words might well have read such native eloquence somewhat differently—as a call for toleration among diverse forms of Protestant religious practice (Red Jacket 1811).

Or Red Jacket's criticism of missionaries could be accepted as a shoe that did not exactly fit, that is, as an indictment of *other* Protestant denominations—not one's own—particularly by Quakers, who came off well in Seneca evaluations of missionaries and who, in fact, had offered humanitarian aid with a minimum of proselytizing. As Red Jacket noted to Reverend Alexander, "Our friends . . . do us great good: They counsel us in our troubles, and tell us how to make us comfortable. Our Friends the Quakers . . . give us ploughs, and instruct us how to use them. They tell us we are accountable beings, but do not say we must change our religion" (Red Jacket 1811; *American Speaker* 378–79). Quaker publishers, like New York's Samuel Wood, were among the first to print Indian speeches. Some whites, no doubt, heard Red Jacket's criticisms as a call from the wilderness—from the lips of a savage no less (a new Christianized noble savage)—for whites to live as true Christians. Finally, Americans with anticlerical leanings or those skeptical or hostile toward evangelicals, including pioneer ruffians and self-interested land speculators who deplored missionaries' sometimes successful advocacy of Native causes, could also delight in presentations of Native rhetoric that undercut self-righteous missionaries.[3]

Red Jacket's apparent evocation of race suggests a sense of a fundamental ethnic difference between Indians and whites, based on "complexions and . . . customs." Yet race in this case, for all of Red Jacket's confidence in and commitment to Seneca autonomy and tradition, had a less irrevocable or biological character to it than the white racist view of African Americans that demonized blacks. Whites typically understood Indians' "red" complexions and "primitive" customs as environmentally determined and reversible, unlike blacks who were more often considered irredeemable. Indeed, on several occasions, Thomas Jefferson even advocated intermarriage with Indians, along with programs in "civilization," to speed the process of uplift and assimilation—"Your blood will mix with ours; and will spread, with ours, over this great island," he told Indian audiences (McLoughlin 34). Such a plan contrasted sharply with his preferred, racist solution to the dilemmas of slavery and black-white tensions within the early republic: colonization, or the removal of freed American blacks to Africa.[4]

From Red Jacket's own words, we similarly observe no sense of a racial fault line between his people and white Americans, certainly nothing like the one that racist whites were constructing to separate whites from African Americans. And Red Jacket's openness to adopt new technologies selectively from white supporters apparently did not strike him as inconsistent with his feelings of ethnic and cultural confidence. Red Jacket's commitment to his race, then, was a nationalist position, not one based on a rigid, racialist adherence to a biological notion of race. His appropriation of that nationalist rhetoric may have made a certain amount of sense to white citizens of the new republic, and it may have been rendered unproblematic by the confidence of white Americans that their own nation would prevail, that Indians could and would be assimilated, or that they would vanish—that is, Indians would not remain undigested nations within the larger United States.[5] But Red Jacket's nationalist rhetoric would not yet approach that of the Methodist minister and Pequot William Apess or those Cherokee leaders who appropriated United States forms of representative democracy and attempted, unsuccessfully, to thwart removal in the 1830s.

Red Jacket's success, not merely as an orator but as a leader and protector of his people, stemmed in part from his ability to play off the divisions, not only among rival Protestant evangelists, but within the early national political world, in which state and federal jurisdictions, and matters of states' rights, remained clouded with some ambiguity. In 1802, for example, Red Jacket challenged the State of New York over its actions in a case against a Seneca man named Stiff-Armed George, who was accused of assault and the murder of a white man, John Hewitt, in an incident that occurred near Buffalo on July 25. In two August addresses to the governor of New York in Albany, Red Jacket argued that Indians and whites were held to unequal standards and, more importantly, that Indians were not answerable to New York state law but only to that of the United States. "Did we ever make a treaty with the state of New-York, and agree to conform to its laws?" he asked. "No. We are independent of that state of New-York. . . . We will never consent that the government of this state shall try our brother. We appeal to the government of the United States" (*Albany Centinel,* September 3, 1802).[6]

Though Stiff-Armed George was convicted on February 23, 1803, jurors in the case surprisingly petitioned the state for a pardon, despite their finding of guilt, as they recognized the existence of extenuating circumstances—including a general pattern of "wanton and unprovoked attacks" inflicted on Senecas near Buffalo, as well as the particular assaults against

Stiff-Armed George that provoked his actions. Even earlier, Secretary of War Henry Dearborn wrote to New York Governor George Clinton recommending such a pardon should the defendant be convicted, and the governor indeed complied with Dearborn's and the jury's wishes. Technically, Stiff-Armed George's conviction signaled a failure for Red Jacket in his efforts to assert Seneca independence, yet clearly he prevailed by pitting federal and state governments against each other, and by appealing to some New York citizens to take his side against their fellow (if unsavory) citizens. Following a paper victory, Clinton's pardon sought to avoid a jurisdictional confrontation and trouble, both with Senecas and the United States federal government. If the state of New York saved face, and if its citizens' act of mercy allowed them to think well of themselves, Red Jacket managed to save the life of Stiff-Armed George and a measure of autonomy for his people (Densmore 61–63; Dennis "Sorcery amd Sovereignty").

During the War of 1812, the Senecas sought to remain neutral—the initial goal for the Iroquois, articulated by the United States government—but as the war along the US-Canadian frontier came to the Senecas, by the summer of 1813 they joined the American side as allies. In a speech of October 21, 1813, Red Jacket affirmed Seneca participation while asserting their independent status, as equals: "Let us unite, . . . and in one season more we will drive the Red Coats from this Island. They are foreigners. This country belongs to us and the United States" (Densmore 85). While recognizing the sovereignty and territorial claims of the United States, Red Jacket challenged not only those of the British but implicitly those of State of New York as well. Ultimately, Senecas involved themselves in the war to preserve their lands. Red Jacket recognized Seneca vulnerability to the white rhetoric and practice of conquest. As he told the US Indian agent Erastus Granger early in the war, "It is necessary now for us to take up the business [of war], defend our property, and drive the enemy from it. If we sit still upon our seats, and take no measures of redress, the British (according to the custom of you white people) will hold it by conquest—and should you conquer the Canadas, you will claim it upon the same principle, as conquered from the British" (Densmore 82). Here Seneca actions were required to support Seneca words.

Red Jacket and his Seneca kinspeople continued to face the threat of dispossession, not only from nations and states but from private land companies. Beginning in 1810, their chief adversary was the Ogden Land Company, which had purchased the preemptive right to purchase Seneca lands in western New York, should Senecas and Tuscaroras be willing to sell.

In this battle, as in others, Red Jacket deployed his rhetorical skills while playing white interests against each other. In May 1811, he replied to the Ogden Company agent, a Mr. Richardson, in one of his most famous speeches, which marked the first of many encounters between the Senecas and the company. Calling Mr. Richardson's proposal to buy Seneca lands "very extraordinary" and "crooked," Red Jacket rejected the agent's proposition. He noted that it lacked federal sanction. "You have no writings from the President," he observed, thus enlisting the United States' chief executive on the Seneca side against both private and state interests. He recounted the process that had eroded Seneca holdings, purchased by Yorkers "piece by piece for a little money," until very little remained. Red Jacket characterized the Ogden Land Company's claims as "false rights to our lands": "the lands do not belong to the Yorkers; they are ours, and were given to us by the Great Spirit." He told Richardson "to go back with your talk to your employers, and to tell them and the Yorkers that they have no right to buy and sell false rights to our lands" (Red Jacket 1811; *American Speaker* 379–81).

In an often-reprinted speech, Red Jacket depicted his people as victims caught between powerful forces on the eve of the War of 1812:

> At the treaties held for the purchase of our lands, the white man with sweet voices and smiling faces told us they loved us, and that they would not cheat us, but that the king's children on the other side of the lake [that is, British authorities, across Lake Erie in Canada] would cheat us. When we go on the other side of the lake the king's children tell us your people will cheat us, but with sweet voices and smiling faces assure us of their love and they will not cheat us. These things puzzle our heads, and we believe that the Indians must take care of themselves, and not trust either in your people or in the king's children (Red Jacket 1811; *American Speaker* 379–81).

Red Jacket's rhetoric reflected real fears of being caught between the clashing imperial ambitions of Great Britain and the United States, but it also betrays his use of the clever tactic of playing one power against another, which Iroquois diplomats had employed since the seventeenth century.[7] And in the orator's manipulation of the language of sensibility—lamenting the apparent lack of real love, sincere countenances, heartfelt smiles, and frank, authentic voices—he invited self-consciously virtuous white Americans to fulfill their specific promises to Seneca people as well as their general promise as new men and citizens of a new nation, unlike the unfeeling subjects of the king.

We have seen in Red Jacket's replies to the Reverend Cram in 1805 and the Reverend Alexander in 1811 that the orator's apparently anti-Christian rhetoric sought to preserve Seneca cultural and religious integrity against intrusive white missionaries while he attempted to protect his peoples' homelands from land-hungry speculators and developers. The two designs were not unrelated, and both involved versions of Red Jacket's dangerous but necessary game of playing off one side against the other. By the 1820s, Red Jacket was widely recognized by whites as a leader of a "Pagan" party, divided against a so-called Christian party among the Senecas. The orator may have told Cram in 1805, "we never quarrel about religion," but in fact no such consensus existed among nineteenth-century Senecas buffeted by unsettling Christian missionaries and Native prophecies. As a so-called Pagan, Red Jacket nonetheless acquired considerable support, not only among like-minded Senecas but among whites as well. Quaker Friends offered political and diplomatic advocacy as well as technical assistance to Seneca efforts to acculturate economically and socially. Even DeWitt Clinton, governor of New York, seemed to take the "Pagan" side in questioning the usefulness of missionaries and expressing his preference for the more circumspect "civilizing" project of the Quakers. In 1821 Clinton responded favorably to Red Jacket's complaint against, among other irritants, missionaries who created discord among the Senecas. The New York State Legislature passed an "Act Respecting Intrusions on Indian Lands" in March 1821, which prohibited non-Indians from "settling or residing on Indian land" in New York. To promote enforcement of the act, Red Jacket obtained the support of local Quakers to help expel unwanted missionaries. In 1824 a Quaker visitor to the Seneca settlement of Cattaraugus confirmed the accuracy of Red Jacket's understanding of factionalism within American Protestantism—and the opportunities it presented to Senecas—with his warning about "hireling priests" sowing division among white Christians. At the eye of this storm was Red Jacket, hoping his people could survive in the relatively calm center defined by the surrounding turmoil (Densmore 93–94).

As in the Cherokee case in the following decades, this storm brought the threat of removal to the Senecas. In his speech to Mr. Richardson in 1811, Red Jacket rejected such a course, for both its likely short- and long-term effects. "If we should sell our lands and move off into the distant country, toward the setting sun, we should be looked upon in the country to which we go as foreigners, and strangers, and be despised by the red as well as the white men, who will there also kill our game, come upon our lands, and try to get them from us" (Red Jacket 1811). Removal was no idle threat. By the early 1820s, the Senecas' kinspeople, the Oneidas, had begun their removal to Wisconsin, pressured by the Ogden Land Company, government authorities, and Christian missionaries' hopes that conversion and "civilization" would proceed more successfully in the West.[8] Among the Oneidas, factionalism—particularly based on religious divisions—and the successful evangelizing of Eleazar Williams, a part-Mohawk Episcopal missionary, unsettled social and political order to the extent that resistance to removal became impossible. The Oneida experience could only increase Seneca suspicion of Christian missionaries. If leaders like Red Jacket enlisted whites—one missionary magazine termed them "white pagans"—in their struggle against other whites, they nonetheless remained aware of their own internal, factional struggles and the ultimate dangers of failure in their complicated playoff game.

Red Jacket's rhetorical magic worked to disorient the white sages and citizens of New York, finding for his people a certain refuge in the gaps created by contradictions within the early national social, political, religious, and legal world of New York and the United States. Red Jacket had the measure of his white friends and foes. He appealed to both their heads and their hearts, while he implored them to keep their distance. "We have other things to do, and beg you to make your mind easy and not trouble us," Red Jacket told the Reverend Alexander in 1811, "lest our heads should be too much loaded, and by and by burst" (Red Jacket 1811). As white Americans groped to define a national identity, amid budding anxieties about unsettling social, economic, and political trends, they were challenged to evaluate the relative merits of tradition and progress, stability and flux, sense and sensibility, rationality and revelation, staid religion and enthusiasm, law and violence. In this context, Red Jacket's rhetoric helped to conjure a measure of Seneca autonomy.

Notes

1. Note, however, that such kinship terms could be contested. Iroquois negotiators often insisted that they were brethren rather than children, and white diplomats sometimes adopted this terminology.

2. Emphasis added here. Note the echo of the Mingo Chief Logan's familiar lament: "Who is there to mourn for Logan?—Not one." Ironically, Red Jacket's

obituary in the *Niles Weekly Register,* February 13, 1830, 411, would nominate him as the "last of the Senecas." Of course, the newspaper was wrong.

3. Samuel Wood was the publisher of an 1810 pamphlet, *Speeches Delivered by Several Indian Chiefs*; it contained Red Jacket's 1805 speech and a similar one by an anonymous Indian to a Swedish missionary in 1710. See also *Indian Speeches delivered by Farmer's Brother and Red Jacket* (1809); *Native Eloquence* (1811). Between 1822 and 1824, these speeches were reprinted by an explicitly anti-Calvinist and anti-missionary magazine, *Plain Truth,* published in Canandaigua, New York.

4. Jefferson wrote similarly to Benjamin Hawkins, agent to the Creeks, February 18, 1803: "In truth, the ultimate point of rest & happiness for them is to let our settlements and theirs meet and blend together, to intermix, and become one people" (*Writings* 1115). And see Sheehan 174–80. On comparisons between Indians and African Americans, see Jefferson's *Notes on the State of Virginia,* Query 14 (*Writings* 266).

5. Jefferson put it this way to Hawkins in 1803: "The wisdom of the animal which amputates & abandons to the hunter the parts for which he is pursued should be theirs [that is, the Indians'], with this difference, that the former sacrifices what is useful, the latter what is not." Assimilation and amalgamation, then, was the best course for Native people to follow, in Jefferson's view, the best of "the various ways in which their history may terminate, . . . the one most for their happiness" (*Writings* 1115).

6. These events were covered in the *Albany Centinel* editions of August 20, August 24, and September 3, 1802. At the end of the September 3 story, reprinted from the *Ontario Gazette* of August 12, the reporter added, "At these and subsequent meetings, they [Seneca and other Iroquois leaders] still continue to insist, in long speeches, upon their entire independence of the state of New-York."

7. On "The Play-off System" of the Iroquois in the late seventeenth and eighteenth centuries, see Wallace, esp. 111–14.

8. On Oneida removal, see Campisi and Hauptman, esp. 48–64. The Senecas themselves faced removal as a result of the Treaty of 1838, which sold the remaining Seneca lands in New York as a step preliminary to migration west to Kansas. The fraudulent treaty was revoked in 1842, and Senecas thereby retained a portion of their New York lands, but some did remove in 1846; see Abler and Tooker, 511; Sturtevant, 537–43.

Works Cited

Abler, Thomas E., and Elisabeth Tooker. "Seneca." *Handbook of North American Indians: Northeast*. Ed. Bruce G. Trigger. Washington, DC: Smithsonian Institution, 1978. Vol. 15, 505–17.

Albany Centinel. 1801–1802.

American Speaker. 3d ed. Philadelphia: Abraham Small, 1816.

American State Papers. Documents, Legislative and Executive, of the Congress of the United States: Indian Affairs. Ed. Walter Lowrie and Matthew St. Clair Clark. 2 vols. Washington, DC: Gales and Seaton, 1832.

Berkhofer, Robert F., Jr. *Salvation and the Savage: An Analysis of Protestant Missions and American Indian Response, 1787–1862*. Lexington: U of Kentucky P, 1965.

———. *The White Man's Indian: Images of the American Indian from Columbus to the Present*. New York: Random House, 1978.

Burstein, Andrew. *Sentimental Democracy: The Evolution of America's Romantic Self-Image*. New York: Hill and Wang, 1999.

Campisi, Jack, and Laurence M. Hauptman. *The Oneida Indian Experience: Two Perspectives*. Syracuse, NY: Syracuse UP, 1988.

Campisi, Jack, and William A. Starna. "On the Road to Canandaigua: The Treaty of 1794." *American Indian Quarterly* 19 (1995): 467–90.

Dennis, Matthew. *Cultivating a Landscape of Peace: Iroquois-European Encounters in Seventeenth-Century America*. Ithaca: Cornell UP, 1993.

———. "Sorcery and Sovereignty: Senecas, Citizens, and the Contest for Power and Authority on the Frontiers of the Early American Republic." *New World Orders: Violence, Sanction, and Authority in the Colonial Americas*. Ed. John Smolenski and Thomas J. Humphrey. Philadelphia: U of Pennsylvania P, 2005. 179–99.

Densmore, Christopher. *Red Jacket: Iroquois Diplomat and Orator*. Syracuse: Syracuse UP, 1999.

Fliegelman, Jay. *Declaring Independence: Jefferson, Natural Language, and the Culture of Performance*. Stanford: Stanford UP, 1993.

Indian Speeches delivered by Farmer's Brother and Red Jacket, two Seneca chiefs. Canandaigua, NY: James D. Bemis, 1809.

Jefferson, Thomas. *Thomas Jefferson: Writings*. Ed. Merrill D. Peterson. New York: Library of America, 1984.

McLoughlin, William G. *Cherokee Renascence in the New Republic*. Princeton: Princeton UP, 1986.

Native Eloquence: being public speeches delivered by two distinguished chiefs of the Seneca tribe of Indians . . . . Canandaigua, NY: James D. Bemis, 1811.

Ontario Gazette. 1802.

Plain Truth. Canandaigua, NY, 1822.

Prucha, Francis Paul, ed. *Documents of United States Indian Policy*. 2nd ed. Lincoln: U of Nebraska P, 1990.

Red Jacket. "Indian Speech." *Monthly Anthology and Boston Review* 6 (April 1809): 221–24.

———. "Indian Speech; The Speech of Sagona Ha . . . , [or] Red Jacket, . . . delivered at a Council, held at Buffaloe-creek, in May, 1811." Broadside Collection, American Antiquarian Society. Worcester, MA; Boston, n.d.

Red Jacket Obituary. *Niles Weekly Register*, February 13, 1830. 411.

Severence, Frank H., ed. *Narratives of Early Mission Work on the Niagara Frontier and Buf-*

falo Creek. Publications of the Buffalo Historical Society. Buffalo, 1903. Vol. 6, 163–380.

Sheehan, Bernard W. *Seeds of Extinction: Jeffersonian Philanthropy and the American Indians*. Chapel Hill, NC: U of North Carolina P, 1973.

Speeches Delivered by Several Indian Chiefs. New York: Samuel Wood, 1810.

Sturtevant, William C. "Oklahoma Seneca-Cayuga." *Handbook of North American Indians: Northeast*. Ed. Bruce G. Trigger. Washington, DC: Smithsonian Institution, 1978. Vol. 15, 537–43.

Tooker, Elisabeth. "Iroquois since 1820." *Handbook of North American Indians: Northeast*. Ed. Bruce G. Trigger. Washington, DC: Smithsonian Institution, 1978. Vol. 15, 449–65.

Waldstreicher, David. *In the Midst of Perpetual Fetes: The Making of American Nationalism, 1776–1820*. Chapel Hill: U of North Carolina P, 1997.

Wallace, Anthony F. C. *The Death and Rebirth of the Seneca*. New York: Knopf, 1970.

Washington, George. *George Washington: Writings*. Ed. John Rhodehamel. New York: Library of America, 1997.

White, Richard. *The Middle Ground: Indians, Empires, and Republics in the Great Lakes Region, 1650–1815*. Cambridge: Cambridge UP, 1991.

Wilkinson, Charles F. "Indian Tribes and the American Constitution." *Indians in American History*. Ed. Frederick E. Hoxie. Arlington Heights, IL: Harlan Davidson, 1988. 117–34.

(NATIVE) AMERICAN JEREMIAD

THE "MIXEDBLOOD" RHETORIC OF WILLIAM APESS

✦

Patricia Bizzell

WILLIAM APESS identified himself in his writings as an Indian.[1] He was perhaps the most successful activist on behalf of Indian rights in the antebellum United States. At the same time, he adopted the European religion of Christianity, and used the European language of English for all of his published works and public addresses.[2] Thus he can be described as what literary historian Bernd Peyer calls a "transcultural individual" (17), incorporating elements from different cultures into his identity. Peyer emphasizes that this internal integration process can be empowering: "Rather than being incapacitated by a disturbed personality, the transcultural individual can, given the right social conditions, develop a 'new multiracial consciousness' that is culturally complex and still psychologically sound" (17). Not only is this cultural mixing a rich source of development for the individual, but as Peyer points out, it can confer social power: "Whenever societies come into contact there will emerge a group of individuals who move back and forth between them and whose services as cultural brokers become essential for both sides" (16).[3]

Comparative literature scholar Mary Louise Pratt enriches our view of this kind of contact situation with her now-familiar concept of the "contact zone": "I use this term to refer to social spaces where cultures meet, clash, and grapple with each other, often in contexts of highly asymmetrical relations of power, such as colonialism, slavery, or their aftermaths as they are lived out in many parts of the world today" (34). Pratt makes explicit what is implicit in Peyer's discussion, namely that contact zone situations are places of conflict, where groups with competing interests and unequal social and political power struggle together. Such struggles, of course, are conducted by many means, sometimes with armed force, but Pratt is most interested in the ways they are conducted in language. For her, above all, a contact zone is a place where different groups are struggling for the power to interpret what is going on. This struggle necessitates the crossing of linguistic and cultural boundaries that Peyer describes. Pratt's prime example is a seventeenth-century South American Indian who wrote a long letter to the King of Spain in Spanish, protesting the brutal treatment of his people, while at the same time interlacing the text with passages in his own language, Quechua, and illustrations in Indian cultural style. Guaman Poma thus exemplifies Peyer's "transcultural" individual, using his cross-cultural knowledge in an attempt to represent the interests of his own, oppressed group.

Pratt's model, however, is further enriched by the work of mixed-blood rhetorician Scott Lyons. Almost five hundred years after Guaman Poma, the situation for Native people in South, and North, America has changed drastically. As Lyons has argued, it is no longer adequate to think of the cross-cultural individual as one who leaves a "pure," homogenous cultural community of one kind and travels into another homogenous community; no longer adequate to think of him or her as one who simply adds to the set of home-community linguistic and cultural practices in his or her head another set belonging to the community newly entered. Rather, what is more typical now after centuries of contact-zone struggle is that different cultural communities have interpenetrated one another to a large degree. Lyons describes how such cultural mixing can be seen in the culture of early nineteenth-century Cherokees, for example. Moreover, individuals themselves have become culturally "mixed"—not only because people in these interpenetrated communities increasingly do not inherit any one cultural legacy in a "pure" or unmixed form, but also because, increasingly, even in their own bodies, people represent cultural mixing, being of mixed biological background, which mingles what were once thought of (and anxiously maintained as) separate races. Therefore, Lyons goes even further than Pratt in his model of the kinds of discourse employed in cross-cultural communication situations. He refers to it as "mixedblood rhetoric," a hybrid discourse in which linguistic, cultural, and cognitive-affective elements are even more thoroughly mixed and mutually influential than in Guaman Poma's complex and moving letter.[4]

We need the help of Peyer, Pratt, and Lyons to understand the complex situation of William Apess. He was of biologically mixed racial background, but chose to identify himself as Indian. He was a convert to European religion, but used its precepts to criticize European Americans for their treatment of Indians. He preached the Christian gospel to New England Indians in Algonquian, but used the English language and English cultural elements masterfully to present an Indian point of view to European American audiences and to serve Indian political ends. He was one of the few persons of color in the antebellum United States who saw all forms of racial oppression as historically determined by the colonial experience and as necessitating the union of all people of color to combat them. The contact zone in which Apess found himself, 1830s New England, was a hotbed of contention over just who had the right to be considered a full participating citizen of the United States. In the context of agitation over citizen rights for African Americans and white women and over the abolition of slavery, Apess advocated for the inclusion of Indians and all other people of color in the US body politic.

I would like to analyze two texts by Apess in which he pursued this advocacy by using a literary form of traditional and deep religious importance to the Puritan-descended white audiences he confronted in New England, namely what American literature scholar Sacvan Bercovitch has called the "American jeremiad." Bercovitch distinguishes between the European jeremiad, ultimately derived from the prophet Jeremiah in the Bible, and what English Puritans made of this genre in their New World. A jeremiad typically invokes the audience's cherished values and prophesies dire consequences for the community if these values are not served. According to Bercovitch, however, the European jeremiad prophesies disaster without really holding out much hope that reform and salvation can actually happen. The status quo is ultimately reinforced. The American jeremiad, in contrast, he argues, clearly intends to spur people to action and imagines that a better civil state can be achieved. Bercovitch summarizes this point:

> The European jeremiad developed within a static hierarchical order; the lessons it taught, about historical recurrence and the vanity of human wishes, amounted to a massive ritual reinforcement of tradition. Its function was to make social practice conform to a completed and perfected social idea. The American Puritan jeremiad was the ritual of a culture on an errand—which is to say, a culture based on a faith in process. Substituting teleology for hierarchy, it discarded the Old World ideal of stasis for a New World vision of the future. Its function was to create a climate of anxiety that helped release the restless "progressivist" energies required for the success of the venture. (23)

Apess was well read in Puritan literature, as the references in the *Eulogy on King Philip* reveal. Indeed, as I have argued elsewhere, he makes detailed strategic use of his knowledge of Puritan historical archives. Thus Apess would have been aware of the "errand" that Bercovitch discusses above, the Puritan sense of their own mission to found a superior society. I am suggesting here that he made use not only of the content of Puritan historical writings but also of their rhetorical techniques, adapting these for Indian purposes. As a Christian, Apess would have shared the most universally applicable of Puritan ideals, and as an American, he would have shared their faith that society could move toward these ideals. At the same time, as an Indian, Apess was in a good position to know how far short of these ideals New England society had fallen. He was thus strategically located culturally to turn the American jeremiad genre to Indian interests, using "mixedblood" rhetoric, as he does in "An Indian's Looking Glass for the White Man" and the *Eulogy on King Philip*.

"An Indian's Looking Glass for the White Man"

"An Indian's Looking Glass for the White Man" was first published in 1833 as an appendix to The Experiences of Five Christian Indians of the Pequot Tribe, a collection of conversion narratives edited by Apess and prefaced by his own conversion story. Apess's modern editor, Barry O'Connell, points out that all six accounts dramatize the difficulty of finding a secure religious identity in the face of white supremacist racism. The essay's placement in the context of conversion narratives emphasizes that its critique should be as universally applicable as the values of the Christian religion are supposed to be. At the same time, the very specific New England context of both the conversion narratives and many of the essay's illustrations emphasizes that these values are to be lived out in the here and now, the social and political milieu of Apess and his audience, in this case mainly white people.

The overarching structure of this essay reflects that of the jeremiad, pointing out that Apess's audience is not behaving in accordance with their own professed principles and that this inconsistency has produced and will continue to produce dire consequences. Apess begins by stating the principle of equality endorsed by both the Christian religion and American democracy; he addresses his readers as "fellow creatures who are traveling with me to the grave, and to that God who is the maker and preserver both of the white man and the Indian, whose abilities are the same and who are to be judged by one God, who will show no favor to outward appearances but will judge righteousness" (155).[5] Egalitarian religion is invoked with the image of the one God for all people, regardless of race, but also with the use of language that invokes egalitarian civil rights, references to the need to judge people equally who are of equal abilities. These are the values that should obtain in a nation that prides itself on both its Christianity and its democracy: but do they? Apess suggests not, by following this opening immediately with a dismal picture of life on New England Indian reservations. Most of the men are absent on a desperate search for work, the women left behind have become prey to white seducers and purveyors of alcohol, and the children are neglected and starving.

Apess then points out that this degradation arises from white people's refusal to live up to their own political and religious principles. Concerning civil rights, he says: "I know that many say that they are willing, perhaps the majority of people, that we should enjoy our rights and privileges as they do. If so, I would ask, Why are not we protected in our persons and property throughout the Union?" (156). It is important for the effect of the jeremiad that Apess testifies to white people's expressed desire that Indians should have the same civil rights as they do. The problem, then, is that the white people are betraying their own expressed principles, as Apess proceeds to illustrate with many examples.

The offense is even more serious in the case of Christianity. Apess warns: "we will strive to penetrate more fully into the conduct of those who profess to have pure principles and who tell us to follow Jesus Christ and imitate him and have his Spirit. Let us see if they come anywhere near him and his ancient disciples. The first thing we are to look at are his precepts . . ." (157). Apess proceeds to quote numerous New Testament passages on the importance of love of neighbor. He emphasizes, too, that the gospel was preached to all nations: "Jesus Christ and his Apostles never looked at the outward appearances. Jesus in particular looked at the hearts, and his Apostles through him, being discerners of the spirit, looked at their fruit without any regard to the skin, color, or nation . . . "(158). And yet, says Apess, what do we find? "Everybody that is not white is treated with contempt," people of color are denied education and relief from poverty that Christian love should dictate, and even when they do succeed against all odds at qualifying as ministers of the gospel, they are rejected from white pulpits" (138, passim). In typical jeremiad fashion, Apess hammers home the evidence of hypocrisy: "How are you to love your neighbors as yourself? Is it to cheat them? Is it to wrong them in anything? Now, to cheat them out of any of their rights is robbery. And I ask: Can you deny that you are not robbing the Indians daily, and many others?" (160).

The jeremiad also threatens dire consequences if the betrayal of values it uncovers is not corrected. We find that strategy in Apess through his denunciation of white racism. He argues that the reason why white people betray their political and religious principles is simply that they are prejudiced against people of color. They "take the skin as a pretext to keep us from our unalienable and lawful rights" (156) and claim that the services of a minister of color "well performed are not as good as if a white man performed them" (159). Apess attacks white supremacist racism by arguing that God finds nothing disgraceful in skins of color: "If black or red skins or any other skin of color is disgraceful to God, it appears that he has disgraced himself a great deal—for he has made fifteen colored people to one white and placed them here upon this earth" (157). Carrying out this theme of the larger numbers of people of color, Apess further imagines: "Assemble all nations together in your imagination, and then let the whites be seated among them, and then let us look for the whites, and I doubt not it would be hard finding them; for to the rest of the nations, they are still but a handful" (157).

At this point, the evocation of the difference in numbers begins to look like a veiled threat to Apess' s primary audience, the "white man" of his title. Apess depicts all people of color as a single group, on the basis of their common interests, amid whom white people appear isolated and vulnerable. Moreover, Apess suggests that white people, given their crimes, should have something to fear from the people of color who outnumber them so greatly:

> Now suppose these skins were put together, and each skin had its national crimes written upon it—which skin do you think would have the greatest? . . . Can you charge the Indians with robbing a nation almost of their whole continent, and murdering their women and children, and then depriving the remainder of their lawful rights, that nature and God require them to have? And to cap the climax, rob another nation to till their grounds and welter out their days under the lash with hunger and fatigue under the scorching rays of a burning sun? (157)

Abolition literature of the day often promised a dire retribution for white participation in the monstrous crime of slavery. Apess may well have known, for example, African American David Walker's *Appeal . . . to the Coloured Citizens of the World*, published in Boston in 1829, which concludes with a ring-ing denunciation of white American hypocrisy and a promise of divine retribution. Apess takes such threats one step further, subtly invoking the specter of retribution in this world by the victims themselves, and making common cause among all people of color, as writers against the enslavement of African Americans seldom did. Presumably the more people who can be enlisted in the army of retribution, the more powerful and terrible it will be.

The American jeremiad, as Bercovitch points out, however, cannot end simply with predictions of disaster (even if they are comfortably vague as to time of arrival). There must be some spur to action in the present day, some hope that reform can come and avert the wrath of both God and human beings. Apess does not omit this step from his jeremiad, concluding with mention of the white people who have already spoken up for Indian rights. They are like "the Good Samaritan, that had his wounds bound up, who had been among thieves and robbers" (160). This is an apt allusion, since the point of the Good Samaritan story is usually adduced to be that the Samaritan's actions are praiseworthy precisely because he helps someone from an ethnic group other than his own, and between which and his own there is enmity. An additional fillip here is that the "thieves and robbers," of course, are the prejudiced white people Apess has been denouncing earlier. Apess exhorts good-hearted white people to continue their efforts on behalf of the Indians, and, implicitly, all other people of color who suffer from white supremacist racism: "pray you stop not till this tree of distinction shall be leveled to the earth, and the mantle of prejudice torn from every American heart—than shall peace pervade the Union" (160–61). These are the essay's last words, invoking an image of peace that is, perhaps, attainable.

Eulogy on King Philip

The *Eulogy on King Philip* was first delivered as a public lecture in Boston in January 1836 and published later that same year. O'Connell has not been able to discover much information about why this speech was given. Apparently Apess was not sponsored by any activist group, as abolition speakers often were, but simply decided to hire the hall and give the address on his own. We do know that he had read drafts of some portions of this address at Mashpee while inspiring the people there to protest against their white overseers and minister, and newspaper notices about the speech suggest that its contemporary audience saw it primarily as a protest against exploitative missionary efforts (see Apress 275). Certainly Apess had denounced the

Mashpees' white minister as an exploiter, and he was involved for much of his adult life in controversy about religious authority, having experienced some difficulty himself in getting ordained and having expressed strong views on the need for Indians to be served by Indian ministers. Apparently his address attracted some notice, because after its initial delivery, public interest stimulated him to give it a second time, and then to publish it.

I would like to suggest that in the *Eulogy*, Apess raises the whole question of religious authority to a broader plane in an argument about European Americans' understanding of what they were doing in New England. In other words, he plays upon the very premises of the American jeremiad as described by Bercovitch: this immigrant community wished to believe that it was engaged in God's work, and constantly, anxiously looked for signs that it was doing the right thing. Apess uses the very narratives that the early English settlers constructed to convince themselves of their rightness to demonstrate how very wrong they were and how terrible the consequences of their actions have been not only for Indians, but for all Americans.

To fully appreciate the *Eulogy*, it helps to be as well read in Puritan literature as Apess was. Evidently he knew not only such well-known authors as William Bradford and Increase Mather, but also more obscure texts such as *Mourt's Relation* and the war narrative of Benjamin Church. The basic structure of his essay is a chronological tour through early New England history, from English-Indian contacts before settlement began to King Philip's War and its aftermath. He cites episode after episode from the white accounts, and then gives a revisionist Indian version.

For example, Apess reviews a passage from Bradford in which the English make a night raid on an Indian dwelling in search of an Indian man who had supposedly threatened their ally Tisquantum, or Squanto. Bradford's own account reports that no one was found at the house but some women and children who fled when the English opened fire. Apess emphasizes that Bradford's own account calls into serious question Bradford's claim that this dwelling sheltered anyone posing any threat to the English: "Now, it is doubtless the case that these females never saw a white man before, or ever heard a gun fired. It must have sounded to them like the rumbling of thunder; and terror must certainly have filled their hearts" (285). This picture of the Indian women's terror gives a very different cast to the episode than Bradford's attempt to emphasize the courage of the English men venturing into the woods after dark.

To give another example from a later point in history, Apess takes up the claim, cited in many English accounts, that the Indians made war with unusual ferocity, thus justifying genocidal measures against them. To refute this claim, Apess uses the captivity narrative of Mary Rowlandson. He points out:

> . . . even Mrs. Rowlandson, although speaking with bitterness sometimes of the Indians, yet in her journal she speaks not a word against him. Philip even hires her to work for him and pays her for her work, and then invites her to dine with him and to smoke with him. . . . Was it known that [the English] received any of their female captives into their houses and fed them? No, it cannot be found upon history. Were not the [English] females completely safe, and none of them were violated, as they acknowledge themselves? But was it so when the Indian women fell into the hands of the Pilgrims? No. (300)

In other words, Apess implies, it is not the Indians who are ferocious and cruel, but the English, who far from entertaining their female captives politely as the Indians do, rape them.

One final example can be taken from Apess's treatment of Benjamin Church's account of the death of King Philip. Church rather gleefully relates that after Philip's death, Church and his soldiers cut up the body and distributed the parts, the head being put on display in Plymouth and one hand in Boston. Apess calls this a "savage triumph," deplores the denial of a decent burial to Philip, and points out that "no such evil conduct is recorded of the Indians" (302–03).

Obviously, Apess's revisionist history is intended to undermine English claims that they were doing God's work in attempting to exterminate the Indians. Apess is not content to let this refutation remain merely an implication, however. He repeatedly directly attacks the English religious interpretation of history. For example, Apess cites Increase Mather: ". . . he says, during the bloody contest [King Philip's War] the pious fathers wrestled hard and long with their God, in prayer, that he would prosper their arms and deliver their enemies into their hands. And when upon stated days of prayer the Indians got the advantage, it was considered as a rebuke of divine providence" (303). Of these days of "rebuke," Apess remarks ironically, "We suppose the Indian prayed best then" (303). His undercutting goes further, however, just a few lines later, when he quotes Mather to the effect that when Philip died, the English had "'prayed the bullet through his heart'" (304). Apess again uses wry humor, begging to "be excused" from being the recipient of such blasphemous prayers, and then denouncing the interpretation outright, on Biblical authority:

> If I had any faith in such prayers, I should begin to think that soon we should all be gone. However, if this is the way they pray, that is, bullets through people's hearts, I hope they will not pray for me; I should rather be excused. But to say the least, there is no excuse for their ignorance how to treat their enemies and pray for them. If the Doctor and his people had only turned to the 23rd of Luke, and the 34th verse, and heard the words of their Master, whom they pretend to follow, they would see that their course did utterly condemn them. . . . (304)

And Apess then cites several Biblical texts on the need to forgive one's enemies and pray for their welfare. The damning point, from the perspective of the American jeremiad, is that in Christian terms the English actions are not justified: "their course did utterly condemn them." Furthermore, if their actions really were justified, one would expect, as Apess ironically observes, that the Indians would now all be gone—but the very fact that he is speaking today refutes that claim.

Apess fulfills his function as a (Native) American Jeremiah by linking these past evil deeds to evils of the present day: "I do not hesitate to say that through the prayers, preaching, and examples of those pretended pious has been the foundation of all the slavery and degradation in the American colonies toward colored people" (304). The fundamental abandonment of cherished values—claiming to be Christian and yet treating others in a most un-Christian fashion—has had, and still has, dire consequences. If the Indians were the enemies of the English, yet Christianity dictates that enemies are to be treated very differently than the Puritans behaved. And other people of color who have been persecuted by the European Americans—such as the enslaved African Americans, to whom Apess makes frequent reference—can hardly be construed as enemies. They never raised arms against the English before they were kidnapped and enslaved.

Apess accuses his white American contemporaries of maintaining the Puritan legacy of prejudice and hatred:

> Christians, can you answer for those beings that have been destroyed by your hostilities, and beings too that lie endeared to God as yourselves, his Son being their Savior as well as yours, and alike to all men? And will

> you presume to say that you are executing the judgments of God by so doing, or as many really are approving the works of their fathers to be genuine, as it is certain that every time they celebrate the day of the Pilgrims they do? Although in words they deny it, yet in the works they approve of the iniquities of their fathers. And as the seed of iniquity and prejudice was sown in that day, so it still remains. . . . (286–87)

Examples of the "works" to which Apess refers here are dotted throughout the essay, but especially clustered at the end, where contemporary instances of prejudice are cited, ranging from racial slights that Apess himself has endured (e.g., 304–05) to the forced removal of the Cherokee people from their lands in Georgia (306–07) and the murder of Indians who had allied themselves with the English, such as the family of Chief Logan (309).

The retribution threatened for such crimes, clearly, from Apess's point of view, will come from divine displeasure. The very terms of the American jeremiad guarantee it, if the European settlers have indeed violated divine will as atrociously as Apess argues that they have. Apess's 1830s audience would have been familiar with such threats from abolition literature, such as Walker's *Appeal*, mentioned above. But Apess suggests that evil consequences will take a political form as well, affecting the American democracy in the here and now. He hints at a dissolution of the political compact by announcing that people of color cannot celebrate holidays central to the US identity, the day the Pilgrims landed and the day the Declaration of Independence was signed:

> . . . let the day be dark, the 22nd day of December 1622; let it be forgotten in your celebration, in your speeches, and by the burying of the rock that your fathers first put their foot upon. For be it remembered, although the Gospel is said to be glad tidings to all people, yet we poor Indians never have found those who brought it as messengers of mercy, but contrawise. We say, therefore, let every man of color wrap himself in mourning, for the 22nd of December and the 4th of July are days of mourning and not of joy. (286)[6]

These holidays are characterized by Apess as "your" days, not "ours," invoking a technique of distancing to be found in abolition oratory such as Frederick Douglass's 1852 address "What to the Slave is the Fourth of July?" As in "An Indian's Looking Glass for the White Man," Apess insists on making common cause, both religiously and politically, with other people of color, calling here not only on Indians, but on "every man of color" to question his participation in the American body politic. And as in the earlier essay, Apess invokes the specter of race warfare, a deadly threat to American political ideals.

As I noted earlier, however, the American jeremiad must not end with a prophesy of doom. There must be some hope offered for amendment and improvement. Do we find that hope in the *Eulogy*? Perhaps. Apess does not appear to be as hopeful here as he was in the "Indian's Looking Glass." No contemporary benefactors of people of color are named. Instead, Apess speaks of a "minority" of people whose "feeble voice" is hardly enough to quench the spread of the flames of prejudice:

> What, then, is to be done? Let every friend of the Indians now seize the mantle of Liberty and throw it over those burning elements that has spread with such fearful rapidity, and at once extinguish them forever. It is true that now and then a feeble voice has been raised in our favor. Yes, we might speak of distinguished men, but they fall so far short in the minority that it is heard but at a small distance. We want trumpets that sound like thunder, and men to act as though they were going at war with those corrupt and degrading principles that robs one of all rights, merely because he is ignorant and of a little different color. Let us have principles that will give everyone his due; and then shall wars cease, and the weary find rest. (307)

Again, the threat of war is raised, almost overpowering any hope that might be gleaned from the image of the few, feeble defenders of the Indians. Nevertheless, Apess's final words in the *Eulogy* do appear to forgive white people for their crimes against people of color, and to hold out the prospect of peace for those who renounce earlier crimes of prejudice: ". . . you and I have to rejoice that we have not to answer for our fathers' crimes; neither shall we do right to charge them one to another. We can only regret it, and flee from it; and from henceforth, let peace and righteousness be written upon our hearts and hands forever, is the wish of a poor Indian" (310). Although he has just been doing so at length, Apess promises now not to charge the crimes of the whites' ancestors against them. He offers the possibility of going on from here with a better mutual understanding.

I remember that the first time I read the *Eulogy*, I was shocked by the last two words. I was stunned that Apess would describe himself, seemingly pathetically, as a "poor Indian," after he has just spent many pages denouncing white crimes most vigorously. Of course, Apess likes wry humor, and this could be another example of it. But I am now more inclined to see these words as an instance of a different rhetorical strategy, an attempt to placate the white audience or at least, perhaps, to disarm some of the alarm they may be feeling at being addressed so forthrightly by a man of color, alarm that if unmoderated, might lead them to reject his message. In short, this strategy might be seen as one of the techniques that qualifies the *Eulogy* as "mixedblood rhetoric."

The *Eulogy* is "mixed" in a number of ways. My entire analysis up to this point has worked to show how Apess represents an Indian viewpoint here on New England history, the Christian religion, and the prospects of American democracy. He inserts Indian cultural material directly into the essay as well, both by repeating a speech of Philip's in English translation (295) and by providing a version of the Lord's Prayer in Algonquian (308). At the same time, this linguistic mixing is illustrative of the contact zone in which he finds himself—a text originally in Algonquian is rendered in English, and a text originally in English (or Hebrew) in Algonquian. Of course, the entire *Eulogy*, except for the prayer just mentioned, is in English, and Apess even uses the English name for his subject, calling him King Philip rather than Metacomet. When he wishes to praise Philip most superlatively, he compares him to George Washington, an allusion that his intended white audience will presumably understand. He flatters English sensibilities by demonstrating his familiarity with English history. Although at times threatening violent retribution for white crimes, he usually wraps himself in a mantle of Christian pacifism or the humble guise of a "poor Indian."

I agree with Scott Lyons and Bernd Peyer that this "mixing" does not constitute adulteration or some sort of "selling out." Rather, it comprises immensely creative rhetorical strategies for enforcing an Indian perspective in contested cultural space, in which Indians are at a political and cultural disadvantage. In short, Apess's rhetoric is an example of what mixed-blood rhetorician Malea Powell calls the rhetoric of "survivance"—a discourse that enables resistance while attending to survival. To forbid such adaptive techniques, it seems to me, would be to imitate the Puritans who thought they could pray the Indians out of existence. "We're still here," says Apess, in effect, and still here because Indian culture has developed and changed through contact with the English and other immigrant cultures. Without such change, yes, the culture would die. William Apess's writing shows how that does not need to happen.

Notes

1. Throughout this essay, unless, of course, I am quoting someone else's work, I will use the term "Indian" to refer to the native peoples of North America, because this is the term that Apess preferred.

2. William Apess was born to mixed-blood parents in Massachusetts in 1798. While his father was probably a full-blooded Pequot, his mother was probably of mixed racial background, including African American, European American, and Wampanoag blood. Apess identified himself as a Pequot but also traced his lineage through his mother to the Wampanoag leader Metacomet, or King Philip, whom he eulogized in his last published work. As will be seen, he often made common cause with all people of color in his writings. Apess's parents separated when he was a baby, and he was raised at first by his grandmother, a violent alcoholic. After she beat him almost to death, white neighbors removed him from her home and placed him with a white family as an indentured servant. (Such placements of Indian children, for purposes of exploiting their labor and assimilating them to European religious and social norms, had been common in New England since the seventeenth century.) Although Apess was not entirely happy in this placement, he did receive six years of schooling and some introduction to Christianity before running away to join the army as a teenager. While in the army, he learned to drink alcohol, and he struggled with alcoholism the rest of his life. As a young man, he returned to his home neighborhood, became an ardent convert to Methodism, one of the more egalitarian Protestant sects, and eventually, in 1829, was ordained a Methodist minister. He married a woman of mixed racial background, similar to that of his mother, and preached to Indian congregations around New England while seeking means to support his family. Apess's religious conviction seems to have fueled his social activism on behalf of Indian rights. He published five books between 1829 and 1836 that variously presented the Indian point of view on Christianity and American politics. From 1834 to 1837, he lived in the Mashpee Christian Indian community on Cape Cod, and lead them in regaining control of their community from oppressive white overseers and an unwanted white minister appointed by the Massachusetts government, suffering jail and a substantial fine himself in the process. In spite of his remarkable career as a writer and political leader, Apess continued to struggle with poverty and alcoholism, and died of the effects of both in 1839. He was only forty-one years old. For information on Apess's life, see Peyer, O'Connell.

3. Many references could be given on the topic of the transcultural individual. This form of mixed cultural experience has been discussed in scholarship on the effects of colonialism, and on the cultural identities of people of color in the United States. Particularly influential on my own thinking have been Gloria Anzaldúa (*Borderlands/La Frontera: The New Mestiza*), Victor Villanueva Jr. (*Bootstraps: From an American Academic of Color*), and bell hooks (*Talking Back: Thinking Feminist, Thinking*

Black). I have chosen to cite Peyer here, however, for several reasons. His opening chapter, "The Indian Writer and the Colonial Situation," provides an especially complete overview of scholarship that draws together various strands on the topic of the transcultural individual and applies them specifically, not only to American Indians in general, but to the Indians of New England in particular. It is important to remember that when Apess was born, New England had already been a site of cultural mixing for two hundred years. Peyer is especially helpful in establishing this context.

4. Literary scholar Cheryl Walker has also noted the "hybrid" quality of Apess's writing (41) as he attempts to reinterpret American history and claim a place for Indians in a truly democratic nation. She discusses both "An Indian's Looking Glass for the White Man" and the *Eulogy on King Philip*, and provides helpful bibliography on the still scanty scholarly attention that Apess has received. But she is more interested in Apess's manipulation of American political concepts, while I focus on his uses of literary genres and rhetorical strategies.

5. All references to the works of Apess in this essay are taken from the Barry O'Connell edition.

6. Apess makes a slip of the pen here in giving the date that the Pilgrims landed on Plymouth Rock as 1622; elsewhere in the *Eulogy*, he gives the correct year of 1620. The exact date of the Pilgrims' first landing at Plymouth is difficult to determine, since, among other obstacles, William Bradford used a different calendar from that employed today, but the historical consensus is that it occurred around December 21 or 22. The tradition that the Pilgrims did indeed land on Plymouth Rock is now disputed, but the rock in question remains a potent symbol, and today it is buried every Thanksgiving by Indians protesting the dominant sanitized account of New England's English settlement and ongoing discrimination against Indians.

Works Cited

Anzaldúa, Gloria. *Borderlands/La Frontera: The New Mestiza*. San Francisco: Aunt Lute Books, 1987.

Apess, William. *On Our Own Ground: The Complete Writings of William Apess, a Pequot*. Ed. and intro. Barry O'Connell. Amherst: U of Massachusetts P, 1992.

Bercovitch, Sacvan. *The American Jeremiad*. Madison: U of Wisconsin P, 1978.

Bizzell, Patricia. "The 4th of July and the 22nd of December: The Function of Cultural Archives in Persuasion, as Shown by Frederick Douglass and William Apess." *College Composition and Communication* 48 (February 1997): 44–60.

hooks, bell. *Talking Back: Thinking Feminist, Thinking Black*. Boston: South End Press, 1989.

Lyons, Scott. "A Captivity Narrative: Indians, Mixedbloods, and 'White' Academe." *Outbursts in Academe: Multiculturalism and Other Sources of Conflict*. Ed. Kathleen Dixon. Portsmouth, NH: Boynton/Cook-Heinmann, 1998.

O'Connell, Barry. "Introduction." In Apess, William. *On Our Own Ground: The Complete Writings of William Apess, A Pequot*. Ed. and intro. Barry O'Connell. Amherst: U of Massachusetts P, 1992.

Peyer, Bernd C. *The Tutor'd Mind: Indian Missionary-Writers in Antebellum America*. Amherst: U of Massachusetts P, 1997.

Powell, Malea. "Listening to Ghosts: An Alternative (Non)Argument." *ALT DIS: Alternative Discourses and the Academy*. Ed. Christopher Schroeder, Helen Fox, and Patricia Bizzell. Portsmouth, NH: Boynton/Cook-Heinemann, 2002.

Pratt, Mary Louise. "Arts of the Contact Zone." *Profession* (1991): 31–40.

Villanueva, Victor, Jr. *Bootstraps: From an American Academic of Color*. Urbana: National Council of Teachers of English, 1993.

Walker, Cheryl. *Indian Nation: Native American Literature and Nineteenth-Century Nationalism*. Durham: Duke UP, 1997.

"FORKED JUSTICE"

ELIAS BOUDINOT, THE US CONSTITUTION, AND CHEROKEE REMOVAL

✦

Angela Pulley Hudson

IN the late 1820s, the Cherokee Nation was in the midst of a revolutionary series of sociopolitical changes that would forever change the course of its history. In fifty years, over half of all Cherokee lands had been ceded to the United States and the pressure for them to move to a territory west of the Mississippi River had been steadily increasing. The growing state of Georgia had a particularly strong desire to see the Cherokees removed, and in 1802, the federal government had assured Georgia leaders that the Indian title to remaining lands in and around Georgia would be expeditiously dissolved.[1] By the 1820s, population pressures and a growing impatience among Georgians made conflicts between white Americans and Cherokees more and more common.

As tensions mounted, the Cherokee leadership was simultaneously undergoing a myriad of cultural and political transformations that culminated in the establishment of a republican form of government, a written constitution (1827), and the adoption of a system of courts. A number of the Cherokee headmen could read and write English; some were Christian and several had been educated at missionary schools. Whites taught that the written word was the source of power and knowledge—sacred and permanent. Thus, when the Cherokees were faced with forcible removal, they resisted not only by physical means, but also through the persuasive power of the written word. In 1828, the Cherokee Nation launched the *Cherokee Phoenix*, the first Native American newspaper in the United States, in part to provide a forum for the grievances of the Cherokee leadership against the federal and state governments.[2] The insightful young man who became the editor was Elias Boudinot (or Gallegina "Buck" Watie), a missionary-educated Cherokee who was pivotal in the transformations one historian has termed the "Cherokee Renascence" (McLoughlin 277).[3]

Boudinot's own writings provide a very unique perspective from which to interpret Cherokee Removal as an American historical moment. His editorials charted the unfolding events leading up to the passage of the Indian Removal Act (1830) and the tumultuous months that followed. In his brief pieces, Boudinot interpreted Cherokee Removal by deconstructing the language and actions of the government officials involved, often appropriating the government's own policies and emphasizing the ideals of justice and equality found in the US Constitution. Boudinot's rhetorical strategy employed two key elements: the language and ideals of the Constitution, and the guardian-ward relationship that had traditionally stressed the responsibility of the federal bodies to protect and preserve the Cherokees. Boudinot's reading of the official rhetoric of Cherokee Removal revealed a concise indictment of the United States government for failing to uphold its own professed principles, and within this argument, the language of the Constitution itself becomes a crucial piece of evidence.

Native Americans and the Constitution

The Constitution of the United States was written and ratified by men of European descent in an attempt to forge a union from the disparate states that emerged from the colonial era. The Constitution was not only written *by* a specific group of people, but also *for* a specific group of people. Elias Boudinot and the Cherokees were, on the whole, not addressed by the Constitution. In fact, there are only nominal direct references to Native Americans within the text of the document. There were no Native Americans involved in either the composition or the ratification of the illustrious document, but as critic Eugene Garver notes, unlike contracts, the Constitution is "binding on people other than the ratifying parties" (174). With this in mind, it is useful to delineate those sections of the Constitution that directly and indirectly relate to Native Americans.

In article 1, section 2 of the US Constitution, the issues of taxation and representation are addressed: "Representatives and direct taxes shall be apportioned among the several States . . . according to their respective numbers, *which shall be determined by adding to the whole number of free persons . . . and excluding Indians not taxed, three-fifths of all other persons.*" Although many Native Americans lived within the official borders of the United States, they were not considered citizens.[4] Indian nations were typically treated with as sovereign entities as indicated by article 1, which enumerates the specific powers invested in the Congress, including, in section 8, the ability to "regulate commerce with foreign nations, and among the several States, and with the Indian tribes."

Article 2, section 2 delineates the power of the executive to make and enforce treaties with foreign nations. This duty historically allowed the president a very involved role in the handling of Indian affairs. In addition, the Constitution grants the executive the power to make war, which has been employed both to attack and to defend the Indian nations with which the federal government has engaged. Further, it is the duty of the executive, articulated in article 2, section 3, to ensure that the "laws be faithfully executed" (Deloria and Lytle 34–36).

In article 3, section 2, the powers of the federal judiciary cover "all cases, in law and equity, arising under this Constitution, the laws of the United States, and treaties made, or which shall be made under their authority." The allocation of these responsibilities to the federal judiciary is especially significant with respect to the Cherokee nation, whose path was shaped, in part, by a number of extremely important Supreme Court cases from 1823 to 1832. The judiciary itself does not have the power to enforce its own decisions, which must be implemented and upheld through the powers reserved to Congress and to the executive branch. A number of Boudinot's writings were specifically directed at the failure of the executive (and often the Congress) to uphold Supreme Court decisions, to "faithfully" execute the laws, and to honor treaties made with the Cherokees, all of which are guaranteed by the Constitution.

Cherokee Nation in Transition

From early contact with Spanish, British, and French explorers and settlers through the early nineteenth century, the Cherokee Nation essentially operated as an independent sovereign entity. As noted, the Cherokees were initially treated with and traded with as a foreign nation. In the beginning of the nineteenth century the delicate relationship between the Cherokee Nation and the newly formed United States was founded on two assumptions: that the US government was bound by the Constitution to uphold and enforce its own laws, and that the protection of the US government would be sufficient to prevent the encroachments of frontier settlers across Cherokee borders. The constitutional commitment to the ideals of justice, honor, and republicanism allowed the Cherokees to maneuver the United States into an ethical corner. In the interests of promoting the growth of the American nation, the federal government had agreed to extinguish Indian title to lands claimed by Georgia in the 1802 compact. But the federal government had also been promoting the acculturation of the Cherokees, affirming their movements toward regular law, and rewarding their accomplishments in the "arts of civilization," including individual property ownership and plantation agriculture.

Simultaneously, Christian missionaries and government officials among the Cherokees stressed the reliability and permanence of the written word. Missionaries taught that divine knowledge and salvation comes from study and application of the holy words written thousands of years ago. The government agents insisted that signing one's name or mark to a paper signified an enduring bond and maintained that signing treaties would ensure peace and security for Cherokees and white settlers alike. In addition, during the early 1820s, a Cherokee named Sequoyah had invented a written Cherokee syllabary that enjoyed widespread popularity among the non-English-speaking Cherokee majority.[5] The political and cultural transformations had, in many ways, incorporated the belief in the permanence, even the sacredness, of the written word into Cherokee epistemology. In 1827, the Cherokee Nation adopted and ratified its own constitution, modeled on the US Constitution. The ratification of this document embodied the culmination of over a decade of revolutionary changes in the Cherokee system of governance. In addition, the appearance of a written Cherokee Constitution was a capstone in the construction of a newly literate culture. When the federal and state governments disregarded treaty after treaty in the effort to extinguish the Cherokee title to the land, it became apparent that the written word was much more duplicitous than the whites had been willing to admit.

Reading Cherokee Removal

Elias Boudinot frequently used the columns of the *Cherokee Phoenix* to express his "reading" of the Indian removal situation. His editorial pieces reflected his strong belief in the power of argument and persuasion and a reliance on the strength of the written word as a tool of resistance. Boudinot interpreted not only the US Constitution but also the actions of the officials sworn to uphold the national document. He accused the US government of supreme hypocrisy by illustrating the ways in which the measures taken by state and federal officials were wholly opposite to both the spirit and letter of the US Constitution. Boudinot's own audience—the readers of the *Phoenix* —provided further reason for appropriating the language of the Constitution. Many of his readers were sympathetic whites outside the southeastern United States who were likely to be receptive to a constitutional interpretation emphasizing the will of the people, the rational mind, and the concept of political accountability.

In 1828, Boudinot premiered the first issue of the *Cherokee Phoenix*, which he would edit until 1831. In addition to publishing local and national news, as well as tracts on temperance and Christian living, he used the *Phoenix* to voice his anger and frustration with the unfolding events as the state of Georgia put greater and greater pressure on the Cherokees to abandon or exchange their homeland for territory west of the Mississippi River. In his readings of Indian removal, Boudinot beseeched his audience, Cherokee and white, to consider the travesties committed upon both the spirit and the letter of the Constitution through the actions of the state and federal governments against the Cherokees. He was less concerned with the philosophical implications of interpreting the Constitution than he was with the day-to-day trials of the Cherokee people once its principles had been discarded. The overarching symbolic narrative of the US Constitution, as Boudinot interpreted it, was rooted in the noble language of the Preamble. The ideals of liberty and justice, as well as political responsibility and accountability, formed, in his view, the foundation of the mythic American union.

In the groundbreaking first issue of the *Cherokee Phoenix*, on February 21, 1828, Boudinot wrote of conflicts between the Cherokees and the state of Georgia and urged both sides to display measured and moderate behavior. Just over a year after the first issue left the presses, Boudinot's tone had changed considerably, and it had become clear that the state of Georgia was not likely to be stopped in its attack upon the sovereignty of the Cherokees. The election of Andrew Jackson in 1828 on a platform that included a detailed plan for consolidation of the southeastern tribes to an area west of the Mississippi had warned the Cherokees of the possible backlash among the southern states. Indeed, within months of Jackson's move into office, several southern state legislatures, including Georgia's, passed acts that allowed for the extension of state laws over the Indian nations within their borders (Satz 11). In December of 1828, the Georgia legislature signed into law an act that, in effect, added the territory of the Cherokee Nation to a number of counties in the state (Deloria and Lytle 28).

In the June 17, 1829, issue of the *Phoenix*, Boudinot reacted to this unfolding course of events. Specifically, he directed attention to speeches by

President Jackson to the Creeks and by Secretary of War Eaton to the Cherokees. These addresses rationalized the states' right to extend their purposefully discriminatory laws over Indians who chose to remain in the east by arguing that the states maintained "original sovereignty" (Boudinot 149n39). In addition, the Cherokees were reprimanded for their newly written constitution, which, Eaton claimed, was a gross attack on the sovereignty of the state of Georgia. Boudinot wrote, "It appears now . . . the illustrious Washington, Jefferson, Madison, and Monroe were only tantalizing us, when they encouraged us in the pursuit of agriculture and Government, and when they afforded us the protection of the United States, by which we have been preserved to this present time as a nation" (108).

The founding fathers "tantalized" the Cherokees with the American ideals of republicanism, literacy, liberty, and prosperity, and then betrayed those ideals in their Indian policies. In addition, Boudinot implicated the government's duplicitous efforts to "civilize" the Cherokees by introducing farming techniques, and encouraging political reform, only to claim that their advancing "civilization" threatened the sovereignty of the states. The Cherokees had no rights under the US Constitution and no guarantee, beyond a learned belief in the significance of written agreements, that the federal government would continue to uphold its treaties and respect Cherokee sovereignty. Boudinot implored his readers to demand that the federal government uphold its own laws.

Boudinot specifically seized on the constitutional responsibility of the executive to honor all treaties and agreements, despite demands made by the state of Georgia. The course of action Georgia took at the end of the 1820s reflected the belief that the sovereignty of the state was at stake in the dilemma of Cherokee resistance, and state leaders assumed a defensive posture towards both the Cherokees and the federal government. Boudinot asked:

> Why were we not told long ago, that we could not be permitted to establish a government within the limits of any state? . . . The Cherokees have always had a government of their own. . . . Now, after being fostered by the U. States, and advised by great and good men to establish a government of regular law; when the aid and protection of the General Government have been pledged to us; when we as dutiful "children" of the President, have followed his instructions and advice, and have established for ourselves a government of regular law . . . a storm is raised by the extension of tyrannical and unchristian laws. (108–09)

Boudinot's language reflects a sense of betrayal, particularly with respect to the failed promises to protect the Indians. The Cherokees were "fostered" and "advised," given "aid and protection," and followed the "instructions and advice" of the president—only to be indicted for their compliance. He deftly juxtaposed the "tyrannical" actions of the state of Georgia with the ideals of "regular law" the Cherokees were encouraged to establish in imitation of the US Constitution.

In September of 1829, Boudinot wrote a piece for the *Cherokee Phoenix* in which he reacted to the increasing intrusions of white Georgians onto Cherokee land. This article revealed Boudinot's essential philosophy regarding the US government's responsibility to uphold the Constitution. He wrote, "We were in hopes the executive of the United States would respect the laws entrusted to their administration, although they maybe inclined to question many of our rights. *One right, however, the United States cannot possibly deny us—the right of calling on her to execute her own laws*" [original emphasis] (Boudinot 111). Again, Boudinot focused on a loss of trust between the Cherokees and the United States. The success of continued Cherokee sovereignty depended on the adherence of the US government to its own laws and treaties and the narrative of constitutional principles on which they were based. Boudinot asked only that the US government abide by its own rules.

A significant component of Boudinot's rhetorical strategy regarding the United States Indian policy was the guardian-ward relationship that had been part of the official interactions between Indians and white government officials since the colonial period. Boudinot asked, "Have we not occasion to question his [the president's] fatherly professions, when he has been ordering the military against us, merely because a malicious white child of his has told a falsehood, but will not a raise a hand to protect us from encroachments and insults, under which we have been laboring for months? Is he not dealing out a forked justice to us?" (111).

Boudinot's admonishments reflect the disintegration of the guardianship dynamic in Cherokee–United States relations. The Cherokees were neither enfranchised nor specifically protected under the US Constitution, and the key to their continued assistance from the government was the precedent set by the first presidents. Boudinot's accusatory tone underscores his sense of the extreme injustice done to the Cherokees when precedent was discarded and renowned Indian fighter Andrew Jackson took office. In addition, Boudinot deconstructed the government's traditional parent-child approach to Indian affairs by mocking its condescending language and belittling the state of Georgia, calling it a lying and "malicious white child."

In May of 1830, Boudinot wrote a bitter editorial for the *Phoenix* in which he interpreted the recent congressional action toward Cherokee Removal. Andrew Jackson had displayed his intentions toward an Indian removal plan in his first address to the Congress and, in February of 1830, Senator Hugh L. White from Tennessee introduced a bill that called for exchanging all the territory of the southeastern tribes east of the Mississippi River for land lying west of it (Satz 20–21). The bill passed later that year and several amendments that would have offered some protection were summarily voted down. Boudinot's reaction to the bill was one of bitter resignation. He cast the decision in a moral light and emphasized the loss of resoluteness in the Congress. He wrote:

> It has been a matter of doubt with us for some time, whether there were sufficient virtue and independence in the two houses of Congress, to sustain the plighted fate of the Republic, which has been most palpably sacrificed by the convenience of the Executive. Our doubts are now at an end—the August Senate of the United States of America, (tell it not in Gath, publish not in the streets of Askelon,) has followed the heels of the President, and deliberately laid aside their treaties. (Boudinot 117–18)

In this editorial, Boudinot mockingly portrays the Senate as subservient to the whims of the president, principles of constitutional balance notwithstanding. His reference to 2 Samuel 1:20 ("tell it not in Gath, publish not in the streets of Askelon") enhances the drama of his accusation, and his assertion that the treaties were "deliberately laid aside" highlights the decisive manner in which the United States violated its own written, binding agreements. Boudinot knew that although supporters defended it as a peaceful removal plan involving no coercion, the bill would quickly give license for a show of force against which the federal government could not and would not protect the Cherokees. As portentous was the symbolic importance of the government's willingness to disregard the treaties that had heretofore governed relations between the Cherokee Nation and the United States.

Boudinot described the capricious behavior of the Congress as such: "They have decided that they will not be governed by these solemn instruments, made and ratified by their advice and consent. When it comes to this, we have indeed fallen upon evil times" (119). The treaties had long been considered the Cherokees' constitutional link to justice. As Boudinot came to realize, the desire for Cherokee land outweighed both the promises of the treaties and the solemn honor of the Constitution. The Removal Act epitomizes what Arnold Krupat calls the conflict of "national interest with national honor" (138). In addition, the permanence of the written word seemed to have dissolved in the push to eliminate the Cherokee title to lands in the Southeast. Former agreements were suddenly voided; new land cessions were devised; state laws were extended to protect and then to threaten, all of which violated not only the ideals but also the mandates of the Constitution.

As a result of outcry by those who opposed the Indian Removal Act, an amendment was offered which professed to reiterate that the previous treaties between the Cherokees and the US government were inviolable. In a June 1830 article in the *Phoenix*, Boudinot responded to this "mock show of justice." His frustration and anger became more apparent as he succinctly expressed the inconsistency of the government's course of action. He declared:

> We confess our ignorance, our utter ignorance, of the views of the majority of the members of Congress, so far as they have been developed, on the rights of the Indians, and the relation in which they stand to the United States, on the score of treaties; nor can we discern the consistency of contending for the unconstitutionality of these treaties, and yet at the same time, declaring that they shall not be violated, which a man of common sense would take to be the meaning of the amendment. If a treaty is unconstitutional, it is of course null and void, and cannot be violated. If a treaty may not be violated, it is taken for granted that it is binding; and if it is binding, the parties to it have a right to demand its enforcement. (Boudinot 119)

Boudinot's point here is that the Congress cannot maintain the appearance of consistency when it simultaneously passes an act which abrogates decades of treaties (and treaty rights) and *then* posits that the treaties are not to be violated. As historian William McLoughlin has noted, "To drive the Cherokees off their homeland, the whites would have to subvert their own Constitution" (409). That is precisely what they did. By June of 1830, the Georgia acts extending state jurisdiction over the Cherokees had gone into effect, and all Cherokee laws of governance were essentially voided. The secondary effect of the extension of state laws was that the Cherokees were no longer offered the meager protection of the national army. In addition, a new law in Georgia prohibited Indians from testifying against whites in court, essentially assuring that no whites would be tried for crimes against Indians (Perdue 21).

In February of 1831, Boudinot wrote an article in which he described a recent law passed by the Georgia legislature that prohibited whites from remaining in Cherokee territory and obeying Cherokee laws, unless they swore to an oath of loyalty to the government of Georgia. This law was an obvious attempt on the part of state officials to eliminate contact between the Cherokees and northern missionaries, who many Georgians felt were inciting the Cherokees to resist removal. Having acknowledged that sympathy for the Cherokees was no longer adequate to stop their planned removal, Boudinot broadened his interpretations of the situation to include implications of the government's actions on the sanctity of the Constitution in general. Boudinot claimed:

> It [the law] is certainly oppressive on the whites, even admitting that the state of Georgia has an undoubted jurisdiction over the Cherokee territory. Why is that required of them to take the oath, when by the extension of that jurisdiction, they were admitted as citizens of the state? Is such a requirement made of other citizens? Do the constitution and the laws recognize such a distinction? But what becomes of the liberty of conscience in this case? (121)

Boudinot adopted an urgent and accusatory tone, asking relentless rhetorical questions and invoking both constitutional ideals and moral obligations. His criticism extended beyond the limits of Cherokee affairs as he drew attention to the "oppressive" nature of the law to whites. Settlers and prospectors, eager to steal Cherokee land, had no problem agreeing to the oath and thus felt no reason to protest the law. The only whites who protested the oath of allegiance were the missionaries who, on principle, rejected the state's claim to jurisdiction. Boudinot went on to describe what effect such an act would have on the Cherokees, by asserting that "the tendency of such a law on the Cherokees would be disastrous. It forces from them the very means of their improvement in religion and morals, and in the arts of civilized life" (121). He asserted that the state of Georgia was purposely depriving the Cherokees of the precise contact that had enabled and empowered them to embrace the ideals upon which the nation was founded. And, indeed, the state was trying to do just that. The extension of Georgia's laws over the Cherokee Nation was not an attempt to incorporate the Cherokees as citizens with rights and property. Rather, it was an attempt to cut the Cherokees off from federal assistance, both civil and military, and isolate them in such despicable conditions that they would voluntarily remove.

In an April 16, 1831, article in the *Phoenix*, Boudinot addressed what he saw as the various misconceptions resulting from the ambiguous decision of the US Supreme Court in the case of *Cherokee Nation v. Georgia*, occasioned by Georgia extending its laws over the Cherokee territory. The chief justice had announced that the Cherokees, while not considered a foreign nation, did exercise a sort of limited sovereignty that entitled it to be considered a "domestic dependent nation." As Boudinot wrote, however, this decision was widely misinterpreted to mean that the state of Georgia did indeed have power over the Cherokee Nation "because it was *not* a foreign state in the sense of the constitution" (126).

He further illustrated his perception that an effort was under way "to mislead the public—to produce the impression that . . . the pretensions of Georgia and the views of the Executive have been sustained by the Court. . . . Now we apprehend this is doing injustice to the Supreme Court" (Boudinot 125). Boudinot argued that the implications of miscarrying a Supreme Court decision reach far beyond the Cherokee Removal issue and touch the nature of constitutional law in the United States. As in earlier editorials, Boudinot contended that the repudiation of legal accountability amounts to a complete inversion of the Constitution and the laws founded on it. He wrote: "The opinion plainly intimates that it is the duty of the Executive and Congress of the United States to redress the wrongs, and to guard the rights of the Cherokees if they are oppressed. . . . The rights of the Cherokees are as plain, as sacred, as they have been, and the duty of the Government to secure those rights is as binding as ever" (Boudinot 126). Boudinot portrayed the responsibilities of the chief executive and the Congress not only with respect to the Supreme Court decision in the *Cherokee Nation v. Georgia* case, but also in regard to the Constitution. Throughout, he consistently appropriated and employed the idealistic language of the Constitution to attack the behavior of state and federal officials as hypocritical and unjust.

One of the most significant Supreme Court cases in the history of Indian affairs, *Worcester v. Georgia* (1832), contributed to the infamy of Andrew Jackson's presidency and his policies with respect to the Cherokees. The case dealt with the arrest of Samuel Worcester, a white missionary who had lived in the Cherokee Nation for several years and had collaborated with Boudinot on Cherokee translations of religious texts and portions of the *Cherokee Phoenix* (Boudinot 151n73). He was arrested for remaining in the Cherokee Nation without taking an oath of allegiance to the state of Georgia. Worcester was soon released on a technicality but was arrested again on July 7 and immediately took steps to appeal to the Supreme Court. The

Court, for a variety of bureaucratic reasons, did not consider the test case until February of 1832 and by that time, Boudinot was no longer writing for the *Cherokee Phoenix*. However, the outcome of the case confirmed Boudinot's claims that Georgia's actions were unconstitutional and violated earlier treaty agreements. Basing his decision on the earlier statement of the court in *Cherokee Nation v. Georgia* (1830), Chief Justice John Marshall's judgment in this case declared the extension of Georgia laws over the Cherokee Nation unconstitutional and ordered the Superior Court of Georgia to reverse its decision in Worcester's case (Miles 527). Both the state of Georgia and President Jackson all but ignored the ruling. Jackson is reputed to have remarked of Marshall's 1832 decision, "Well: John Marshall has made his decision: *now let him enforce it!*" (Miles 519). This unconstitutional imbalance in the federal government epitomizes what the Cherokees experienced in their attempts to preserve the title to their lands in the Southeast.

In September of 1831, over a year after Andrew Jackson had signed the removal bill into law, Boudinot described the current situation of the Cherokees, still under the jurisdiction of the state of Georgia. He wrote:

> The Governor [Gilmer] is pleased to say that the rights of liberty, personal security and private property of the Indian are better protected under the laws of the state than heretofore. The Cherokees will laugh at this. They believe, and know by sad experience, the reverse to be the fact. There has been no personal security thus far, and liberty does not exist even in name, and as to property, it is sufficient that many, who may be said to have been under good circumstances heretofore, have been completely ruined since the administration of the Georgia laws commenced. (Boudinot 139)

Boudinot's complaint referred to a specific loss of rights—the rights of liberty, security, and property. By adopting a constitutional government, abolishing long-standing practices such as blood revenge, restructuring the entire political system of the nation, and regulating themselves with a written body of laws, the Cherokee leaders thought they had earned the rights of life, liberty, and the pursuit happiness. Boudinot bitterly testified that the "Cherokees will laugh at this." When the state of Georgia unconstitutionally extended its laws over the Cherokee Nation, it became clear that these rights were not available to the Indians and any agreements made in the past were essentially void. Boudinot remarked upon Governor Gilmer's (Georgia) speech on the condition of the Cherokees in Georgia, "[he] expresses the fullest conviction that the happiness and prosperity of the Cherokees depends upon their removal. It may be so after having made their existence here untolerable *[sic]*; but . . . we presume the Cherokees will judge for themselves . . ." (Boudinot 139).

In November of 1831, Boudinot published a column in the *Cherokee Phoenix* in which he recounted the history of the US government's dealings with the Cherokees. This article was one of his last attempts to show his readers, many of whom were outside the borders of the Cherokee Nation, that the current policy of removal was not in keeping with the precedent established by the Constitution and Andrew Jackson's presidential predecessors. In this piece, Boudinot carefully reconstructed and deconstructed the guardian-ward relationship that had dominated white-Indian relations since the colonial era. He focused on the assimilation efforts of the "Great Fathers" who had convinced the Cherokees that if they established a regular form of government, developed a written language, and adopted Christian doctrines, they might be suitable for inclusion in the array of sovereign states. He attacked the Jacksonian removal plan as a complete betrayal and critiqued the government's policies as self-serving and fraudulent. Boudinot wrote:

> No sooner was it made manifest that the Cherokees were becoming strongly attached to the ways and usages of civilized life, than was aroused the opposition of those from whom better things ought to have been expected. . . . [T]hey [the Cherokees] came in conflict with the cupidity and self-interest of those who ought to have been their benefactors. . . . The *guardian* has deprived his *wards* of their rights—The sacred obligations of treaties and laws have been disregarded—The promises of Washington and Jefferson have not been fulfilled. The policy of the United States on Indian affairs has taken a different direction, for no other reason than that the Cherokees have so far become civilized as to appreciate a regular form of government. (142, original emphasis)

In the phrase "appreciate a regular form of government," Boudinot implies that with this newfound appreciation comes the recognition that the US government does not, indeed, maintain a civilized and "regular" form itself. It was, in the simplest terms, a double standard. He aptly concludes: "A desire *to possess* the Indian land is paramount to a desire to see him *established* on the soil as a *civilized* man" (143, original emphasis).

Facing Removal

Robert Ferguson has asserted, "Political rhetoric contains a basic act in mutual recognition on the part of the leaders and led . . . [and] instills the consciousness of belonging to a particular hegemonic force" (26). The position the Cherokees occupied in the 1820s and 30s was one of political limbo, despite their best attempts to gain recognition as a self-governing, sovereign nation. They had effectively incorporated every aspect of the "civilized arts" only to be confronted with an imminently powerful and persistent metanarrative in which they were depicted as savages unworthy of fair treatment under the law.

By the summer of 1832, Boudinot had become dejected and disillusioned as a result of the federal government's alternate impotence and reticence to protect the Cherokees from the depredations of the white squatters all around them. He began to consider voluntary removal the only option for the Cherokee Nation that would afford any opportunity for survival. His advocacy of removal appears to have been rooted in his genuine belief that removal was the only path to a peaceful resolution. Unlike some of his peers who would also sign the New Echota treaty in 1835, Boudinot had little financial wealth at stake and instead relied on his education and faith to guide him. The decision to sign the treaty was made against the wishes of the Cherokee majority, including Principal Chief John Ross who had dismissed Boudinot from his position as editor of the *Cherokee Phoenix* for expressing opinions in favor of removal (Perdue 25–26).

In 1835, Boudinot met with other members of the so-called treaty party, an influential faction representing only a tiny portion of the Cherokee Nation, to discuss the dwindling options facing the Cherokees. They assembled at New Echota, the capital of the Cherokee Nation and signed a treaty on December 29 that exchanged the remaining Cherokee land in the Southeast for land west of the Mississippi. Boudinot was not unaware of the position in which he put himself by signing treaty. He spoke at the New Echota assembly, telling his fellow signers: "I know that I take my life in my hand, as our fathers have also done. We will make and sign this treaty. . . . We can die, but the great Cherokee Nation will be saved. They will not be annihilated; they can live. . . . Who is there here that will not perish, if this great Nation may be saved?" (Perdue 27, 37n76). In December of 1839, two years after he had removed to the West with his family, Elias Boudinot was killed by members of the anti-treaty party (Perdue 30).[6]

A New Era

From the beginning of the nineteenth century to the mid-1830s, the relationship between the United States and the Native peoples within its borders underwent a momentous transformation. But the United States itself was also changing. The era of Jeffersonian Enlightenment ideals was giving way to a period of romantic nationalism in which the vision of America was dominated by notions of expanding the frontier. Concepts of equality were dissolving as economic opportunities made a distinct racial hierarchy more practical for exploiting non-whites. As William McLoughlin has succinctly noted, "From 1815 to 1833 the people of the United States wrestled with the conflict between their original commitment to integrate Indians and their desire to expand and exploit the land the Indians occupied" (xvii).

Elias Boudinot's arguments from the columns of the *Cherokee Phoenix* are grounded in the same ideals of Enlightenment thinking that helped inspire the writing of the US Constitution. But by the 1830s, those ideals were being subverted daily in the effort to establish an American national identity based on expansionism and romanticism. Boudinot found that his carefully crafted arguments based on reason and moral obligation no longer carried much weight with an American public in love with its frontiers. Boudinot's reading of the Cherokee Removal dramatically illuminates the hypocrisy and deceit on which the nation's federal Indian policies were constructed and maintained for decades following the Trail of Tears (1838–1839). The era of great nation-building demanded broad interpretations of constitutional principles, and that often meant negating both the spirit and the letter of the nation's founding document, delivering a "forked justice" in favor of so-called national interests.

Notes

1. Largely as a result of the Yazoo land frauds, the state of Georgia surrendered its western lands (extending to the Mississippi River) to the federal government in what is known as the Georgia Compact. In exchange, the federal government agreed to dissolve Indian title to lands remaining within the state. See McLoughlin 22.

2. The *Cherokee Phoenix* was published in alternating columns of English and Cherokee, using the syllabary devised by Sequoyah. See Perdue 15–16.

3. Boudinot and his cousin John Ridge were both educated at a mission school in Spring Place, Georgia, before attending the American Board of Commissioners for Foreign Missions school in Cornwall, Connecticut. Both Boudinot and Ridge married white women from the local community. Boudinot and his wife were

burned in effigy on the town green and the school was later closed. See Perdue 6–10.

4. Native Americans were not recognized as citizens of the United States until 1924. See Deloria and Lytle 221.

5. For an alternate view of how the Cherokee syllabary was developed, see Traveller Bird, *Tell Them They Lie: The Sequoyah Myth*, Los Angeles: Westernlore Publishers, 1971.

6. Boudinot was killed in accordance with an 1829 Cherokee law that made cession of tribal land a capital offense. See Perdue 31, 38n85.

Works Cited

Boudinot, Elias. *Cherokee Editor: The Writings of Elias Boudinot*. Ed. Theda Purdue. Athens: U of Georgia P, 1996.

Deloria, Vine, Jr., and Clifford M. Lytle. *American Indians, American Justice*. Austin: U of Texas P, 1983.

Ferguson, Robert A. "'We Hold These Truths': Strategies of Control in the Literature of the Founders." *Reconstructing American Literary History*. Ed. Sacvan Bercovitch. Cambridge: Harvard UP, 1986. 1–28.

Garver, Eugene. "Rhetoric, Hermeneutics, and Prudence in the Interpretation of the Constitution." *Rhetoric and Hermeneutics in Our Time*. Ed. Michael J. Hyde and Walter Jost. New Haven, CT: Yale UP, 1997. 171–95.

Krupat, Arnold. *Ethnocriticism: Ethnography, History, Literature*. Berkeley: U of California P, 1992.

McLoughlin, William G. *Cherokee Renascence in the New Republic*. Princeton: Princeton UP, 1986.

Miles, Edwin A. "After John Marshall's Decision: *Worcester v. Georgia* and the Nullification Crisis." *Journal of Southern History* 39 (1973): 519–44.

Perdue, Theda. Introduction. *Cherokee Editor: The Writings of Elias Boudinot*. 1983. Athens: U of Georgia P, 1996. 3–38.

Satz, Ronald N. *American Indian Policy in the Jacksonian Era*. Lincoln: U of Nebraska P, 1975.

United States Constitution. 1789. Rpt. in *The United States Constitution: 200 Years of Anti-Federalist, Abolitionist, Feminist, Muckraking, Progressive, and Especially Socialist Criticism*. Ed. Jonathan Birnbaum and Bertell Ollman. New York: New York UP, 1990. 306–27.

2

RHETORICAL SELF-FASHIONING

SARAH WINNEMUCCA HOPKINS

HER WRONGS AND CLAIMS

✦

Malea D. Powell

THIS is a story.

In 1883, Sarah Winnemucca Hopkins wrote and published *Life Among the Piutes: Their Wrongs and Claims*. She did so in order to enlist the aid of the American public, particularly the eastern reform communities, in her struggle to find justice for her people, the Northern Paiutes. Winnemucca is frequently cited as the first American Indian woman autobiographer, "the only Indian woman writer of personal and tribal history during most of the nineteenth century" (Ruoff 261). While I agree that Winnemucca's text follows the general rules of autobiography, *Life Among the Piutes* (hereafter referred to as *Life*) is also much more than a simple iteration of events for the purpose of self-expression or ethnographic recording. Primarily, I hear Winnemucca's text as a deliberate performance of the kinds of Indianness that would have appealed to her late nineteenth-century reformist audience, a performance[1] constructed in order to make changes in Bureau of Indian Affairs (BIA) policies that directly (and negatively) impacted the Northern Paiutes. One of the lingering remainders of the ideology of colonization of the Americas is the notion among scholars that Native people, especially pre-twentieth-century Natives, produced texts naively; that is, they were rhetorical innocents who had none but the most straightforward of intentions in the production of a text. This belief about the rhetorical naiveté of indigenous peoples is too often reflected in critical work that refuses to see early Native textual engagements as calculated and negotiated with a specific audience, and a specific goal, in mind. My listenings to Winnemucca here presume a sophisticated and capable rhetorical subject. My claim that Winnemucca's text is a performance is a claim about rhetorical exigency and the creation and presentation of a public self who could respond to that exigency in all the appropriate ways. It is based on an understanding of the discourses about Indians that circulated during the last decades of the nineteenth century and the expectations of the Indian reform groups that comprised Winnemucca's public.

Late nineteenth-century beliefs about "the Indian" were, according to Roy Harvey Pearce, rooted in the ideological systems carried across the ocean by early seventeenth-century colonists. Pearce explains that the "Englishman who became Americans were sustained by an idea of order," an "eternal and immutable principle that guaranteed the intelligibility of their relations to each other and their world" (3). Burdened with an Anglo-French primitivistic belief about "the savage" as a European *manqué*, European, then Euro-American, colonists formulated countless "civilizing" strategies—mission society conversions, genocidal warfare, reservations, boarding schools, legal restrictions, etcetera (Pearce 4). The one principle that held clear for those hundreds of years between initial colonization (1609) and the late nineteenth century was that the sacrifice of the "savage" was necessary for the existence of America, and that it could be justified through the language of Christian conversion.

Like previous reform groups, the Indian reformers of the late nineteenth century believed in the sacrifice of the "savage" to Christianity and civilization, but the members of the Boston Indian Citizenship Committee, the Women's National Indian Association, the Indian Rights Association, and the Lake Mohonk Friends of the Indian conference opposed the reservation protectionism previously mandated by President Ulysses S. Grant's "peace policy" of 1870.[2] These reformers were aggressively anti-reservation and their work "revolution[ized] the relations of Indians with the rest of the nation," forcing Congress into a program of rabid anti-tribalism and private property reform (Prucha 609).[3] The Indian Rights Association, in their *Second Annual Report* (1885), blatantly stated that their intent was to secure "for the Indian" three things: "Law," "Education," and "a protected individual title to land, . . . the entering-wedge by which tribal organization is to be rent asunder" (Indian Rights Association 43). That same year, in the *Seventeenth Annual Report of the Board of Indian Commissioners* (1885), Merrill Gates, who presided over the Lake Mohonk Conference for several years, wrote that "the aim of legislation for the Indian should be to make him as soon as possible an intelligent, useful citizen" and that "Indian reservations . . . insulate Indians from civilization, cultivate vice, and [are] a domain for lawlessness licensed by the United States" (Gates 55–56). The culmination of these reform groups came in the passage of the General Allotment Act, or the Dawes Act, of 1887.[4]

It was into this arena of aggressive anti-tribalism that Winnemucca stepped. Winnemucca clearly understood her audiences' beliefs about Indians, and she also understood how to negotiate those beliefs. She writes: "I have lived a long time with white people, and I know what they do. They are people who are very kind to any one who is ready to do whatever they wish" (*Life* 113). Audience is the crucial term here. In the tellings that follow, I navigate Winnemucca's multiple audiences/authors—the body of historians and literary critics who write about Winnemucca and her text, her turn-of-the-century reformist audience, and myself as a third audience who hears the tellings of those other audiences as part of Winnemucca's accumulated text.

In the first section, "Interpreting the Indian," I listen closely to some of the biographical and literary critical work written about Winnemucca and her text. I do so in order to hear and resist textually what David Spurr calls "the rhetoric of empire"— the "particular languages," both generative and enabling, which belong to "the historical process of colonization" (1). These languages are what Gerald Vizenor identifies as "manifest manners," the "notions and misnomers that are read as the authentic and sustained as representations of Native American Indians" (5). Manifest manners are the strategies whereby certain beliefs about Indians are manufactured and made real. Much of the scholarly work on Winnemucca participates in these manners; that is, Winnemucca's life and her text are often used in the service of constructing new histories and/or new interpretive frames that can then be applied to all Western women's/women's/Indian women's/Indians' lives and texts. The thrust of my argument in this section is that in the competition over the significatory power of an identity category—Native American Woman—which enables the rhetoric of empire, the materiality of Winnemucca's complicated life, her rhetorical sophistication, and her resistance are erased.

In the second section, "Listening," I listen to Winnemucca's textual performance and articulate what I, a mixed-blood Native woman scholar, hear. My focus here is on the tactics that Winnemucca uses to represent herself as a civilized Indian woman, the performance that would be the most persuasive to her audience of reformers and legislators. Primarily, I will revisit a particular cultural and historical moment that is saturated with the desires of her late nineteenth-century public—an 1883 speech given by Winnemucca at Soldier's Hall in Boston wherein she rebuts BIA charges of immorality and answers the semi-official charges against her that disputed her fitness to speak as a Paiute representative. This speech creates a rhetorical moment in which popular discourses of womanhood, Indianness, and reform intersect. Winnemucca's speech is both an acknowledgment and a negotiation of that intersection, one in which she consistently positions and repositions herself as both *apart from* and *a part of* Euro-American and Paiute cultural discourse. My point in all of this is not to rehabilitate or rescue Winnemucca's text, nor to establish my account of her text as better than others. My listenings to Winnemucca are simply different—differently positioned, differently motivated, differently encouraged. My hope is that this difference makes possible an imagining of Winnemucca that focuses on her use of dominant discourse as a practice of survivance.

Interpreting the Indian

Most biographies chronicling Winnemucca's life begin as her own text begins, with her birth around 1844 near the sink of the Humboldt River. Born the granddaughter of Truckee, self-proclaimed chief of all the Paiutes, Winnemucca spent her life as a spokesperson and advocate for the Northern Paiute peoples.[5] She experienced her first contact with whites when she was about four years old. Winnemucca spent much of her life living and working within Euro-American culture, learning Spanish as a young girl during an extended stay with her grandfather in Santa Cruz, and teaching herself to read and write in English while working as a domestic servant in Virginia City. She also worked as an interpreter for the US Army and various Indian agents, and as a teacher at several schools for Indians. Winnemucca had especially close contact with government officials, particularly Indian agents, who, in her mind, often mistreated the Paiutes for their own selfish gain. It was this mistreatment that prompted her first public lectures in San Francisco in 1879, in which she directly criticized the practices of a particular Indian agent—William V. Rinehart—who was stationed at the Malheur Reservation in eastern Oregon where the Paiutes were reserved.

Rinehart's behavior has been cited as one of the major causes of the Bannock War of 1878, when Paiutes joined with Bannocks and, because of the deplorable conditions on the reservations, literally took to the surrounding hills to hide from the government, periodically borrowing supplies from nearby settlers and reservation stores. When the army was called in, General Oliver Otis Howard contacted Winnemucca and asked that she serve as his liaison with these "renegade" Paiutes. For her service and peacekeeping efforts, the army gave her $500, which she promptly spent to travel to San Francisco where her lectures on behalf of the Paiutes concerning the causes of the war were a great success. Within a month, Winnemucca, her brother Natchez, and her father Old Winnemucca were called to Washington DC for a meeting with Carl Schurz, the secretary of the interior in charge of the Bureau of Indian Affairs, and with President Hayes. During this trip Winnemucca was introduced to Elizabeth Peabody, who offered to finance a series of East Coast lectures.[6] Winnemucca was even more of a success in the East than she had been in San Francisco. In her stereotypical Indian Princess regalia, she delivered over three hundred lectures from April 1883 to August 1884.[7] During the lecture tour Winnemucca became determined to write a book. *Life Among the Piutes* was published with Peabody's financial support and Mary Peabody Mann's unobtrusive editing in 1883. Following its publication, the BIA launched an extensive campaign to discredit Winnemucca. Ultimately, she returned to Lovelock, Nevada, and began a bilingual school for Paiute children, again with Peabody's financial support. Winnemucca died in 1891.

The biographical details of Winnemucca's life are often used by contemporary scholars engaged in the project of "collecting women's history" (Ashby and Ohrn xiv) to add some spice to projects that focus on the "real lives of the real people who went West."[8] In this context, Winnemucca's biography is usually situated alongside those of other "mythical" Indian women like Pocahontas and Sacajawea[9] and interpreted as one in a series of heroic figurations that Rayna Green has identified as the "Indian Princess." In short, according to Green, the authenticating device for the Princess, the "good" Indian woman, is her kindness (even her love) toward white men and her ability to see other Indians as "savage," often figured as her conversion to Christianity. She is marked as "more Caucasian than her fellow natives" and more tragic since in order to become the Princess "she must defy her own people, exile herself from them, become white, and perhaps suffer death" without ever a hint of her availability as a sexual object (Green 17–18).[10]

This symbolic interpretation of Winnemucca as a virtuous defender of "truth, justice and the American way" is latched onto by writers like Harriet Sigerman, author of *Laborers for Liberty: American Women 1865–1890*. Sigerman writes Winnemucca as a "witness" to the "forced resettlement of her people" who, despite being a "fearless spokesperson for Native American rights" in her beaded buckskins, is ultimately powerless in the face of government policies that "herded [Native Americans] off their lands and forced [them] onto reservations" (Sigerman 93–94). Sigerman's take on Winnemucca is interesting insofar as it exemplifies a paracolonial typology: the now-common depiction of the "heroic" Native woman coupled with the equally common representation of Native women as essentially more connected to the land. Sigerman, however, uses that landed relationship to establish a link with white women settlers who went west in a statement that is stunning in its pronounance (in Vizenor's term) and the pronouncement it makes about the visibility of Native peoples: "There, before the white invader came, Native American women lovingly tended their stalks of corn and beans. Later on, other women came to use the land for different purposes, to wrest from the dusty soil their livelihood or their families' well-being and to build new communities and the foundations of a new life" (Sigerman 109). The land becomes only the sections of "the West" that were devoted to agriculture pre-contact; Native women are noble earth mothers and whites are "invaders." Yet in the very next sentence, these whites are ambiguously and simply "other women" who take up the task of caring for "the dusty soil" and Natives are important only in their absence from the "new life" that the "white invaders" will establish in "the West."

Of course, not all biographical work on Winnemucca participates in this project of erasure and iconographic replacement to the same degree.[11] For example, Gae Whitney Canfield's full-length biography, *Sarah Winnemucca of the Northern Paiutes,* is excruciatingly detailed and gathered from dozens of archival sources, both public and private. Canfield's text concentrates on Winnemucca's relationship with whites and her relationships within the Paiute community. Through the weight of her documentation alone, Canfield amasses a powerful narrative about the convolutions of Indian-white relations at the end of the nineteenth century. Further, the proliferation of detail works rhetorically at portraying Winnemucca as a complete human being with problems and shortcomings as well as strengths and victories. It also provides an opportunity for this reader to claim that what Winnemucca left out of *Life Among the Piutes* was as important as what she put in, and to see *Life* as more of an extended pamphlet about the claims of the Northern Paiutes than the "truth" of Winnemucca's life.

The use of Winnemucca as a foil for the concerns of colonizing scholarly work is not confined to the writing of biography or history; there is also a small body of literary criticism on *Life*. Much of that work—Gretchen Bataille and Kathleen Mullen Sands's *American Indian Women: Telling Their Lives*, H. David Brumble's *American Indian Autobiography*, and LaVonne Ruoff's "Three Nineteenth-Century American Indian Autobiographers"[12]—looks at Winnemucca's text as a part of larger projects that engage the question of autobiographical materials produced by Native writers. While I want to emphasize that studying American Indian autobiography is an important and critical project, I think it is a mistake to try to shove rhetorical performances like Winnemucca's into definitive categories that do not take into account the possibility that Winnemucca was trying to resist the material effects of colonization. For example, Bataille and Sands deal briefly with Winnemucca in what is probably the first book devoted to defining American Indian women's autobiography. Bataille and Sands construct a rubric of classification that unfortunately reinscribes the stereotypical and simplistic trope of an orality/literacy binary that seems all too often to go hand in hand with discussions of American Indian culture. Though they allow that Indian women mix these two cultural understandings in their writings, they lay forth a history of autobiography that begins with "as told to" narratives (oral but culturally tainted through translation) and leads to written, edited recollections (again, tainted by co-writers)—both mostly ethnographic in nature—then moves to the pinnacle of "real" autobiographies that Indian women produce "by themselves." Winnemucca's text becomes less than interesting to their study since it "focuses heavily on cultural disintegration and reflects the [popular] notions of what it meant to be a 'good Indian'" (Bataille and Sands 21). Quite simply, Bataille and Sands spend less than a paragraph on "one of the earliest written autobiographies" because it isn't "Indian" enough (21). They aren't interested in Winnemucca's text for precisely the reasons that I *am* interested in it—its display of notions of "good Indianness" and its rhetorically specific performance as a persuasive text.[13]

Even more problematic is H. David Brumble's study of Winnemucca in *American Indian Autobiography* (1988). Brumble groups *Life* with two other early Native texts—*The Personal Narrative of Chief Joseph White Bull* and *Two Leggings*[14] —that he considers to be strongly influenced by what he calls "preliterate autobiographical traditions among the American Indians" (48). Winnemucca's text differs greatly from the ones attributed to White Bull and Two Leggings, theirs being "as told to" ethnographically gathered tales of warrior life "before the coming of the white man" published by Euro-American editors after both tellers were long dead. However, Brumble claims that they share a common connection to the oral autobiographical traditions of their tribes, a trait that he describes as different from "modern" autobiography in that they are not about discovering "who am I," but are instead are culturally sanctioned tellings that are more about "credentialling" than they are about self-discovery (Brumble 17, 46). In the first chapter of his book, Brumble describes in detail six kinds of "preliterate"[15] autobiographical narratives: coup tales, less formal and more detailed tales of warfare and hunting, self-examinations, self-vindications, educational narratives, and tales of acquisition of powers. He wants to make a link between these "preliterate" forms and published autobiographies because he claims it will "allow us to recognize something that is *ancient* even in the autobiographies of such very literate moderns as N. Scott Momaday and Leslie Silko" (23, emphasis mine). It is this desire for "something ancient" that I find suspicious here. Brumble is clearly searching for authenticity, for the "real" Indianness present in published texts by Indians. In doing so, he mishears a great many of the stories being told, a mishearing that allows him to classify Winnemucca's text, published in her lifetime with little editorial intervention for a specific and identified purpose, as "preliterate," written to "preserve something of 'authentic' Indian life before it vanished utterly from the face of the West" (56).

In an extensive critique of fellow critic LaVonne Ruoff's reading of *Life*,[16] Brumble claims that Ruoff's placement of Winnemucca alongside William Apess and George Copway[17] is a mistake. Also mistaken are Ruoff's claims that *Life* resembles captivity and slave narratives, and these interpretations are mistaken because "Ruoff is telling us more about Winnemucca's audience than about what might have influenced Winnemucca in writing her autobiography" (Brumble 61). As if her audience had no effect on the writing of her autobiography! Despite the fact that *all* archival evidence points to a multiply literate Winnemucca, Brumble claims "it is unlikely that Winnemucca was much aware of literary influences at all" and stubbornly clings to the notion that Winnemucca was probably only a fluent speaker, an imperfect writer, and not a reader, of English (62).[18] Clearly Brumble does not see Winnemucca as rhetorically aware, a portrayal that ignores her work with white people for several years as well as her experience as a performer and speaker for white audiences. This is odd, since his assumption that she was not aware of the cultural discourses of her audience contrasts sharply with his claims for her text as influenced mostly by "preliterate" tribal traditions, traditions that demanded a speaker know, understand, and speak with a cultural understanding of the needs and desires of her/his audience. And while Brumble willingly points out how different Winnemucca's text is from the autobiographies of "literate" Indians like Apess, Copway, and Charles Eastman[19] (all men who "made the journey that Winnemucca made, from the tribal world to the white world"), he never allows for how different her text is from those of White Bull and Two Leggings—men whose texts were not intended to persuade a Euro-American public to take up the Indian cause and influence public policy.

As Green points out, since the Indian Princess is frequently figured as a handmaiden to American independence and civilization, the presence of real Indian women often perplexes the ideological creation of "the Indian," especially in terms of its gendered expectations for particular kinds of Indianness—the Princess/Squaw and the Noble/Ignoble Savage. Winnemucca clearly doesn't fit in Brumble's categories, and her text (and her lecture/performances) is different than that of Apess, Copway, or Eastman—all of whom were educated in more traditional schools than Winnemucca, and all of whom textually perform a particular Euro-American version of masculinity that simply was not an option for Winnemucca. It is this performed masculinity, marked by its participation in certain upper-middle-class ideals, that I hear as what Brumble sees as the "literate" qualities of the autobiographies of Apess, Copway, and Eastman: "these men wrote autobiography in such a way as to describe an individual self and to account for just how that self came to be" (Brumble 63). Winnemucca's text doesn't so much account for the creation of a "self" as it does perform the appropriate concerns of dominant cultural notions of "woman." Her first chapter of *Life*, "First Meeting of Piutes and Whites," emphasizes her childhood fear of white people who she had been told "were killing everybody and eating them," especially children (11). She gives many accounts of violence against the Paiutes perpetrated by white men and offers two events that caused her "to love the white people" (33).

The first such event came during her first journey to California when the traveling Paiutes encountered a group of settlers who were also traveling West. One of the white women gives the Paiute children some sugar to eat; Winnemucca writes: "That was the first gift I ever got from a white person, which made my heart very glad" (23). The second event occurred later in the journey when Winnemucca grew ill from poison oak. She writes, "My face swelled so that I could not see for a long time, but I could hear everything. At last some one came that had a voice like an angel. I really thought it must be an angel" (31). Once Winnemucca regains her sight, she meets the white woman who brought her the medicine that helped make her well: "The first thing she did was put her beautiful white hand on my forehead. I looked at her; she was, indeed, a beautiful angel" (32).

Winnemucca clearly and immediately constructs white men as frightening (her fear of white men is repeated throughout *Life*) and white women as "angels" who bring gifts, a characterization that would have appealed to the nineteenth-century women reformists to whom Winnemucca often spoke. In fact, the second chapter of *Life*, "Domestic and Social Moralities," is clearly aimed at a female audience and is an adaptation of a lecture Winnemucca often delivered to women-only audiences during her tour in the East. Finally, Winnemucca was aware of the importance of her gender in the reform arena. During a San Francisco trip in 1879, she told a *San Francisco Chronicle* reporter that "I have just been thinking how it would do for me to lecture upon the Bannock War. . . . I would be the first Indian woman who ever spoke before white people" (qtd. in Canfield 162). Winnemucca certainly was aware of the audiences for which she wrote and lectured. Further, her text clearly displays what Ruoff points to as a continuing perception of herself "as part of a tribal community, even after conversion and entry into a predominantly Western society," and also presents a "complex blend of influences" from both Northern Paiute and Euro-American culture (Ruoff 265–66, 269). Ruoff's goal in this study is not, as Brumble claimed, to equate Winnemucca's narrative with slave and captivity narratives under the assumption that Winnemucca had firsthand readerly experience with those forms. Instead, it is to "trace the evolution of American Indian written autobiographies in the nineteenth century through the personal narratives of three authors"—Apess, Copway, and Winnemucca—in order to "examine the relation of these works to the history and literature of the age" (Ruoff 251). She uses the changes and developments in narratives produced by former slaves as an analogue to the kinds of discourse that could be produced by Native writers whose audiences were primarily Euro-American.

Ruoff claims that by the time "the first personal narratives by American Indians were published in the late 1820s, the tide of popular taste and of Indian-white relations ensured a ready audience for Indian authors" (252). The "ignoble savage" revealed in captivity narratives competed with James Fenimore Cooper's "noble but doomed" portrayals of Indian peoples during the early nineteenth century, but as Pearce carefully points out, these images weren't contradictory. They were, instead, one of the ways that American writers "tried to argue feelings of guilt and hatred, of pity and censure, out of existence by showing how Indian nobility was one with Indian ignobility" (Pearce 197). The presence of Native authors, then, becomes important in disrupting the ideological configurations of manifest manners. Ruoff's article claims that, like slave narratives, personal narratives written by American Indians moved from spiritual, confessional narratives to ones that openly critiqued certain Euro-American practices. While the spiritual confessions of former slaves centered mostly on flight from slavery, later texts "forthrightly criticized the prejudice they encountered in the North" (Ruoff 261). Ruoff sees a parallel here beginning with the early spiritual conversion narrative of

Apess (though he offers a fair amount of critique as well) and ending with Winnemucca, whose "central theme is Indian-white relations" (263). What is most shared by slave narrators and their Indian counterparts is much rhetorical circumstance—their goals were "to convince their readers that they [the writers] were members of the human race" and to fulfill the "moral obligation to portray the harsh injustices they and their fellows suffers," all the while managing "to avoid antagonizing their white audiences" (Ruoff 252). Ruoff claims, in fact, that "to gain the attention of their audiences," Native writers "structured their narratives to reflect not only native oral traditions but also the forms and themes to which their readers would respond" (269).

It is the "forms and themes" of Winnemucca's age that become the focus of Brigitte Georgi-Findlay's argument in her essay "The Frontiers of Native American Women's Writing." Georgi-Findlay carefully positions Winnemucca within her historical moment and with an understanding that *Life* is "a text of some political impact in the area of Indian policy," in order to "suggest that Winnemucca's identity as a women and the way her womanhood is, so to speak, 'incorporated' into her text, form an important part of Winnemucca's dialogue with her public that should not be underestimated" (227). Georgi-Findlay's acknowledgment that Winnemucca "seems to capitalize" on "the romantic public image" of the "Indian princess" (228), alongside her persuasive argument concerning Winnemucca's use of sentimental discourse in order to reach her audience, are particularly useful. Unfortunately, Georgi-Findlay's astute observations and compelling argument devolve into a vision of Winnemucca as without agency, "trapped" in the discursive conventions of Indianness and sentiment. Instead of remaining a mediating performative subject who moves between discourse communities, Winnemucca is "an individual woman under attack from two sides" who "has never spoken with her own voice, but always in the words of others" (Georgi-Findlay 239). Instead of finding a refigured Indianness in the space of negotiation between cultural literacies, Georgi-Findlay ultimately finds Winnemucca "vulnerable and alone," a "woman between two worlds" (245).

The theme of American Indians "torn between two worlds" is a common tragic representation of the lives of Native peoples on this continent and plays fully into the imperial ideology in which indigenous populations were doomed by fate to disappear. When a historical figure (and I use "figure" in the rhetorical sense here) is consistently read as tragic, then the transformative and imaginative possibilities present in her figuration and refiguration are lost. What I hope to accomplish in my listenings to Winnemucca's text is to see her as an active participant in negotiating and refiguring particular discursive frames. For example, Georgi-Findlay does a fine job of locating Winnemucca's text within late nineteenth-century discourses of morality prevalent in women's reform movements, but she misses entirely the ways in which all "others"—especially Indian men—are feminized through discourses of imperialism,[20] a move that for me becomes important in thinking about the exigencies of Winnemucca's text, and of her representations of herself as performing feats that "only an Indian woman" could do (*Life* 164).

Listenings

So far I've emphasized the ways in which scholars often fail to listen to the nuances of *Life Among the Piutes*, as well as to Winnemucca's life, in a rather single-minded focus on defining the text or Winnemucca herself as "preliterate," "heroine," "Indian," "woman." My goal in offering these scholars' stories and my interventions in them has been to emphasize the importance of listening to Winnemucca and her text, an engagement that requires attention to the particularities of context, to the tactics of representation that *Life* performs, and to the tropes and figures of "savagery" and "civilization" Winnemucca uses to authenticate and authorize herself.[21] I particularly want to pay attention to the ways she tactically negotiates representing herself as a *civilized Indian woman*, an identity category that has complicated valences and that demands different rhetorical performances than that of Native American Woman/Indian Princess. Women, both white and Paiute, are important to the story Winnemucca tells in *Life*. Remember, amidst the violence of white men (who looked like owls) Winnemucca is only convinced out of her fear of white people in general by the kindness of white women.

Winnemucca emphasizes the dangerous position of women throughout *Life*. In her chapter on "Domestic and Social Moralities," she writes that "mothers are afraid to have more children, for fear they shall have daughters, who are not safe even in their mother's presence" (48). During her descriptions of the Bannock War, Winnemucca refers again and again to places where she was afraid to stay overnight: "We did not stay long, because I was afraid of the soldiers" (84). Winnemucca explains this fear clearly in the final chapter of *Life*, "The Yakima Affair." Winnemucca and her sister Elma had been staying with a cousin for a few days because heavy snow kept them from traveling. When it is time to leave, the cousin insists on accompanying them, claiming "there were very bad men there," that "sometimes they would throw a rope over our women and do fearful things to them" (228). Though the presence of a family friend at the "horrible place" protect Sarah and Elma during the night, they are followed by "three men [who were] coming after us as fast as they could ride" (228–29). One of the men claims to be a friend of Natchez and leaves the sisters unmolested. That night, they stayed at the farm of a Mr. Anderson, a US mail contractor whom Winnemucca had known for years. Though they slept in Anderson's own room, one of the eight cowboys staying with him tried to molest Winnemucca during the night (231).

Winnemucca clearly attributes her vulnerability to the fact that she is an Indian woman and on the fact that there were "no white women" present to regulate the moral conduct of the men. At the end of this descriptive section, Winnemucca directly addresses her audience again: "thanks be to God, I am so proud to say that my people have never outraged your women, or even insulted them by looks or words" (244). She then asks if the same can be said for white men: "they do commit some most horrible outrages on your women, but you do not drive them round like dogs" (244). What I see Winnemucca doing here is carefully avoiding the "railing against the opposite sex" that Annie Nathan Meyer warns about in her preface to *Woman's Work in America*. At the same time, Winnemucca writes Indian women into the picture that Meyer later draws of the relations between men and women in 1891: "Men and women both are born into the world helpless and unprotected; it may seem an ugly and bitter truth, but it is so, that in this struggle for existence daily going on about us, men and women do indeed stand 'side by side,' [but] not, as with the poet, 'full summed in all their powers'" (Meyer v).

My claim here is that Winnemucca was more than familiar with an understanding of women as the "moral eye of the state" (Ginzberg 174) and that she used this to build equivalencies between her and her female audiences. Again, as part of her chapter on "Domestic and Social Moralities," she talks about the importance of women in Paiute society: "The women know as much as their advice is often asked. We have a republic as well as you. The council-tent is our Congress, and anybody can speak who has anything to say, women and all" (*Life* 53). At the bottom of that same page, she writes: "If women could go into your congress I think justice would soon be done to the Indians" (53). Elizabeth Palmer Peabody, Winnemucca's Boston patron, would echo this sentiment in an 1885 letter to Rose Cleveland: "You & I must have *another* hour of conference on this [Indian] matter & who knows but we may begin a new era? Women's *wit* is need in administration . . ." (reprinted in Ronda 423). This hardly seems coincidental to me, especially considering that this chapter contains much of the lecture that Winnemucca delivered "exclusively to women" in Boston in the spring of 1883, a lecture that Peabody claims "never failed to arouse the moral enthusiasm of every woman that heard it, and seal their confidence in her own purity of character and purpose" (Peabody 28). Peabody often makes reference to this "women-only" lecture in her correspondence with various friends and associates and in both of her "reports" on Winnemucca's school. Further, Peabody cites the "inherited domestic moralities" that Winnemucca talks of in her women-only lecture as the "wild healthy stock" upon which Winnemucca, like a mother, will be able to "graft a Christian civilization worthy of the name" (Peabody 8–9).

Winnemucca's role as the Christian/Indian mother of the Paiutes is reinforced in her own text. In the final chapter of *Life*, "The Yakima Affair," Winnemucca describes what happens after she returns to Pyramid Lake from Washington DC with Secretary Schurz's letter in hand. Old Winnemucca tells the gathered Paiutes, "they have given us a paper which your mother will tell you of" (225). Later at Yakima, rumor of the letter spread long before Winnemucca arrived. When she did arrive and didn't read the letter, in the incident I refer to earlier in this chapter, the Paiutes believed Winnemucca had betrayed them, while she claims that she hesitated out of shame, "because we came and told them lies which the white people had told us" (225). Leggins, the leader of the Paiutes at Yakima, berates Winnemucca to the gathered Paiutes, "you all see that our mother has sold us to Father Wilbur" (235). The references to Winnemucca as the "mother" of the Paiutes are constant throughout this part of the text. Winnemucca addresses Leggins's Paiutes, "My dear children," she begins, "I know that I have told you more lies than I have hair on my head. I tell you, my dear children, I have never told you my own words; they were the words of white people, not mine" (236). Winnemucca clearly configures herself as the responsible parent, able to represent the Paiutes to the people in Washington but unable to stop the BIA from its dishonesty.

It is because of Winnemucca's success at gaining a champion such as Elizabeth Peabody and at speaking to audiences like Senator Dawes that I am particularly interested in an incident that occurred after Winnemucca's book was published in 1883, when the Bureau of Indian Affairs initiated a print campaign aimed at discrediting Winnemucca that was, in large part, based on the points at which Winnemucca did not comply with the bureau's imagined behavioral "norms" for that reformist "public" with which she had allied herself. In the midst of her successful lecture series in Boston, the BIA's charges claimed that Winnemucca was no decent woman, and that her only interest in speaking for her people was for her own material gain. The charges leveled at Winnemucca appeared in the magazine *Council Fire* and were based on a report that Rinehart had written criticizing Winnemucca. It reads:

> AN AMAZONIAN CHAMPION OF THE ARMY
>
> In the February Council Fire notice was taken of the fact that a Piute woman, known as Sarah Winnemucca, had written a letter to Senator Logan thanking him for his opposition to the Indian appropriation bill and opposing the system of Indian education, abusing civil Indian agents, &c. We then expressed the opinion that Sarah was being used as a tool of the army officers to create public sentiment in favor of the transfer of the Indian Bureau to the War Department. Sarah is now on a lecture tour East. She opens in Boston, and the newspapers inform us that General O. O. Howard and other officers of the army were among her chief supporters, and that Senator Dawes wrote a letter to be read at her meeting expressing regret at not being able to be present, and endorsing her views.
>
> To those who know that General Howard is fully informed as to the character of Sarah Winnemucca it seems incredible that he should give her any countenance, and as Senator Dawes has heretofore claimed to be a champion of the peace policy his action is unaccountable on any hypothesis consistent with such claim. In view of the effort being made to use this Indian woman as an instrument to aid the army in its selfish scheme to overthrow the present Indian policy, and again return to the barbarous policy in vogue before 1869 [. . .] we deem it a duty to tell the readers of the Council Fire what sort of woman this Amazonian champion of the army is. We shall make no statement that is not sustained by irrefutable testimony (most of it in the form of affidavits) now on file in the Indian office, copies of which were sent to Colonel Meacham two years ago.
>
> According to this testimony she is so notorious for her untruthfulness as to be wholly unreliable. She is known to have been for some time an inmate of a house of ill-fame in the town of Winnemucca, Nevada, and to have been a common camp follower, consorting with common soldiers. It is a great outrage on the respectable people of Boston for General Howard or any other officer of the army to foist such a woman of any race upon them. (*Council Fire*, May 1883, 69)

Marked copies of *Council Fire* were sent to those influential peoples who had been supporting Winnemucca and her cause. Rumors and newspaper editorials, coupled with negative reviews of Winnemucca's book, made up the second front of attack against Winnemucca's character. What is rhetorically interesting is that the anonymous claims against Winnemucca—later attributed to Rinehart-influenced sources within the BIA—seem to focus on the points at which Winnemucca did not "fit" with the supposed behavioral norms for the public inside which she was participating—she was being figuratively marked as an "unruly body" in that, although she was currently married to Lewis Hopkins, she had been married and divorced (to a white man) previously; she had spent a lot of time in the company of male military officers during her prolonged working stays at Fort McDermitt; and she was prone to "unseemly" fits of temper.

In short, the attack characterized Winnemucca's behavior as immoral and unwomanly—a characterization they supposed would be the kiss of death among Peabody and her women friends. Fortunately for Winnemucca, and probably not anticipated by the BIA, there were several ways for her to counter their representation. She could deal with the factuality of their attack: The BIA didn't claim that the Paiutes hadn't been treated the way that Winnemucca claimed, just that she wasn't a "reliable" narrator of that treatment; the treatment of the Paiute peoples, and Winnemucca's work on their behalf could easily be proven through letters written by the army officers (most notably General O. O. Howard) to whom Winnemucca had often turned for help. Further, she had never actually hidden her previous marriage; she had only presented it as too painful to talk about since the relationship had come to an end because her husband had been a drunk. And she was currently married to a respectable white man, proof that she understood and participated in the sanctity of marriage within a Euro-American cultural framework. Add to that the fact that she and Hopkins were staying with Peabody—a woman whose belief in traditional women's roles was widely known, and whose own prolonged celibacy spoke for her own compliance with the moral and ethical codes constructed for women within Victorian society. On a factual basis alone, Winnemucca could have countered the Bureau's slander, but she wasn't content to let the facts speak for themselves.

On the night that the attack on Winnemucca was made public, she was scheduled to speak to a large crowd at Soldiers' Hall in Boston. Winnemucca's negotiation of the discourse conventions of the reformist public and her skill at constructing the ethos to which that public would respond is evident in that lecture:

> Dear Friends, after my people were driven away from reservations by starvation, and after having every promise broken and all kinds of falsehoods told them by agents, there was no one to take their part but a woman. Everyone knows what a woman who undertakes to act against bad men must suffer.
>
> My reputation has been assailed, and it is done so cunningly that I cannot prove it to be unjust. I can only protest that it is unjust, and say that wherever I have been known, I have been believed and trusted. Those who have maligned me have not known me. It is true that my people sometimes distrust me, that is because words have been put into my mouth which have turned out to be nothing but idle wind. Promises have been made to me in high places that have not been kept, and I have had to suffer for this in the loss of some of my people's confidence. I have not spoken ill of others behind their backs and said fair words to their faces. I have been sincere with my own people when they have done wrong, as well as with my white brothers. Alas! How truly our women prophesied when they told my dear old grandfather that his white brothers, whom he loved so much, had brought sorrow to his people. Their hearts told them the truth. My people are ignorant of worldly knowledge, but they know what love means and what truth means. They have seen their dear ones perish around them because their white brothers have given them neither love nor truth. My heritage is from a people who know nothing about the history of the world, but they can see the Spirit-Father in everything. The beautiful earth talks to them of their Spirit-Father. They are innocent and simple, and they are brave and patient, and they know that black is not white. Thank you. (*Life* 259)

Winnemucca begins by pointing out that she did not seek out her position as spokeswoman for the Paiute nation, but that it fell into her lap—probably because she had been given the opportunity to live among whites, and could therefore speak, read, and write in their language. She then seems to draw on the tradition of women working for some kind of social reform—abolition of slavery, temperance, women's rights, education—in pointing out the dangers that are possible for women who speak out against "bad" men. This successfully establishes a connection between herself and the women in the audience; she establishes a connection between herself and the men in the audience in that they can not be "bad" men if they have come to support her cause.

She then goes on to deal with the rhetorically delicate situation of protesting the charges against her reputation. First, that she cares about her reputation would speak well of her to her audience—she shows herself to be "civilized." Second, that she points out the horrible situation of being a woman accused would speak to those people that understand the powerlessness of women's situations in a society where they weren't even allowed to vote. Finally, she points out how this attack came from people who do not know her. The implication here is that the audience, her "friends," *do* know her and can be a better judge of her worth and morality—her "right" to speak for her people. That she highlights her own participation in some sort of idealized Christian charitableness (by saying that she doesn't talk behind people's backs and that she always tells the truth) is very important to maintaining her balance between white and Indian culture here since she goes on to speak of Paiute prophecy.

I find it significant that she tells of the Paiute *women* prophesying in ways that contradict the feelings of their male leader. The women, she alludes, always know the truth in their hearts; the men may believe that what they know is true, but it's really often just what they want to believe that they see as truth. Winnemucca seems to be making a gesture toward some sort of essential womanhood that would cut across cultural divides, and she does so as a way to establish herself as part of Peabody's network of women reformists. Again, this positioning of herself as part of the group is necessary since she is about to represent her people as innocent and naive in a way that she would not choose to represent herself—she is the "civilized" Indian. She uses this positioning to open a space in which she is like white women but is not white, at the same time that she is like Indian women but is not "primitive." This is the space of her textual authority—the space from which she establishes her own representations as "truth" because she, unlike others in the room, can see both positions—white and Indian—clearly because of her position between them.

Next, Winnemucca conjures the "primitive" relationship to language that Peabody had theorized about, except she uses it as a way to gain sympathy for the Paiutes and, more importantly, to finalize herself as a member of Peabody's reformist public. Winnemucca can be read here, in Peabody's terms, as the primitive who gains access to the analytical, but instead of spiritually transcending the analytical, Winnemucca *remembers* and *speaks* for the primitive (in the form of the "innocent" Paiute peoples). Peabody herself says as much in two of her letters, one written to her close friend Amelia Bolte in 1886: "the customs etc. of the Piute's the tribe of Indians who never knew of Whites till 1848 confirms wonderfully [the] idea of the primitive men" (qtd. in Ronda 433); and another written to Rose Elizabeth Cleveland in 1885: "no tribe had the advantage of this one in having one of themselves civilized with the language—so as to be able to deal first hand with the government" (qtd. in Ronda 422).

In this speech, and in much of her writing, Winnemucca positions herself in very specific ways in relation to how her experience has led her to construct Peabody's reformist public. This is contrary to the way that the BIA positioned their attack of Winnemucca and is, perhaps, one of the reasons that instead of being ruined, Winnemucca became even more popular. That is, the BIA positioned its attack within an imagined construction of the conventions that counted in Peabody's reformist public. This was an idealized construction, based on men's views of a women-based group. That Winnemucca understood how to navigate within this public is not surprising, given her contact with white women during her work as a teacher and domestic in the West. That the men in the BIA did not understand that same public should not be surprising either, given that few of them would have had the kind of face-to-face experiences with reformist white women that Winnemucca had. What I want to make clear here is that in Winnemucca's relationships to white women, however friendly and supportive they might have been, she was the subordinate, while the BIA men's relationships to white women would have been ones in which they were, at least in their minds, dominant. Those who are relegated to the subordinate position often must, in order to survive, learn the language of their "betters"; those who are already betters need not bother to learn any other language at all. And while Winnemucca was able to negotiate the language of the reformist public, it is important to note that her acceptance into their circle would have always been contingent on her Otherness, on her value as a cause; her negotiations certainly made her membership less difficult than it could have been, but her authenticity was what made that marginal membership possible.

Winnemucca's membership in that circle can be clearly seen in their immediate response to the slanders on her character. The *Silver State*, one of Winnemucca's home newspapers, immediately published an article supporting Winnemucca, claiming that "now, because she states, before an audience in Boston, what the whites in Nevada and on the frontier generally know to be facts, the 'Council Fire,' the Washington organ of the Indian Bureau, roundly abuses her . . . without attempting to refute or disprove her assertions," and ending with "the 'Council Fire' ought to know that scandalous charges against this woman, based on false affidavits of rascally Indian agents and their paid tools, are not arguments, and are no answer to her indictment of these agents" (reprinted in *Life* 267–68). In the July/August issue of the *Council Fire*, there is reprinted a long letter from Mary Mann that includes a letter from M. S. Bonnifield (Winnemucca's Nevada attorney) as well as one from Lewis Hopkins, both protesting the characterization of Winnemucca as immoral and untrustworthy. The *Council Fire* responded with less than a paragraph of justification for printing the original charges—"being convinced that she is an Indian, and a woman of talent and education, she could wield great influence for evil" and a reiteration of the presence of affidavits "on file in the Indian office" (99). In the September issue of *Council Fire* there is yet another letter vouching for Winnemucca, this time from Alfred Love, president of the Universal Peace Union. Love takes an entirely different tact than Winnemucca's other defenders:

> even if the statements you make be true, would it not be kind to keep them from the public. Suppose she had been attracted by the soldiers with their gay trappings, and perhaps their promises of favors; they are called Christians, she is styled savage. What wonder if she went astray? Of whom should we expect the most? Who were more to blame? . . . Rather should we applaud this woman for now coming forth in all womanly dignity and earnestness and upholding justice, virtue, peace. (134)

Though no amount of persuasive appeal would change the minds of the editors of the *Council Fire*, a journal "devoted to the civilization and rights of the American Indian" (January 1883, 1), Winnemucca did have a great deal of influence on Senator Dawes while he was writing the Dawes Act, which passed only seven months before Winnemucca died at the age of forty-three in Henry's Lake, Idaho, while living with her sister Elma. And, eventually, the single piece of policy that had been so important to Winnemucca and her father—a reservation for the Paiutes on the traditional lands near Fort McDermitt—did come to pass in July of 1889. Winnemucca's text is much larger than *Life Among the Piutes*; it encompasses her lectures/performances and her personal correspondence, as well as all the stories that have been told about her, scholarly and otherwise.[22] Winnemucca is an important figure in the history of rhetoric in the United States, and in the history of resistance to the manifest manners of empire. Brought about by the contingencies of imperial conquest on the continent of North America, Winnemucca's rhetorical negotiations and performances open up questions of ethnicity and gender that Native peoples are still answering, questions that have deep import in our survivance. In this way, Winnemucca provides an important cornerstone to future work in American Indian rhetoric, and an important lesson for those of us who propose to tell the stories of Native peoples within the academy.

Notes, or Other Stories

1. The understanding of "performance" used here is a combination of Judith Butler's theories concerning the production of gender and sexuality from her essay "Imitation and Gender Insubordination" and Gerald Vizenor's arguments about Indians, articulated most clearly in *Manifest Manners*. In short, our participation in identity categories requires a certain kind of production or performance of the "rules" for those categories, and it must be understood that those rules frequently elide the presence of material peoples even as they "produce" an iteratable identity.

2. For more information on Indian reform, see Christine Bolt's *American Indian Policy and American Reform* (Boston: Allen and Unwin, 1987), Henry Fritz's *The Movement for Indian Assimilation, 1860–1890* (Philadelphia: U of Pennsylvania P, 1963), Frederick Hoxie's *A Final Promise* (see works cited), Robert Keller Jr.'s *American Protestantism and United States Indian Policy, 1869–1892* (Lincoln: U of Nebraska P, 1983), Robert Mardock's *The Reformers and the American Indian* (Columbia: U of Missouri P, 1971), Valerie Mathe's *Helen Hunt Jackson and Her Indian Reform Legacy* (Austin: U of Texas P, 1990), and Francis Paul Prucha, *The Great Father*.

3. Under Grant's "peace policy" the attempt was made to force all Indian nations, even those exempt from removal, onto reservations for their own "protection" and allowed religious groups (Quakers, Catholics, Methodists, etc.) control of both BIA-appointed offices and the Board of Indian Commissioners. For more information see Prucha.

4. The Dawes Act was designed to allot a quarter section of 160 acres to the head of each Indian family. Indians who refused or failed to select an allotment would have one selected for them by the Secretary of the Interior. The new land "owner" would not, however, receive a patent for the land until it had been held in trust for twenty-five years by the Office of the Secretary of the Interior; the land could not be sold or its title encumbered by its "owner." Further, when the land patent was finally issued, the landowner became subject to state and federal laws, and US citizenship would be granted to those Indian landowners who had "resided separate and apart from the tribe" and had "adopted the habits of civilized life," thus eradicating treaty obligations and cultural distinctiveness in one fell swoop. All reservation lands left over after the initial allotment were to be purchased by the government, the moneys from that purchase being held in trust "for the education and civilization of the former tribe members" (Berkhofer 174). Unfortunately,

an 1891 legislative act enabled allotted lands to be leased for agriculture, mining, and lumbering while other provisions of the Act—reservation courts and police and citizenship for "reformed" Indians—did not come about in any substantial manner before the 1930s. Before the Dawes Act went into effect, Native nations held 138 million acres. Sixty percent of that land was lost through sale of "surplus" lands, 20 percent was lost through "disposal of allotments," and an unknown amount was leased in perpetuity (Berkhofer 175).

5. There is a good deal of controversy about this point. Truckee was probably only the recognized leader of a few bands, since the Northern Paiutes did not have any leader who spoke for all bands; however, as Frances Karttunen has pointed out, Winnemucca most likely created her grandfather as chief of all the Paiutes since "she knew that white people thought in terms of great chiefs and Indian princesses" (46).

6. Elizabeth Peabody and her sister, Mary Peabody Mann, were Winnemucca's staunchest defenders and advocates. Peabody frequently defended Winnemucca to her detractors. In a letter to the *Boston Daily Advertiser*'s editor, Edwin Munroe Bacon, Peabody acknowledges that while Winnemucca "has been misrepresented in some quarters," "every thing has been thoroughly investigated & every thing is perfectly right about her," adding that "she has shared our bed & board for months this last summer and fall" (415). Peabody's association with intellectual spheres, like the Transcendentalists, and with political spheres, in her acquaintance with Rose Cleveland and with several congressmen's wives, put her in a uniquely powerful position from which to lobby for Winnemucca.

7. Winnemucca's attire—fringed buckskin and beads with a gold crown and an embroidered wampum bag—can hardly be described as traditionally Paiute, though many eastern newspapers did just that. Pre-contact Paiute women wore a skirt of tule fiber and were often bare-chested; after contact they often combined the traditional skirt with men's shirts or wore European-style skirts, blouses, and dresses (Canfield 7, 201).

8. For example, see Christiane Fischer's *Let Them Speak for Themselves*. Fischer uses Winnemucca as contrast to the other women in her text who are all settlers in a West that is a "wasteland," devoid of "civilized life" (17, 13). Others, like Ruth Ashby and Deborah Gore Ohrn, repeat this usage, representing Winnemucca as "an eloquent defender" and role model "for later Native American movements" (137) among a panoply of "women who changed the world" (Winnemucca is sandwiched between Mary Cassatt and Carry Nation)—a veritable buffet of difference.

9. For example, in *Three American Indian Women* (New York: MJF Books, 1995), excerpts from biographies on Pocahontas (Grace Steele Woodward), Sacajawea (Harold P. Howard), and Sarah Winnemucca Hopkins (Gae Whitney Canfield) are offered one after the other with no introduction or commentary on what these women might, or might not, have in common. This lack of context makes it difficult

to not read the excerpts of these three biographies as literal depictions of the "real."

10. Green's argument is significantly more complicated than I am able to represent here. In it, the companion to the Princess is "the Squaw"—a figure signified by "the presence of overt and realized sexuality" and by "the same vices attributed to Indian men" like drunkenness (19).

11. Two notable short exceptions are Gayle Hardy's entry on Winnemucca in *American Women Civil Rights Activists* (Jefferson, NC: McFarland, 1993), which offers a soundly contextualized biographical and bibliographical sketch of Winnemucca against a backdrop of no less than twelve other American women who worked for Native rights, and Catherine Fowler's excellent biographical essay on Winnemucca in the *American Indian Intellectuals* collection. Fowler's essay, "Sarah Winnemucca, Northern Paiute, ca. 1844–1891," is particularly important since it offers solid critical commentary and corrects Katherine Gehm's fictionalized biography of Winnemucca, *Sarah Winnemucca, Most Extraordinary Woman of the Paiute Nation* (Phoenix: O'Sullivan, Woodside and Co., 1975), which focuses on Winnemucca's life as a sentimental romance/tragedy, and precedes Doris Kloss's predictable but not blatantly fictionalized account of Winnemucca's life, *Sarah Winnemucca* (Phoenix: O'Sullivan, Woodside and Co., 1981).

12. These are all fairly dated essays but they are influential in shaping the ways in which the scholarly community, particularly in American Indian literature, could think about Native autobiography in general, Winnemucca in particular.

13. Winnemucca is also briefly mentioned in Hertha Dawn Wong's *Sending My Heart Back across the Years: Tradition and Innovation in Native American Autobiography* (New York: Oxford UP, 1992). Tacked on to the end of a chapter on Black Elk and Charles Eastman, Wong claims Winnemucca as part of "the autobiographical tradition of Euro-American influenced native people . . . who wrote their life stories in English without the aid of an amanuensis" (152).

14. White Bull (1849–1947) was one of the chiefs of the Miniconjou and was rumored to have been at the Battle of Little Big Horn. In 1931 he was persuaded to tell his story to Usher Burdick, including pictographs and an account written in Lakota. In 1957, James Howard published a translated version entitled *The Warrior Who Killed Custer: The Personal Narrative of Chief Joseph White Bull.* Two Leggings was a River Crow Indian (1847–1923). He is rumored to have led the last Crow war party in 1888 and in 1919 began to tell his story to William Wildschut, a Dutch-born amateur ethnologist. *Two Leggings* was not published until 1962 when Peter Nabokov put out a re-edited version of the 480-page manuscript

15. I am at a loss to explain this label of "preliterate," which is why it appears in quotation marks here. Clearly Brumble is defining literacy as print literacy only. My own working definition of literacy refers to education and general knowledgeability in cultural systems and in the ways to negotiate those systems. Constructing and interpreting, for example, a winter count is a "literate" act in that it

requires culturally specific knowledge and education in particular systems of interpretation.

16. In my discussion of Brumble, I offer his readings of Ruoff's article (unpublished at the time of his reading) "Three Nineteenth-Century American Indian Autobiographers," though they differ greatly from my own understandings of her essay as well as from her understandings of her essay. In the final note to that text, she writes "Brumble misinterprets the thrust of my argument. . . . The presence of aspects of popular literature in their autobiographies . . . may well mirror the taste of the age rather than the literary background of the narrators" (269).

17. William Apess, a mixed-blood Pequot, is credited as having written the first published full life history written by an Indian—*Son of the Forest: The Experience of William Apes, a Native of the Forest* (1829). Because Apess was not raised in a tribal community but was bound out, by age five, to a series of white families, and later became a Methodist minister, his narrative is markedly different from that of later Indian writers who often describe idyllic tribal childhoods. While *Son of the Forest* reads most like a spiritual confessional, Apess's other writings, most notably his *Eulogy of King Philip* (1836) can easily be classified as Indian protest literature. (Both works are available in *On Our Own Ground*, ed. Barry O'Connell [Amherst: U of Massachusetts P, 1992].) George Copway (Ojibway) wrote the first published book-length history of the Ojibways written by an Indian, *The Traditional History and Characteristic Sketches of the Ojibway Nation* (1850), as well as his autobiography, *The Life, History, and Travels of Kah-ge-ga-gah-bowh* (George Copway) (1847). Copway was a converted Methodist who "seemed to represent what the Indian man must become in order to survive": a mixture of noble savage and European virtues (Ruoff 256).

18. As Frances Karttunen points out, and as anyone can see who has looked at any of the archived letters written by Winnemucca, her "mastery of English spelling and punctuation" was "a good deal better than average and much better than that of William Clark" of Lewis and Clark (*Between Worlds* 46).

19. Charles Alexander Eastman was one of the first Native men to become a medical doctor and was the physician at Pine Ridge during the 1890 Battle of Wounded Knee. He was widely published in the early twentieth century; his most well-known works are *Indian Boyhood* (1902), *From the Deep Woods to Civilization* (1916), and *The Soul of the Indian* (1911).

20. See Jenny Sharpe, *Allegories of Empire: The Figure of the Woman in the Colonial Text* (U of Minnesota P, 1993) for a full discussion of this phenomenon in East Indian literary texts.

21. I focus more fully on *Life* in my essay "Rhetorics of Survivance: How American Indians Use Writing," *College Composition and Communication* (February 2002).

22. Significantly, the last twenty pages of *Life* are comprised of an appendix of letters, most in support of Winnemucca's cause or speaking directly to her good character.

Works Cited

"An Amazonian Champion of the Army." *The Council Fire and Arbitrator* 6.5 (May 1883): 69.

Ashby, Ruth, and Deborah Gore Ohrn, eds. *Herstory: Women Who Changed the World.* New York: Viking, 1995.

Bataille, Gretchen M., and Kathleen Mullen Sands. *American Indian Women: Telling Their Lives*. Lincoln: U of Nebraska P, 1984.

Berkhofer, Robert F., Jr. *The White Man's Indian*. New York: Vintage, 1979.

Brumble, H. David, III. *American Indian Autobiography*. Berkeley: U of California P, 1988.

Butler, Judith. "Imitation and Gender Insubordination." *Inside/Out*. Ed. Diana Fuss. New York: Routledge, 1991. 307–20.

Canfield, Gae Whitney. *Sarah Winnemucca of the Northern Paiutes*. Norman: U of Oklahoma P, 1983.

"Explanatory." *The Council Fire and Arbitrator* 6.9 (September 1883): 134–35.

Fischer, Christiane, ed. *Let Them Speak for Themselves: Women in the American West, 1849–1900*. New York: Dutton, 1978.

Fowler, Catherine S. "Sarah Winnemucca, Northern Paiute, ca. 1844–1891." *American Indian Intellectuals*. Ed. Margot Liberty. St. Paul: West, 1978. 33–42.

"From a Zealous Friend of the Indian." *The Council Fire and Arbitrator* 6.8 (July-August 1883): 98–100.

Gates, Merrill E. "Land and Law as Agents of Educating Indians." Seventeenth Annual Report of the Board of Indian Commissioners (1885). Reprinted in *Americanizing the American Indians: Writings by the "Friends of the Indian" 1880–1900*. Ed. Francis Paul Prucha. Cambridge, MA: Harvard UP, 1973. 45–56.

Georgi-Findlay, Brigitte. "The Frontiers of Native American Women's Writing: Sarah Winnemucca's *Life Among the Piutes*." *New Voices in Native American Literary Criticism*. Ed. Arnold Krupat. Washington, DC: Smithsonian Institution P, 1993. 222–52.

Ginzberg, Lori D. *Women and the Work of Benevolence: Morality, Politics, and Class in the Nineteenth-Century United States*. New Haven: Yale UP, 1990.

Green, Rayna. "The Pocahontas Perplex: The Image of Indian Women in American Culture." *Massachusetts Review* 16 (Autumn 1975).

Hopkins, Sarah Winnemucca. *Life Among the Piutes: Their Wrongs and Claims*. Boston: privately printed, 1883. Reprint. Bishop, CA: Chalfant P, 1969.

Hoxie, Frederick E. *A Final Promise: The Campaign to Assimilate the Indians, 1880–1920*. Lincoln: U of Nebraska P, 1984.

Indian Rights Association. "Statement of Objectives" from Second Annual Report of the Executive Committee of the Indian Rights Association (1885). Reprinted in *Americanizing the American Indians: Writings by the "Friends of the Indian"*

1880–1900. Ed. Francis Paul Prucha. Cambridge, MA: Harvard UP, 1973. 42–44.

Karttunen, Frances. *Between Worlds: Interpreters, Guides, and Survivors*. New Brunswick, NJ: Rutgers UP, 1994.

Meyer, Annie Nathan. Editor's Preface. *Woman's Work in America*. New York: Henry Holt and Co., 1891. iii–vi.

Peabody, Elizabeth Palmer. *Sarah Winnemucca's Practical Solution of the Indian Problem: A Letter to Dr. Lyman Abbot of the "Christian Union."* Cambridge: John Wilson and Son, 1886.

Pearce, Roy Harvey. *Savagism and Civilization: A Study of the Indian and the American Mind*. Rev. ed. of *The Savages of America*. 1953. Berkeley: U of California P, 1988.

Prucha, Francis Paul. *The Great Father: The United States Government and the American Indians*. 2 vols. Lincoln: U of Nebraska P, 1984.

Ronda, Bruce A. *Letters of Elizabeth Palmer Peabody, American Renaissance Woman*. Middletown, CT: Wesleyan UP, 1984.

Ruoff, A. LaVonne Brown. "Three Nineteenth-Century American Indian Autobiographers." *Redefining American Literary History*. Ed. A. LaVonne Brown Ruoff and Jerry W. Ward Jr. New York: MLA P, 1990. 251–69.

Sigerman, Harriet. *Laborers for Liberty: American Women, 1865–1890*. New York: Oxford UP, 1998.

Spurr, David. *The Rhetoric of Empire: Colonial Discourse in Journalism, Travel Writing, and Imperial Administration*. Durham, NC: Duke UP, 1996.

Vizenor, Gerald. *Manifest Manners: Postindian Warriors of Survivance*. Hanover, NH: Wesleyan UP, 1994.

RESISTANCE AND MEDIATION

THE RHETORIC OF IRONY IN INDIAN BOARDING SCHOOL NARRATIVES BY FRANCIS LA FLESCHE AND ZITKALA-SA

✦

Ernest Stromberg

IN the preface to his autobiographical narrative *The Middle Five: Indian Schoolboys of the Omaha Tribe*, Francis La Flesche provides a poignant sense of the rhetorical context in which he and other early authors of boarding school narratives wrote: "[N]o native American can ever cease to regret that the utterances of his father have been constantly belittled when put into English, that their thoughts have been travestied and their native dignity obscured" (xix). In this brief passage, La Flesche indicts a history of misrepresentations of American Indians and specifically English as the vehicle for conveying these distorting and belittling representations. As historian Robert Berkhofer observes, from the early reports of Christopher Columbus and Amerigo Vespucci emerged a long "line of savage images of the Indian as not only hostile but depraved" (7). While exceptions to these negative representations of Indians exist within the historical record, the general trend was toward a discourse of Indianness that had the rhetorical effect of persuading a non-Indian audience of the inherent inferiority of America's indigenous peoples. Evidence of the persuasiveness of this rhetoric can be found in works of art, literature, and perhaps most clearly in government policy.

Within and against this well-developed discursive field, in the late nineteenth and early twentieth centuries, American Indian writers such as La Flesche of the Omaha, Dakotan Zitkala-Sa, Santee Sioux Charles Eastman, and Lakotan Luther Standing Bear, to name but a few, wrote and published accounts of their own conflicted acquisition of literacy in spoken and written English. While many of these writers have garnered attention in recent times for their literary achievements—both Eastman and Zitkala-Sa are included in the *Norton Anthology of American Literature*—more attention is needed in terms of their place within "Native intellectual history of the past one hundred years" (Warrior 3). In addition, as many of these writers were political activists who wrote and spoke publicly on a variety of Indian-related issues, their work must also be seen as part of an ongoing Native American rhetorical tradition, dedicated, in Scott Lyons's words, to the "political, pan-Indian pursuit of social justice" (153). Furthermore, any attempt to develop a coherent sense of the United States' multicultural rhetorical tradition without attention to these writers will remain incomplete.

To understand the exigencies propelling the narratives of these Indian writers requires a glance backward at a sampling of representative textual depictions of America's indigenous peoples. From the advent of their arrival on the shores of the American continent, European settlers and their descendants have employed various means to "educate" the indigenous people. For instance, Columbus, in one of the first recorded encounters between Europeans and Native Americans, articulates a perspective that remained stunningly contemporary for over four centuries: "They should be good and intelligent servants . . . and I believe that they would become Christians very easily. . . . [A]t the time of my departure I will take six of them from here . . . in order that they may learn to speak" (qtd. in Greenblatt 90). Columbus articulates a hierarchical social place for Indians as servants, an easy conversion to Christianity, and the necessity of teaching of them an acceptable European language. To understand how enduring this construction of indigenous identity and capability was, compare Columbus's entry with the following descriptions of the primary goals of missionary and later government-sponsored Indian boarding schools established in the late nineteenth century: "[T]o teach [Indian] children English, Christianity, and the moral superiority of a clean life of honest labor" (Lomawaima 2). Resting beneath these goals are a number of unstated assumptions: the compelling need for the children to learn English because their first language is inadequate; their need to be converted to Christianity because their own traditions are unclean and immoral; and finally, their future role as "good servants" to white people. Indeed, at the majority of church and public boarding schools emphasis was placed on "manual skills for boys and domestic skills for girls over academic training" (Lomawaima 2–3). To achieve these goals, fully in line with Columbus's original plan to seize "six of them," Indian children were removed from the influences of their families and home in order to be weaned from their own culture and taught "to speak" and write in English.

Between Columbus's seminal opinions and the pedagogical goals of the boarding schools remains a consistent desire to transform Native people. The desire to transform America's indigenous peoples was fueled in large part by representations that defined Indians "in terms of . . . [their] lack of White ways" (Berkhofer 26). The duty of good Christians and civilized Americans, therefore, was to compensate for this Indian lack. By the middle of the nineteenth century, one of the primary mechanisms for enacting this compensation would be the Indian boarding school.

The notion of indigenous "lack" coalesced around the rhetoric of "civilizing and assimilating." While diverse and varied in its specific expressions, the rhetoric of assimilation, too, remained consistent in several basic assumptions. The primary assumption was the inferiority of Native American cultures, including spiritual beliefs, language, and material practices. While occasionally romanticized, the ways of Indians were by the late nineteenth century equated with a disappearing primitive past, and for Indian people to survive and progress into the future, they must abandon their traditions and take up the ways of Western and Christian civilization. Richard Pratt, the founder of the first government-sponsored off-reservation school at Carlisle, Pennsylvania, expresses this perspective quite clearly: "[For] the complete civilization of the Indian and his absorption into our national life . . . the Indian . . . [must] lose his identity as such, [and] to give up his tribal relations. . . . The sooner the Indian loses all his Indian ways, even his language, the better. . . . To accomplish that, his removal and personal isolation is necessary" (qtd. in Lomawaima 5).

The discourse of civilization and assimilation, the answer to the so-called Indian problem, was clearly rhetorical in its dimension. It was via the discourse of "civilizing" that missionaries persuaded church congregations and administrations to provide funds to establish boarding schools. In response to the same discourse "in 1870 Congress authorized the first appropriation for Indian education" (Adams 48). The discourse of civilization and assimilation also shaped the pedagogy of these schools. Under Daniel Dorchester, the superintendent of Indian schools from 1889 to 1893, "[a] sincere effort was made to develop the type of school that would destroy tribal ways" (56). And, according to some scholars, this discourse was used to influence the students at the boarding schools who would then assist in the assimilation among their own people "from within" (Noriega 379). As Thomas J. Morgan, commissioner of Indian affairs in 1889 explained, "a fervent patriotism should be awakened in their minds. . . . They should be taught to look upon . . . the United States Government as their friend" (qtd.

in Coleman 42). Yet the awakening of this fervent patriotism seemingly could only come at the denigration of Native cultures. As Roy Harvey Pearce argues in *Savages of America: A Study of the Indian and the Idea of Civilization*, the idea and image of the Indian as savage served as the negative mirror for the construction of the idea and image of whites as civilized.

I dwell upon the discourse of civilization and assimilation for two reasons. The first is to underscore the ideology upon which both missionary and government boarding schools were established. It was clearly a paternalistic ideology that both assumed the superiority of Western culture and a knowledge of what was in the best interests of Native Americans. My other purpose is to highlight the rhetorical context in which the utterances of the two writers I examine develops and participates. In examining the published accounts by two Native American writers, Francis La Flesche of the Omaha tribe and Lakota Zitkala-Sa, the question at issue concerns how they engage this discourse. That is, to what extent do their texts affirm, contest, or supplement the dominant discourse's positioning of American Indians as a primitive type in need of civilizing and for whom abandonment of cultural heritage and complete adoption of so-called white ways is the best answer?

Before fully engaging with these questions, I want to qualify the scope to this paper. The boarding school narratives under consideration cannot be said to fully represent the experiences of all Indian boarding school students. These texts reflect boarding school experiences ranging from the late eighteen sixties to the eighteen nineties and were both published between 1900 and 1901. As examples of a genre, these texts are also distinct in that they are the works of writers whose acquisition of English literacy enabled them to achieve a great deal of success in the terms of the dominant culture. La Flesche possessed a law degree and established a reputation as an ethnographer. Zitkala-Sa first published her accounts in *Harpers* and the *Atlantic Monthly*. Because they were Indian public figures, even public intellectuals, and also given that thousands of Native Americans attended boarding schools, it would be reductive to consider their testimonies as representative of the boarding school experience. And an examination of a variety of boarding school narratives reveals a range of ambivalent and "highly mixed" responses to the experience (Coleman x).

Yet confronting all American Indian writers at this time was the need to establish that America's indigenous peoples were fully human. Arguments over indigenous humanity go back at least as far at the debate between the Spaniards Bartolomé de Las Casas, who argued on behalf of indigenous virtues, and Juan Gines de Sepulveda, who argued that in America's indigenous peoples, "you will scarcely find traces of humanity" (qtd. in Berkhofer 11). Even by the dawn of the twentieth century, United States Indian policies, while operating under the assumption of an Indian humanity that could be assimilated, still defined Indians as an underdeveloped or immature people. Furthermore, concepts of racial difference applied to American Indians rendered them an "other," significantly different from "white" people of European stock. Thus, Carlisle Indian School founder Richard Pratt could infamously assert that the function of his school was to "kill the Indian and save the man." Pratt's slogan exemplifies Kenneth Burke's point that "the killing of something is the changing of it" (20).

The desire to change Indians is a response to difference as division. American Indians cannot join US society until they have been changed, the differences eradicated. The issue of difference confronting Native writers made one of their first rhetorical requirements the bridging of these differences and the establishment of an identification with white readers. As Kenneth Burke explains in *A Rhetoric of Motives*, "Identification is compensatory to division. If men were not apart from one another, there would be no need for the rhetorician to proclaim their unity" (22). It is in this sense that La Flesche, Zitkala-Sa, and many other Indian authors of the period were exemplary rhetoricians. Given the historical context for their writing, one primary objective of their discourse was to establish the human "consubtantiality" of Indian peoples. That is, these writers were required to establish a common ground of shared humanity with a non-Indian audience imbued with images of Indian savagery. Thus, the decision to write accounts that focus on the experiences of children serve the rhetorical function of establishing identification. All readers, regardless of race, have at one time been children. The writers can also assume that the majority of their readers will share a concern with the welfare of children and respond with condemnation to acts of cruelty inflicted upon children. La Flesche makes this point rather explicit in dedicating his book "To the Universal Boy" (v).

Of course in dedicating his book to an idealized "universal boy," La Flesche and the other authors of childhood memoirs who seem to emphasize the universal aspects of childhood can be seen as effacing the unique aspects of their respective indigenous cultures. Indeed, scholar Robert Warrior identifies the writing produced by the Indians of La Flesche and Zitkala-Sa's era as "Christian and secular assimilationist" (4). According to Warrior, "The purpose of these authors . . . was to gain sympathy from white audiences for the difficult, but to the authors necessary, process of becoming American citizens" (8). While Warrior effectively demonstrates that these authors were in favor of American Indians receiving a "white man's" education and that many advocated for US citizenship for Indian people, this does not necessarily lead to the conclusion that they were assimilationists in the ways in which educators such as Pratt understood the term. Rather, their texts reflect a rhetorical situation in which to even be heard they needed to establish a speaking position that would be recognized by a mainstream audience. Thus the acquisition of written literacy in English would enable Native writers to be read and their problems made part of the public discourse. The advocacy of citizenship would further confer recognition upon American Indians and entitle them to the same rights and protections afforded other citizens. This is not to deny the limitations of these positions, but to note that given the historical and rhetorical contexts, they are very understandable positions.

Because it is the first of the two accounts to be published, I begin with La Flesche's autobiography, *The Middle Five: Indian Schoolboys of the Omaha Tribe.* Published in 1900, *The Middle Five* reflects upon a particularly liminal period in recent American Indian history. Only ten years earlier, the massacre at Wounded Knee had effectively ended Indian military resistance to the United States' conquest of the continent. Indian communities had been forced onto reservations and increasing numbers of Indian children were being removed from their homes for education in boarding schools. In this period, for La Flesche and others of his generation, there were difficult choices to be made. Traditional Indian ways of living appeared less viable and engagement with Euro-American culture unavoidable. La Flesche's own father, E-sta'-ma-za or "Iron Eyes," had recognized the need for Omaha people to be educated in the ways of white people and had sent Francis to attend the Presbyterian missionary boarding school. In one sense, his father's decision paid off as La Flesche went on to obtain a law degree and compose a number of ethnographies on the Omaha and Ponca. His successes in mainstream terms might render understandable La Flesche's promotion of the type of education he received at the boarding school. Indeed, among La Flesche's family his sister Susette Tibbles would also become a published author as well as a leading lecturer on behalf of Indian rights. Another sister, Dr. Susan Picotte, is considered to be the first Native American woman to earn a degree in medicine. Nevertheless, almost in spite of these successes, La Flesche's autobiography, read rhetorically, is not an endorsement of the boarding school. While it is not a polemic indictment, his childhood memoir develops a subtle yet effective and ironic critique, not only against the pedagogical practices of the boarding schools but more importantly against the fundamental assumptions about race and culture that underlie those practices.

I identify La Flesche's rhetoric as subtle and discreet in that he does not write a vitriolic assault upon the boarding school and the missionary system. This subtlety may reflect that his overall memory of the experience was not negative. It may also be that a rhetorical concern with audience explains La Flesche's temperate account. At the time of the book's publication, he was an employee of the American Bureau of Ethnography, and he may not have wished to alienate his white employers and co-workers. He may also have wished to avoid appearing ungrateful for the education that enabled his later successes in the white world.

Regardless of the precise explanation, La Flesche's subtlety recently led Michael Coleman to write, in his study *American Indian Children at School, 1850–1930*, "I was disappointed in La Flesche the pupil. He should have resisted the missionary contempt for the Omaha culture characteristic of these decades of assimilationist education" (ix). Ignoring the question of whether it is reasonable or fair to expect a child to "resist" the adult missionary teachers, I want to show how Coleman's observation misses the subtle but frequent ironic critiques of the "missionary contempt" that the adult La Flesche has rhetorically sutured into his narrative.

From the first pages of his preface, La Flesche assumes an ironic stance toward the civilizing discourse. In explaining how the names of the children were changed in part because "the aboriginal names were considered heathenish, and . . . should be obliterated," he adds this reminder: "No less heathenish in their origin were the English substitutes, but the loss of their original meaning and significance through long usage had rendered them fit to continue as appellations for civilized folk" (xvii). In this passage, La Flesche highlights the unintended irony of the missionaries' intentions in changing the children's names. La Flesche assumes the role of instructor to remind readers of the historicity of those "Christian" names and Christianity itself. In the scope of human existence, Christianity remains a fairly recent development, and the supposedly Christian names have pagan roots that predate Christianity. In essence, the missionaries' efforts to "obliterate" signs of heathenism were in effect replacing one heathen sign with another.

A few pages later, La Flesche comments upon the language used by the children at the school. Whereas the children's presence at the school was designed to acculturate them through exposure to a superior civilized people, in fact the language of the Indian children was corrupted by the "slang and bad grammar picked up from uneducated white persons employed at the school" (xviii). La Flesche observes that "Oddities of speech, profanity, localisms, and slang were unknown in the Omaha language, so when such expressions fell upon the ears of these lads they innocently learned and used them without the slightest suspicion that there could be bad as well as good English" (xviii). The boarding school, built to civilize and Christianize, has had the ironically unintended effect of instructing the children in decidedly "uncivilized" uses of language.

In the narrative itself, La Flesche's masterstroke is to use the voices of the young schoolboys to mimic the discourse of civilization. One of the first examples of this "signifying" involves a retelling of one of the most popular American national origin stories. In La Flesche's work, a version of American history is told "sincerely" by the one of the boys to comic effect. This rendering makes the familiar story strange and undermines its heroic authority. In the scene, one of the Omaha boys asks, "Why don't the 'Mericans have a king?" Another boy responds,

> They had one . . . but they didn't like him because he put a terrible big tax on tea. The 'Mericans are awfully fond of tea, and when they saw they'd have to pay the trader and the king, too, for their tea, they got mad; and one night, when everybody was asleep, they painted up like wild Indians, and they got into a boat and paddled out to the tea ship and climbed in. They hollered and yelled like everything, and scared everybody; then they spilted the tea into the ocean. . . . Then the 'Mericans made General George Washington their president because he couldn't tell a lie. (51)

In this retelling of a patriotic national narrative, La Flesche reduces it to the level of a comic story, emphasizing the slapstick imagery of our great patriots howling like "wild Indians" at the Boston Tea Party. There is a further irony. Not only is the story reduced from authoritative epic to comedy, but the patriots' glorious deeds are performed in imitation of the very "Indian" manners the boys are being urged to shun. In La Flesche's hands, one of our cherished narratives of national identity becomes a comic cultural drag performance.

Throughout *The Middle Five*, La Flesche reveals a profound interest in the role of stories. Implicitly, the text reveals an understanding that the boys are being coerced into rejecting one system of cultural narrative and to assume the truth of a new system. At the missionary boarding school La Flesche attended, one of the primary goals was to supplant the children's Indian spiritual traditions with the Christian narrative. In the chapter "The Splinter, the Thorn, and the Rib," La Flesche provides an ironic retelling of a Christian myth in order to contest its claims to ultimate truth.

The chapter begins with a description of young Frank (La Flesche the child) having a thorn removed from his foot by one of his aunts. La Flesche uses this incident to call into question another assumption of Western civilization, superior hygiene and medical knowledge. As she removes the thorn from his foot, his aunt remarks on the dirty bandage covering the wound. When Frank informs her it contains pig fat she asks, "Why did they put pig-fat on your toe; who put it on? Bah it's nasty!" Frank replies, "The white woman who takes care of the children, she put it on to draw the splinter out." His aunt responds,

> "To draw the splinter out!" . . . Then she tossed up her fine head, gave shouts of laughter, and said . . . "Oh this is funny! This is funny! Your White-chests might as well hitch a bit of pig-fat to their wagon and expect it to draw a load up the hill! . . . If this white woman takes as much care of the other children as she has of you,—I'm sorry for them. No children of mine should be placed under her care." (55)

The laughing of La Flesche's aunt becomes ironic, even sarcastic, laughter at white culture's claims to superior medical knowledge and hygiene. And his aunt's suggestion that the White-chests hitch the fat to a wagon can further be read as accusation of a superstitious white belief that the pig fat has "magical" properties to draw the thorn out. As an ethnographer employed by the American Bureau of Ethnography, La Flesche is well aware that many Americans regarded Indian spiritual and healing rituals as foolish pagan superstitions; the voice of his aunt provides an ironic reversal of that belief.

The removal of the thorn leads to one of the other boy telling an Omaha story of how first woman was created from a thorn. As the story advances, some of the boys compare it with the Biblical story of Eve's creation from Adam's rib. This in turn leads to a humorous rendition of Eve's temptation:

> "Well, one morning she [Eve] went down to the creek to swim, and just as she was going to step into the water . . . she saw a snake in the tree with a man's head on, and the snake—" "It wasn't a snake," interrupted Warren; "it was the serpent. . . ." "Well, it's the same thing,—the snake and the serpent is the same thing." "No they're not. The serpent is the kind that's poisonous . . . and the snake is like those that don't poison.". .

> "Well, the serpent was Satan, and Sa—" "how can Satan be a serpent and a snake?" asked Lester. "First you said it was a snake; then you said it was a serpent; now you say it was Satan!". . . "Well, the Devil spoke to Eve and said—" "Your snake has turned into a devil now," sneered Edwin. (61–62)

The scene ends with all the boys laughing derisively at the story. The teller of the story, Brush, who in the narrative has most fully embraced the ideology of the school, mutters "There's no use talking to you boys" (63). In this scenario, La Flesche has taken one of Western culture's most sacred texts and rendered it comic. The apparently naive questioning of the boys exposes the contradictions in the story, denies its realism, and ultimately makes it the subject of mocking laughter. It is laughter of the kind theorist Mikhail Bakhtin terms "Rabelaisian laughter . . . [which] destroys traditional connections and idealized strata . . . [and] brings out the . . . connections between things that people otherwise seek to keep separate" (170). The boys' laughter subverts the cultural authority of the Christian story; simultaneously, La Flesche has brought the Christian narrative into intimate proximity with the Omaha story of first woman, in effect bringing together what the missionaries strove to separate.

These examples from La Flesche's text indicate his rhetorical sophistication in engaging and ironically undermining the discourse of civilization. La Flesche's narrative ends on a powerful appeal to pathos that is rich in symbolism and irony. Throughout La Flesche's account, Brush, the most assimilation identified of the boys, has been young Francis's best friend. It has been Brush who urges the boys to obey the headmaster of the school, who has memorized the Bible stories, and who plans to become a Christian preacher. Thus, it is with a rich and sad poignancy that the story ends with Brush's death. While La Flesche may not have intended any irony with this ending, one effect of the conclusion is to suggest that the way of life is not the assimilationist way embraced by Brush. His death serves as a cautionary note to readers wondering what paths and policies will be best for Indians.

The irony of Zitkala-Sa's text varies somewhat from that of La Flesche. An activist who would later champion Indian rights, Zitkala-Sa constructs her narratives with less of the humor that marks La Flesche's autobiography. Her rhetoric appeals more to pathos, pity, and indignation for the abuses and isolation she experienced first as a student and later a teacher in Indian boarding schools. This is not to say that her engagement with the discourse of civilization lacks subtlety. For instance, in the concluding chapter of her book "Impressions of an Indian Childhood," she tells of how she was persuaded by the missionaries to come east with them to attend their boarding school. The image that tantalizes and tempts young Zitkala-Sa into accepting is of "the great tree where grew red, red apples; and how we could reach out our hands and pick all the red apples we could eat. I had never seen apple trees. . . . [A]nd when I heard of the orchards of the East, I was eager to roam among them" (41–42). For irony to function, one requirement is a shared knowledge. In this case it is knowledge of the apple as the symbolic fruit of temptation, knowledge that Zitkala-Sa comes to learn from her boarding school education. It is also a symbol she can trust her audience to be familiar with. In her account, however, the tempting apple is held ironically in the hands of the missionaries who come to save her. In her story, the Christian missionaries occupy the slot of Satan. And like Eve, Zitkala-Sa's acquisition of knowledge will result in alienation, cruelty, and profound loneliness. Her life among her people and with her mother she will come to regard nostalgically as a prelapsarian paradise. She goes East to eat of the tree of knowledge, but it exacts a heavy price.

Because one of the shared aims of most of the boarding schools in the nineteenth century was the Christian conversion of the Indian children, it should come as no surprise that both La Flesche and Zitkala-Sa engage the Christian narrative. Like La Flesche, Zitkala-Sa ironizes the discourse of civilization in what amounts to a performance of linguistic ventriloquism. In her discussion of Satan, Zitkala-Sa appropriates the voice of ethnographic authority. She writes, "Among the old legends the old warriors used to tell me were many stories of evil spirits. But I was taught to fear them no more than those who walked about in material guise. I never knew there was an insolent chieftain among the bad spirits who dared to array his forces against the Great Spirit, until I heard this white man's legend from a paleface woman" (62). Like La Flesche, she has brought the Christian narrative into proximity of her Lakota traditions, and she actually conflates the narrative traditions by identifying Satan as an enemy of the Lakota Great Spirit. She also undermines the absolute truth claims of the Christian narrative by referring to it as a "white man's legend."

Lest we overlook the ironic edge of this use of the term "legend," a bit later in the story she directly challenges the truth claims of Christianity. The scene is the deathbed of one of her Indian schoolmates. "Among the bedclothes I saw the open pages of the white man's Bible. The dying Indian girl talked disconnectedly of Jesus the Christ. . . . I grew bitter. . . . I blamed the hard-working, well-meaning, ignorant woman who was inculcating in our hearts her superstitious ideas" (67). The critique is sharp and direct. Yet underlying it is an ironic edge. For the "well-meaning woman" is symbolic of the so-called friends of the Indians who were instrumental in acquiring support for the boarding schools. Against the discourse of civilization, with its images of ignorant and superstitious Indians, Zitkala-Sa reverses the order, portraying the faithful Christian white woman as ignorant and superstitious. A bit later, after she has returned to her reservation, she will speak of wanting to burn the Bible, "which afforded me no help and was a perfect delusion to my mother" (73). Her critiques of Christianity serve to level the hierarchy between Western European beliefs and indigenous belief and undermine "the evangelical foundation" of the boarding school education (Bernardin 217).

Zitkala-Sa's narrative holds additional interest because not only did she receive the boarding school education designed to expunge her Indian identity, she went on to become an agent of this education as a teacher at Pratt's Carlisle boarding school. In her essay "An Indian Teacher Among Indians," Zitkala-Sa launches a final thrust at the entire structure of boarding school education and its supporting ideology. In this essay, she negotiates a delicate balance between her desire to expose the corruption she witnesses among those who assume the role of teachers and her need to maintain an audience of white readers who have supported the very system that employs these teachers. She describes one teacher as "an opium eater"; another she accuses of torturing an "ambitious Indian youth." However, she then aligns herself with her non-Indian readers by noting how she was "nettled by this sly cunning of the workmen who hookwinked *[sic]* the Indian's pale Father at Washington" (95–96). The implication is that Zitkala-sa's readers are not the "men of small capacity . . . the dwarfs" who prey upon the system of Indian education. In her stance as witness, Zitkala-Sa calls upon her non-Indian readers to cleanse a system that serves the self-interests of whites at the expense of Indian students.

Ultimately, in this essay, her indignation overcomes any concern for the sensibilities of her white audience. Perhaps believing that the instances of abuse she has recounted will justify her anger in the eyes of her readers, she concludes by calling into question the assumptions of white "civilization's" superiority: "I remember how, from morning till evening, many specimens of civilized peoples visited the Indian school. The city folks with canes and eyeglasses, the countrymen with sunburnt cheeks and clumsy feet forgot their relative social ranks in an ignorant curiosity. Both sorts of these Christian palefaces were . . . astounded at seeing the children of savage warriors so docile and industrious" (98).

The final reference to "children of savage warriors" must, I think be taken ironically. Given her critique of the palefaces' "ignorant curiosity" and weighed against her other respectful accounts of her elders, it seems hardly possible that she really regards the parents of the children of the school as "savage warriors." Rather, this is a case of what Wayne Booth terms "stable irony" (19), leaving little doubt that her ironic edge is directed at the "whiter visitors [who were] . . . well satisfied they were educating the children of the red man!" (98). And in case any doubt lingers of her ironic intent, she closes by observing, "But few [white visitors] there are who have paused to question whether real life or long-lasting death lies beneath this semblance of civilization" (99). Zitkala-Sa's conclusion reverses the assumption of Indian lack that guided the educational system of the boarding schools and suggests that it is white culture and values that lack the ingredients needed for growth and progress.

While contemporary readers such as Robert Warrior have characterized Zitkala-Sa's writing as part "the integrationist legacy of post-Wounded Knee existence" (7), it is crucial to note the delicate rhetorical context she negotiated. Warrior notes her staunch opposition to the spiritual use of peyote by American Indians as an example of her assimilationist leanings (10). Yet I would argue that the problem in terms of understanding figures such as Zitkala-Sa and La Flesche arises from a neglect of the specific historical situation from which their writings emerge. Both writers were thrust into educational systems over which they had no control. To label either of these writers as "assimilationist" reduces the complexity of what they actually wrote. Evidence that Zitkala-Sa's essays and stories were not seen as forwarding the agenda of many white policy makers of her time can be found in the following response published in the Carlisle school's newspaper: "By this course she injures herself and harms the educational work in progress for the race from which she sprang. In a list of educated Indians whom we have in mind, some of whom have reached higher altitudes than Zitkalasa *[sic]*, we know no other case of such profound morbidness" (qtd. in Fisher viii). Clearly, the writer of this review did not see the rhetoric of Zitkala-Sa's fiction supporting their assimilationist educational goals. Yet these seemingly contradictory appraisals of Zitkala-Sa's point of view highlight the very complexity of the times she, La Flesche, and other Indian writers inhabited. In many ways they were archetypal border subjects. Pulled from indigenous communities and traditions and thrust into indoctrination programs, prepared to live in a white culture that did not want them, it should come as no surprise if their rhetorical stances appear at times paradoxical or inconsistent.

From a rhetorical perspective, both writers display a remarkable understanding of the values of their audiences. Both employ the sentimental literary tropes familiar to readers in the late nineteenth century. It is the knowledge and mastery of the discourse of the dominant culture—knowledge of United States history and heroic narratives, knowledge of the Bible—that enables both writers to employ irony in ways that are by turns razor sharp and sledgehammer blunt in their critiques. Theorist Linda Hutcheon describes this use of irony as one "that functions to repeat and yet revise white discourses." It is an irony that "deconstructs and decenters" authority (31–32). As members of marginalized and colonized communities, both writers demonstrate great rhetorical effectiveness in crafting documents that forge an identification with the values of their white readers. The need for this identification has been created by nearly five hundred years of dividing America's indigenous peoples from Europeans and Euro-Americans and by the establishment of policies that further solidify these divisions. Indeed, the perception of division is the "characteristic invitation to rhetoric" (Burke 25). Both La Flesche and Zitkala-Sa respond to this invitation. Their stories of childhood, their appeals to sentimentality, and their displayed understanding of their audience function to create the identification needed for effective communication. Yet neither ends with the goal of identification. Both employ a sophisticated irony to critique and persuade their readers of the injustices perpetuated in the name of education.

With an irony that ranges from the almost unnoticeable to the biting edge of sarcasm, both La Flesche and Zitakala-Sa rhetorically engage the question of what lies beneath this discourse of civilization. As important as these narratives are for understanding the educational histories of Native Americans, the lessons and insights they offer have implications that extend beyond their local contexts. For all teachers, especially teachers of writing—a teaching of literacy—it behooves us to consider how the lessons offered by La Flesche and Zitkala-Sa are not just artifacts out of history. We need to consider the ways, in an era of standards and standardized assessments of learning, that we may unconsciously position our students as uncivilized "savages." And we need to reflect on the extent to which our own pedagogical practices are unintentionally coercive as we seek to assimilate students to the scholarly community via an acquisition of literacy in academic discourse.

Works Cited

Adams, Evelyn C. *American Indian Education*. New York: King's Crown P, 1946.

Berkhofer, Robert F., Jr. *The White Man's Indian*. New York: Vintage, 1978.

Bernardin, Susan. "The Lessons of a Sentimental Education: Zitkala-Sa's Autobiographical Narratives." *Western American Literature* 3 (1997): 212–38.

Booth, Wayne. *The Rhetoric of Irony*. Chicago: U of Chicago P, 1974.

Burke, Kenneth. *A Rhetoric of Motives*. 1952. Berkeley: U of California P, 1969.

Coleman, Michael C. *American Indian Children at School, 1850–1930*. Jackson: UP of Mississippi, 1993.

Fisher, Dexter. Foreword to *American Indian Stories*, by Zitkala-Sa. Lincoln: U of Nebraska P, 1985. v–xx.

Greenblatt, Stephen. *Marvelous Possessions: The Wonder of the New World*. Chicago: U of Chicago P, 1991.

Hutcheon, Linda. *Irony's Edge: The Theory and Politics of Irony*. London: Routledge, 1994.

La Flesche, Francis. *The Middle Five: Indian Schoolboys of the Omaha Tribe*. 1900. Reprint, Lincoln: U of Nebraska P, 1978.

Lomawaima, K. Tsianina. *They Called it Prairie Light: The Story of Chilocco Indian School.* Lincoln: U of Nebraska P, 1994.

Lyons, Scott Richard. "The Incorporation of the Indian Body: Peyotism and the Pan-Indian Public, 1911–23." *Rhetoric, the Polis, and the Global Village: Selected Papers from the 1998 Thirtieth Anniversary Rhetoric Society of America Conference*. Ed. C. Jan Swearingen. Mahwah, NJ: Lawrence Erlbaum Associates, 1999. 147–53.

Noriega, Jorge. "American Indian Education in the United States: Indoctrination for Subordination to Colonialism." *The State of Native America*. Ed. M. Annette Jaimes. Boston: South End P, 1992. 371–402.

Warrior, Robert. *Tribal Secrets: Recovering American Indian Intellectual Traditions*. Minneapolis: U of Minnesota P, 1995.

Zitkala-Sa. *American Indian Stories*. 1921. Reprint, Lincoln: U of Nebraska P, 1985.

SUN DANCE BEHIND BARS

THE RHETORIC OF LEONARD PELTIER'S PRISON WRITINGS

✦

Janna Knittel

LEONARD PELTIER has been in prison for just under thirty years. Accused of killing two FBI agents during a confrontation at Wounded Knee, South Dakota, in 1973, Peltier has argued for his innocence. His supporters say that he is a political prisoner, held for upholding Native rights. Conversely, more recent researchers into the American Indian Movement (AIM) and the death of activist Anna Mae Pictou Aquash have sketched AIM's own politics as self-aggrandizing and masculinist,[1] and some historians suggest that Peltier's importance as a political figure has been exaggerated.[2] Amid these conflicting views, Peltier has published *Prison Writings: My Life Is My Sundance* (1999), discussing his life story, his prison sentence and trials, and Native activism.

This article seeks neither to lionize nor to vilify Leonard Peltier the man, but to investigate the rhetoric of those prison writings. Such an investigation certainly cannot claim to be apolitical or divorced from history, and so acknowledgement of Peltier's case and discussion of historical incidents are vital. Ultimately, placing *Prison Writings* within the larger body of Native literature is the task at hand. While some of Peltier's strategies are similar to the strategies employed by the American Indian Movement, this article emphasizes the rhetorical variety Peltier employs, including historical parallels, metaphorical references to the Lakota Sun Dance ceremony, and features of oral storytelling.

Introduction to Peltier's Case

The events surrounding Peltier's arrest are complex. What follows is a very brief overview of incidents that led up to his accusation of murder.

These incidents include a demonstration at Wounded Knee, South Dakota, in 1973 by American Indian Movement activists. The site was chosen to commemorate the 1890 massacre of Big Foot's band by the United States cavalry, an event notorious in Native history for the deaths of unarmed elders, women, and children. The massacre has been described as the result of "the unwarranted panic of an Indian agent, caused by the ghost dances" (Matthiessen 21); the Ghost Dance ritual was part of the political and spiritual revival that swept multiple tribes in response to the quality of life on reservations. "Wounded Knee II" was organized to protest a history of broken treaties and injustices against Native peoples of North America. The federal government responded with a military assault.

The Federal Bureau of Investigation (FBI) spent the next three years harassing AIM and traditional Lakotas on the Pine Ridge Reservation. The bureau also collaborated with tribal chairperson Dick Wilson and his followers, known as Guardians of the Oglala Nation, or GOONs. Wilson and his GOONs favored ceding land for uranium mining on the reservation, while AIM members and traditional Lakotas argued in favor of retaining tribal land. The tensions and violence mounted, "resulting in 66 documented violent deaths and 200 murders overall" (Messerschmidt xix). The FBI investigated and decided that "paramilitary assault" was necessary to overcome AIM and its supporters (xix).

On June 26, 1975, while AIM members camped on private property owned by a couple named Jumping Bull, having been asked there for protection from the GOONs, two FBI agents, Jack Coler and Ronald Williams, entered the property in pursuit of a Native man believed to have stolen a pair of boots. A shootout ensued between the AIM members defending the Jumping Bull property and the two agents. In the end, the agents were dead, shot at close range. The alleged thief was never found, but in the rain of bullets a Native man, Joe Stuntz, was also killed.

Whether or not Peltier is innocent, the injustices related to these events are many. One is that "Four Indians were charged with the murders of the FBI agents. No one has ever been charged with the murder of Joe Stuntz" (Sanchez, Stuckey, and Morris 41). In addition, though the original prosecutor admitted in 1985 that the government does not know who killed the two agents (Clark xx), Leonard Peltier has remained in prison. Peltier himself has called for retrials based on new evidence, yet each time the evidence was claimed by the court to be insufficient. As Joseph C. Hogan III argues, the rhetoric of justice has been reversed in Peltier's case, for "Due to stringent standards and the ease with which crucial evidence may be concealed,

Leonard Peltier has become one of the victims of a sublegal system where citizens are functionally guilty until proven innocent" (934). The lives of the two agents who died should not be minimized. However, as Peter Matthiessen has shown in his extensive study of the case, the evidence leveled against Peltier remains dubious. Peltier's supporters believe that he is a political prisoner rather than a murderer, held as an example to anyone who would threaten to assert the rights of Native people.

How someone like Peltier could be imprisoned and how a group like AIM—who insist that their primary mission is spiritual revival[3] and who do not intervene in tribal affairs unless invited[4]—could be treated as disgruntled militants becomes clear when one studies the rhetoric of the opposition. In their article "Rhetorical Exclusion: The Government's Case Against American Indian Activists, AIM, and Leonard Peltier," John Sanchez, Mary E. Stuckey, and Richard Morris analyze the rhetoric employed by US politicians, government agents, judicial figures, and the media whenever they confront dissidents:

> [P]rotectors of the status quo come to rely upon a variety of communicative tactics designed to foreclose debate without appearing to engage in undemocratic actions. One such tactic is "rhetorical exclusion," a rhetorical strategy that defines those who seek inclusion into the larger polity on their own terms as inherently destructive of that polity, questioning the motives of those who challenge governmental power, and a presumption that those involved in such challenges are inherently guilty of crimes against the polity. (28)

Sanchez, Stuckey, and Morris add the following with regard to Leonard Peltier and AIM:

> Because of their unique legal, cultural, and political status, Indian challenges are well-suited to expose the masks of government and thus represent a particularly potent threat to that government. In the social context of the 1960s and 1970s, the nature and extent of that threat was clear to all participants. The government's response to this threat at that time is thus a particularly good example of rhetorical exclusion. (29)

The authors describe specific features of rhetorical exclusion and pinpoint uses of it in the words of politicians and press releases. They argue convincingly that "Alterity becomes equivalent to malevolence" (30), meaning that "efforts aimed at the protection of indigenous traditions, cultures, religions, values, sovereignty, and land are 'subversive' by definition because those efforts run counter to the perpetuation of a single, monolithic hegemony" (30). They conclude, "The insinuation here is that AIM emerged not as an effort to address serious grievances, including those conditions that encourage the incarceration of Indian people, but as a matter of felonious intent. Such insinuations fit with the exclusionist conclusion that Indians who resist assimilation must be guilty of something" (32).

In pointing out the occasional collaboration between AIM members and members of other ethnic protest groups, they say that exclusionist rhetoric "leads not to the conclusion that individuals and organizations confronting similar situations sometimes momentarily coalesce, but to the inevitable conclusion that malevolent people congregate to conspire" (33). Because of this assumed malevolence, "The words and deeds of Indian activists cannot be believed" (33).

These assumptions of guilt and of lying on the part of activists is important to Peltier's *Prison Writings* as he remains aware of his opposition's rhetoric and responds with a more inclusive rhetoric, a rhetoric that invites his readers to understand and even participate in his story.

Peltier's Rhetoric and Responses to Rhetorical Exclusion

Peltier responds to such rhetorical exclusion in *Prison Writings*. For instance, his name for the exclusionist notion that "Indians who resist assimilation must be guilty of something" is "Aboriginal Sin" (15). He states many times, in multiple ways, that his only crime is in being Indian.[5] Peltier says that "when you grow up Indian, you don't have to become a criminal, you already *are* a criminal. You never know innocence" (67, original emphasis). Peltier's statement is not hyperbolic. Recall the statement made by Sanchez, Stuckey, and Morris, that "alterity becomes equivalent to malevolence" (30) and it becomes clear that Peltier is well aware of the rhetorical strategies used by his opposition. The punishment for being Indian began for Peltier in a Bureau of Indian Affairs (BIA) boarding school in Wahpeton, North Dakota. In reference to being punished for speaking Lakota, Peltier says, "you could say that the first infraction in my criminal career was speaking my own language. There's an act of violence for you!" (78).

Peltier's first arrest was after watching a Sun Dance with some friends. The charge was drunkenness, a claim Peltier states was untrue. This Sun Dance occurred in 1958, when ritual piercing was still illegal. According to Peltier,

> [the BIA police] were afraid to arrest the Sun Dancers, who would surely have put up a fight, but we young teenagers were there, and we were Indian, so why not arrest us? They did. Here I was, not yet fifteen, and already I was getting firsthand experience in government-fabricated criminal charges and false imprisonment. I began to realize that my real crime was simply being who I was—an Indian. (83–84)

In response to such false charges, Peltier turns to the reasons for the violence on the Pine Ridge Reservation, making clear that AIM was at Pine Ridge not only to protect Lakota traditionals from the violence of the FBI and the GOONs, but also to show resistance to uranium mining on the reservation:

> I have no doubt whatsoever that the real motivation behind both Wounded Knee II and the Oglala firefight, and much of the turmoil throughout Indian Country since the early 1970s, was—and is—the mining companies' desire to muffle AIM and all traditional Indian people, who sought—and still seek—to protect the land, water, and air from their thefts and depredations. In this sad and tragic era we live in, to come to the defense of Mother Earth is to be branded a criminal. (117)

Thus, fighting against corporations and for the environment create additional categories of Aboriginal Sin.

Peltier concludes his original "Pre-Sentencing Statement," included in *Prison Writings*, with the assertion that "The only thing I'm guilty of, and which I was convicted for, was being of Chippewa and Sioux blood—and for believing in our sacred religion" (232). The importance of traditional religion to Peltier is made clear, as I will show below, in discussions of the Sun Dance.

While in many places Peltier claims the crime of Aboriginal Sin, in his writing he also attests to his innocence of the crime of killing two FBI agents. The rhetoric of innocence is more difficult to assess than Aboriginal Sin. The reader expects Peltier to assert his innocence and must ask if such rhetoric can ever be believable, or if it merely folds back on itself, calling attention to Peltier's incarceration and the fact that somebody has determined that he is guilty. As he says, "I suppose every man proclaims himself innocent, whether innocent or not" (20). Peltier makes claims for his innocence in a variety of ways, for instance, taking the rhetorical stance of speaking to the families of Coler and Williams: "I state to you absolutely that, if I could possibly have prevented what happened that day, your menfolk would not have died. I would have died myself before knowingly permitting what happened to happen. And I certainly never pulled the trigger that did it. May the Creator strike me dead this moment if I lie" (15). He swears he is innocent as many individuals would similarly swear, but swearing before the Native Creator rather than the Judeo-Christian God; he does not capitulate entirely to a judicial system that acknowledges only the latter.

He claims shock as his reaction to the FBI agents' deaths, and this is certainly believable given his emphasis on Aboriginal Sin, that the deaths of government agents at the hands of dissident Indians would certainly be punished, and harshly:

> After a while, when we realized that the drivers of the two shiny cars were apparently already dead, slouched beside their vehicles in pools of blood, and that they weren't GOONs but FBI men, we could only look at each other in shocked disbelief. We each knew what that stunned and vacant look in the others' eyes meant. If those agents were dead, we—those of us Indians at the Jumping Bull property that day, whether man, woman, or child—were as good as dead, too. Even if they'd only been injured, we were goners. We knew we wouldn't be taken alive even if we tried to surrender. (126)

Ultimately, Peltier asserts, he has been imprisoned because somebody had to be: "If the feds couldn't get the real killer, they were damn sure going to get me. And they did" (162). Even when he retells the story of an attempt to escape prison, he asserts, "I've never killed anyone and I never will" (167), speaking as a peaceful activist rather than the murderer he knows his opposition perceives him to be. Acknowledging how powerful rhetoric can be, he shows how little it would take to free him: "So simple an act by the courts as changing my 'consecutive' sentences to 'concurrent' sentences would give me my freedom and return to me at least a fraction of my life, if only my old age" (171).

Historical Analogies

According to Elizabeth Rich, who analyzes the rhetoric of the slogan "Remember Wounded Knee" developed by AIM, reference to history has been a useful tool for Native activism:

> *Wounded Knee*, then, is a metonymy in which the massacre of 1890 stands for more than one event, the basis for a host of stories, values, and historical characters. It links the gold rush in the Black Hills of South Dakota, which gave rise to the conflict that prompted both the signing and later abrogation of the Black Hills treaty of 1868, and the effort by the U.S. government to allow corporations to mine for uranium in the Black Hills in the early 1970s. . . . AIM's metonymic narrative not only allowed the 1970s activists to shed light on past injustices but also to direct contemporary acts of resistance, which is evident in AIM's action at Wounded Knee on the Pine Ridge Reservation. (78)

Furthermore, "The invention of *Wounded Knee*," says Rich, referring specifically to the trope, "marks a new effort to organize discursively as well as politically" for Native people (71). The strength of this trope rests on the fact that "AIM's focus on *Wounded Knee* also provides access to documented American Indian resistance to colonization" (74).

A similar tactic, one that Peltier and AIM use, is making historical parallels. These parallels can be helpful for readers unfamiliar with the issues facing Native peoples today, but such parallels have their limits. The most common references Peltier makes are to the Holocaust of World War II and the US war in Vietnam.

Peltier grew up in the Eisenhower era and in the fear of the government terminating the reservations and relocating Indians to the cities. He calls attention to the political language of that era:

> Those suddenly became the most important, the most feared, words in our vocabulary: "termination" and "relocation." I can think of few words more sinister in the English language, at least to Indian people. I guess the Jews of Europe must have felt that way about Nazi words like "final solution" and "resettlement in the East." To us, those words were an assault on our very existence as a people, an attempt to eradicate us. (80)

Peltier also sets up this comparison earlier in the book by describing the massacre at Wounded Knee in December of 1890 as a "holocaust" (50).

Comparisons of any situation to the Holocaust can seem hyperbolic at best, inflammatory at their worst. However, Peltier's analogy is apt in significant ways. In recounting the Eisenhower era he shows how abstract language can veil more ominous intentions. Adolf Hitler based his own expansionist politics on "Lebensraum," simply meaning "living space"; this concept sounds uncannily similar to the United States notion of Manifest Destiny, or westward expansion, which justified eradication of indigenous people.

To describe how the FBI and the GOONs' zeal developed, Peltier compares the manhunt on Pine Ridge to "a Vietnam-style search-and-destroy operation" (133), thereby aligning his opposition's cause with what has become known in popular culture as an unjust and fruitless war. He also links the Vietnam War and the Holocaust at one point, arguing for a memorial wall similar to the Vietnam Veterans Memorial:

> I would like to see a red stone wall the like black stone wall of the Vietnam War Memorial, which I've only seen in pictures. Yes, right there on the Mall in Washington, D.C. And on that red stone wall—pigmented with the living blood of our people (and I would happily be the first to donate that blood)—would be the names of all the Indians who ever died for being Indian. It would be hundreds of times longer than the Vietnam Memorial, which celebrates the deaths of fewer than sixty thousand brave lost souls. The number of our brave lost souls reaches into the many millions, and every one of them remains unquiet until this day. Just as effective might be a Holocaust Museum to the American Indian to recall the voices of those who were slaughtered. (21)

This passage is effective in that it gives the reader a visual image of a wall that would overshadow the Vietnam Veterans Memorial because of the number of Native people who have died since European contact. Further, the length of this wall visually connects that early contact to the continuing struggles in which Native people continue to die. On the other hand, the image of this wall clashes with the alternative monument, the proposed "Holocaust Museum to the American Indian." If we can establish the relationship between the Holocaust and federal Indian policy in the United States, and between government military action on Pine Ridge to the Vietnam War, what, if anything, connects the Holocaust and Vietnam? Conflating different historical phenomena can be problematic when it elides differences between historical conflicts and cultures. Rich mentions in her study of the phrase "Remember Wounded Knee" that cultural critics must "understand how cultural difference as well as cultural hegemony come into play" (77), and that "while the *Wounded Knee* metonymy recovers the 1890 events and important Lakota values, it also obscures an important Lakota value that was evident in the Ghost Dance Movement, which was adaptability. The Lakota adapted spiritual beliefs to suit a political aim" (79–80). This adaptability is lost when contemporary activists try to fix too rigid or specific meanings on historical events.

The value of linking federal Indian policy to the Holocaust is that it reveals genocide to be, not an anomaly in human history, but instead, something humans face every day. Genocide is not something that happened only in the past, but continues to happen around the world, in places as far apart as El Salvador and Rwanda. Such linking must be problematized, however. The word "holocaust" means destruction by fire and thus specifically refers to the use of gas ovens in exterminating Jews and others in World War II. To apply the word "holocaust" to federal Indian policy, or to any instance of genocide, for that matter, erases the cultural specificity of the Holocaust and may desensitize us to other forms of human rights abuses. This desensitization is precisely the reason calling an event a holocaust sounds hyperbolic in the first place.

The fact that Peltier calls attention to the words "termination" and "relocation," as mentioned earlier in this section, overlaps with another technique that demonstrates Peltier's interest in the power of language. Peltier redefines and refines familiar words and phrases in order to drive home his arguments. In the following example, he explains how views of Native activism have been skewed by those in power: "When the oppressors succeed with their illegal thefts and depredations, it's called colonialism. When their efforts to colonize indigenous peoples are met with resistance or anything but abject surrender, it's called war. When the colonized peoples attempt to resist their oppression and defend themselves, we're called criminals" (44). In a similar vein, he retells the events of the 1890 massacre of Big Foot's Band of Lakota at Wounded Knee Creek in South Dakota, in which elders, women, and children counted among the dead: "Afterward, the proud butchers of the Seventh Cavalry were awarded twenty-six Medals of Honor for their heroics. White man's history books still call it a 'battle,' as if to give some dignity to what had none. It was a slaughter, pure and simple" (53).

Near the end of his book, Peltier makes a striking statement in a section titled "A Message to Humanity." Writing about the ways that relations between Native and non-Native people have caused both groups suffering, he states, "To heal we will have to come to the realization that we are *all* under a life sentence together . . . and there's no chance for parole" (209, original emphasis). This use of metonymy signifies in multiple ways. Humans are all under a "life sentence" together if we consider the fact that we have but one planet to share. If Earth is our collective prison, then Peltier makes a case for conservation of the Earth's natural resources, understanding between cultures, and forgiveness of the past, all in one sentence.

The Sun Dance as Rhetorical Strategy

The title of Peltier's book comes from the traditional Lakota religious rite the Sun Dance, which was once outlawed (along with all other spiritual practices) until freedom of religion was granted to Native people in 1978. In Lakota, the rite is *wiwanyag wachipi*, translated as "dance looking at the sun" (Brown 67). It is traditionally performed in early summer. The purposes of the Sun Dance are renewal and sacrifice.

In an early account of the practice, the Lakota elder Black Elk cites the importance of the rite to renewing the people. First, the practice came to the Lakota as "a new way of prayer" in a time of strife (Brown 68); secondly, "much strength would be given to the life of the nation" for each Sun Dance performed (Brown 100).

Luther Standing Bear, one of the first Lakota to write about Lakota culture in his own words, describes the element of sacrifice. The warriors sacrifice themselves for the good of all their people:

> During the winter if any member of the tribe became ill, perhaps a brother or a cousin would be brave enough to go to the medicine man and say, "I will sacrifice my body to the Wakan Tanka, or Big Holy, for the one who is sick." Or if the buffalo were beginning to get scarce, some one would sacrifice himself so that the tribe might have something to eat. (Standing Bear 113)

In preparation for the Sun Dance, the dancers purify themselves in the *inipi*, or sweat lodge. Respected people venture out to select the sacred cottonwood tree that the dancers will encircle. The dancers stare at the sun from sunrise to sunset, taking no food or water during the dance (Standing Bear 120). In the second phase of the Sun Dance, men young and old have the flesh of their breasts pierced. Leather thongs tied to the piercing sticks that remain in the breast are then tied to the cottonwood pole or, sometimes, to a buffalo skull. The dancers must dance, straining against the thongs, until the flesh tears and they break free.

Peltier refers to the Sun Dance throughout his book and these references function in several ways. The Sun Dance to which he refers is sometimes literal, because he himself has danced in this sacred dance, the first time in 1973. He had wanted to participate ever since secretly observing a Sun Dance as a child. The Sun Dance functions as a literal reference as well when Peltier uses it to describe the circumstances of his imprisonment: he has sacrificed freedom, comfort, health, and the presence of his children and grandchildren during his stay in Leavenworth. The reward for such a sacrifice is an indirect one, the attention his case has brought to Native people's issues. As a modern warrior who no longer has the option of hunting buffalo to feed his people or of counting coup[6] on his enemies, Peltier had to find a new meaning for the Sun Dance. For him, that meaning was in his growing political activism. He describes his sacrifice thus: "Now I had given not just my time and my effort and my dedication to my People's cause; I had given my flesh" (109).

Peltier describes another purpose of the Sun Dance that has benefited him in prison: "Sun Dance is our religion, our strength. We take great pride in that strength, which enables us to resist pain, torture, any trial rather than betray the People. That's why, in the past, when the enemy tortured us with knives, bullwhips, even fire, we were able to withstand the pain. That strength still exists among us" (11). Part of the commitment a participant makes is to remember the pain of the Sun Dance as he goes through life's difficulties, and Peltier claims, "So Sun Dance made even prison life sustainable for me" (12).

Peltier suffers from the results of a childhood case of lockjaw and has endured three prison surgeries that have failed to ease his pain or even correct his bite. He relates that, "When the pain screaming in my jaw gets too bad, I just close my eyes and think of Sun Dance" (25). Thus the Sun Dance has helped him to endure physical pain even as he remains in prison. Peltier also uses humor to describe his tenacity: "Sun Dance sends us out into the world hardened against pain the way a charred stick is hardened against fire. That doesn't mean you can't break or kill us, but you're sure going to have to work like hell to do it" (147). The memory of the Sun Dance has also given him strength in the face of emotional pain. Describing how he was challenged to escape by a harassing, hateful guard, Peltier remembers that fear turned to strength when he recalled what he had endured during his Sun Dance: "My strength and courage suddenly came roaring back inside me like a hot volcanic tidal wave" (156). This example of mixed metaphor sounds confusing at first, but it follows a vision of Peltier's that makes the conflation of volcano and ocean sound apt, for in it, he sees the face of the guard change: "I swear, I saw his face and head turn into a serpent's" (156). In a belief system in which vision and reality can commingle like this, discussed further below, such mixing of metaphors may be the only way to express one's own spiritual transformation.

The Sun Dance itself must also operate metaphorically here. Peltier is no longer free to participate in a traditional Sun Dance. Living behind bars, his life has become a sacrifice that he hopes will benefit his people, but the leather thongs have become iron bars around him. He says, "Sun Dance takes place inside of me, not outside of me" (10), to acknowledge the spiritual practice of the Sun Dance as well as the fact that he cannot literally perform the Sun Dance anymore.

He recounts the many ways he wants to help Native people and that "It's so frustrating to hear over and over again about teen suicide, drug abuse, unemployment, and seemingly eternal poverty among my people" (38). Wondering if his imprisonment has accomplished anything as a sacrifice for his people, he states, "And yet I know when this sacrifice ends, a new sacrifice begins. There's always another Sun Dance" (38). Thus, his life in prison is a Sun Dance and he will perform the Sun Dance anew—in other words, sacrifice himself in another way to help his people—outside of prison. In his "Message to Humanity" at the end of *Prison Writings* he asks his opposition, "Can't we resolve this thing between us now, and finally end it? I am praying that we can. My life is an instrument for that purpose" (206). Making his body, his life, an "instrument" sounds metaphorical here, but given the emphasis on the physical sacrifice of the Sun Dance and how Peltier considers his life in prison a sacrifice for his people, the statement signifies literally as well.

Rhetorical Inclusion: Oral Tradition in Peltier's Writing

Aspects of oral tradition are laced throughout Peltier's writing. In an interview, novelist and poet Sherman Alexie says, "I mean, you always get tired of the question, Y'know, of 'How does your work apply to the oral tradition?' It doesn't. I *type* it!" (qtd. in Purdy 6, original emphasis). Alexie acknowledges that focusing on oral tradition with every Native writer reifies stereotypes of Native people as living in the past. Yet, for someone like Peltier who grew up on reservations and was told stories by his grandparents, characteristics of oral performance often infiltrate writing as well as speech.

Some features of oral storytelling are culturally specific. This section emphasizes features that commonly recur throughout the writings of different Native authors. One writer who uses oral tradition even though she also types her stories is Leslie Marmon Silko. In "Language and Literature from a Pueblo Indian Perspective," she acknowledges features such as "stories within stories" and storytelling that "always includes the audience, the listeners" (50). She cites as well what Pueblo storytellers do not do: "We make no distinctions between types of story—historical, sacred, plain gossip—because these distinctions are not useful when discussing the Pueblo *experience* of language" (53, original emphasis). Repetition characterizes virtually all oral storytelling, and Silko argues it has a purpose: "[T]he repetitions are, of course, designed to help you remember. [Information] is repeated again and again, and then [the story] moves on" (57).

While studying the structure of Silko's volume of stories, poems, memories, and photographs entitled *Storyteller*, Bernard A. Hirsch notes additional features than can be attributed to oral tradition. They are "circular design" (2), "episodic structure," and a tendency for the material to reflect back on preceding passages (3); "interrelationships between the various narrative episodes" (3); the tendency for the audience to stop the storyteller and ask questions (7), represented in the book by her reproduction of her grandmother's explanations; a thematic emphasis of the "journey of self-discovery" (14); the presence of "occasional expository digressions" (19); a "conversational tone" (21); asides such as "you know" that give "a sense of [Silko's] immediate audience" (22); a "juxtaposition of different kinds of narratives and subjects" (22) ranging from traditional stories to modern ones, from poems to photographs of life in New Mexico by her father and herself; storytelling as "a way in which people define themselves and declare who they are" (25); and the presence of variations upon stories (26n26). Many of these narrative features permeate storytelling in cultures across North America. For instance, Greg Sarris's analysis of the stories of Pomo medicine woman Mabel McKay underlines some of the features just listed: "Mabel didn't present her stories in chronological sequence. Her stories moved in and out of different time frames and often implicated me as a listener" (1).

Some features of oral storytelling occur in Peltier's writings. One feature is apparent when merely looking at the title page of the book: it is coauthored by Harvey Arden. In academic circles, collaboration is inferior to individual authorship, at least in the humanities, where a coauthored work will not earn tenure for either author. But the implication of the listener in stories and the tendency for stories to change over time suggest that, in cultures that value oral tradition, collaboration is part of the art form. Rather than effacing the collaborative aspect of Peltier's writing, Arden addresses it directly and suggests his role was indeed as collaborator rather than as mere editor: "I want to thank Leonard for the high honor of being chosen to select, edit, arrange, and, on more than a few occasions, to goad him into revealing even deeper levels of his thought and memory" (qtd. in Peltier 220).

Peltier addresses his audience directly several times, making it apparent that this is not the kind of text that assumes a passive and invisible audience. For a reader unused to being addressed, it can be a striking experience to be addressed as "you" while reading, as if the author were speaking directly to the reader. In addition, though, the "you" he addresses changes from context to context. In one example, Peltier refers to Native people who work for the government, and includes them in his struggle: "It's good you're there, my brothers and sisters . . . so they can see us for what we are, human beings, yes, ordinary—and extraordinary—human beings" (19). Other times, the "you" he addresses is clearly not Native. When giving his biography, he says, "I myself was brought up on both Sioux and Ojibway (Chippewa) reservations in the land known to you as America" (63). Here, the reader is the Other, for only non-Native people, Peltier suggests, call Turtle Island by its European namesake, America. Later, when discussing the reign of terror at Pine Ridge and the struggle over uranium on reservation land, Peltier mentions people who "are victims of the energy wars, as were agents Coler and Williams, as am I. And so are you, my friend, and your children and your children's children" (119–20). Again, the reader is part of that larger audience. Peltier's inclusion of the audience shifts according to his purpose.

When reading a published work, one expects the final version to be fully edited and polished. One of the ways Peltier preserves ties to oral tradition in his writing is by letting his revisions be heard, just as they would in speech, where they cannot be erased. In one of the rare vindictive moments in the book, Peltier wishes great suffering on the agents who allegedly killed Anna Mae Pictou Aquash and threatened Myrtle Poor Bear.[8] He stops himself, though, and includes this change of direction in the text, complete with ellipses: "But . . . no . . . there I go, being vindictive and vengeful myself, wishing harm on others as they have wished it on me. I have to watch that in myself. I have to step on the head of that snake every time it rises" (19). He revises his course again when he indicates the limits to the information he can properly give his readers about the *inipi* ceremony: "And when you open that door and pass through into that other realm . . . But, no, please forgive me, I have to stop here. Beyond this point it becomes utterly private, incommunicable" (186).

Shifts among different identities and different realities are also possible in oral tradition, particularly in reference to spiritual states of being. Gloria Anzaldúa, a native Texan, or Tejana, follows a shamanic tradition when she prepares to write stories by entering into a dreamlike state, shape-shifting into different characters, and fighting with and against the urge to write. "I 'trance'" (69) she says: "My 'awakened dreams' are about shifts. Thought shifts, reality shifts, gender shifts" (70). With this precedent, the many names Peltier claims become increasingly significant: "One of my names is Tate Wikuwa, which means 'Wind Chases the Sun' in the Dakota language. That name was my great-grandfather's. Another name, bestowed on me by my Native Canadian brethren, is Gwarth-ee-lass, meaning 'He Leads the People'" (61).

His Christian name holds particular value for him because his mother thought the name Leonard sounded like "lion-hearted"; Peltier did not know until much later that is the literal meaning of his name. The most striking name Peltier holds is his prison identity, or what we might see as his lack of name and lack of identity in prison: "Here at Leavenworth . . . my official name is #89637-132. Not much imagination, or inspiration, *there*" (62, original emphasis).

Names in and of themselves may not seem significant, but Peltier carefully explains the importance of all of his names. His many names are not mere labels; they signify the many roles he plays in his life. He has been a leader of Native American people and, as United States prisoner #89637-132, he remains an exemplary prisoner despite constant denials of parole. Since the rigors of boarding school and forced assimilation are recent in Native memory, the correlation between names and identity is apt. Luther Standing Bear's birth name was Ota Kte or "Plenty Kill" (6); it was only after being asked to choose a name that he became Luther Standing Bear. The teacher asked his father's name and that name became his last or paternal name; the name Luther he chose by taking his turn pointing a stick at a blackboard full of many "white man's names" (137). Taking this new name becomes part of the process of Standing Bear's assimilation; his new identity is an ambiguous one. As he says, regarding concern for his future, "[My people] wanted me to marry in the right way, but, as I had been educated, they could not just figure out what was the right way in my case" (195).

Along with identity shifts come reality shifts, to use Anzaldúa's phrase. Peltier has experienced ambiguous states of reality many times. He describes the *inipi* ceremony that the Native inmates of Leavenworth are allowed every Saturday. Despite the tight security and multiple head counts, Peltier experiences a kind of freedom; at the end, it is "Back to Leavenworth after seven hours of blessed freedom. And those guards in their gun towers never even realized we'd escaped!" (198). Such ambiguous states as being free while in prison occur with striking regularity in Peltier's writing. They are part of Native spirituality:

> Am I dreaming or am I being dreamed? Sometimes I'm not sure. Anyway, here's one of my dreams that I've written down. I've had it in various forms many times. Often it comes to me in that state between waking and sleeping. My grandmother told me that was the holiest time, that little moment between waking and sleeping, that little luminous crack between this world and that other, greater reality that contains this little reality we call our lives. (175)

Peltier's acceptance of differing realities originated early in his life and he associates his acceptance of them with being multilingual: "As a child, I became fluent in *métis*—a French-Indian mixture—as well as English, and I also spoke some Sioux, Ojibway, and French words. Since every language gives you a different view of reality, I soon saw that there were many realities you had to cope with in this life, most of them unpleasant" (72).

He further conveys the value placed on transformation rather than stasis in oral tradition when he describes the importance of keeping ritual experiences private: "To put those [experiences] into words is to freeze them in space and time, and they should never be frozen that way because they're continually unfolding, changing with and adapting to each passing moment" (184).

Repetition is one of the most noticeable features of oral tradition. Peltier's best demonstration of repetition for emphasis and for building tension is the text of a speech included in his prison writings. In his "Pre-Sentencing Statement," delivered in 1977, Peltier argued in favor of serving his two life terms simultaneously while knowing that the judge was biased and would order the terms served consecutively. Peltier emphasizes this over and over again in this speech so that almost every paragraph ends with a similar phrase: "[Y]ou will run my two life terms consecutively. . . . [Y]ou will sentence me to two life terms without hesitation. . . . [Y]ou will call me heartless, a coldblooded murderer who deserves two life sentences consecutively. . . . [Y]ou know and always knew you would sentence me to two consecutive life terms" (240–42). The repetition in this speech exerts one last bit of power, for here Peltier speaks to a judge as a storyteller might speak to a child, emphasizing a lesson over and over again. In this way, a basic rhetorical technique becomes an act of defiance.

Peltier's prison writings make a powerful case for his freedom. They accomplish more, though, by articulating Native values such as spirituality. They also connect his writing to a tradition of Native rhetoric, characterized by recognition of the government's own ironic use of language, historical analogies, and oral tradition.

It is difficult, however, to imagine a happy ending to Peltier's story and therefore difficult to create a happy ending for this essay. Yet the power of writing and speaking in Native cultures cannot be denied. One of the songs within Silko's novel *Ceremony* contains the following lines: "Their evil is mighty / but it can't stand up to our stories" (Silko 1977, 2).

Notes

1. I refer, in particular, to Devon A. Mihesuah's article, "Anna Mae Pictou Aquash" in *Sifters: Native American Women's Lives*, ed. Theda Perdue (New York: Oxford UP, 2001), 204–22. Mihesuah emphasizes that male AIM members felt threatened by Aquash's perceived adoption of masculine roles and suggests that AIM may have been responsible for her subsequent murder.

2. In fact, some historians have called attention to Peltier's case primarily to show how inflated Peltier's reputation has become. Paul Chaat Smith and Robert Allen Warrior, for instance, strive to demythologize the man:

> Most . . . young people knew of AIM's glory days, but were confused in the details. By the late 1980s an AIM dog soldier named Leonard Peltier had arguably become more famous than any AIM leader. Peltier was *[sic]* serving two life sentences after being convicted of murdering two FBI agents in a 1975 shoot-out on Pine Ridge. A national campaign that gave him equal billing with Nelson Mandela toured college campuses, and documentaries cast him as a symbol of Indian resistance. He was often referred to as an AIM leader, though he would be more accurately described, before the shoot-out, as a not particularly beloved AIM regular. The 1975 incident [at the Jumping Bull Compound] and Wounded Knee, though two years apart and occurring in vastly different circumstances, had become conflated with time, and Leonard Peltier, to many young Indian activists, was vaguely understood to be a key AIM leader who was framed for shooting FBI agents during the occupation of Wounded Knee. (276–77)

Matthiessen says Peltier "was recognized increasingly as a leader" (142), in contrast to Warrior's dismissal of him.

3. "The movement was founded to turn the attention of Indian people toward a renewal of spirituality which would impart the strength of resolve needed to reverse the ruinous policies of the United States, Canada, and other colonialist governments of Central and South America," according to Laura Waterman Wittstock and Elaine J. Salinas in "A Brief History of the American Indian Movement" (par. 3). The American Indian Movement Grand Governing Council states that

"AIM is first, a spiritual movement, a religious re-birth, and then the re-birth of dignity and pride in a people" in the "AIM-GCC Profile" (attributed to Birgil Kills Straight).

4. According to Sherry Means, "Principle/Rule Four: We don't get involved with tribal politics or any other community politics unless invited to do so. A written letter must be sent to any AIM chapter before AIM will get involved."

5. A similar claim has been made by another writer. In the film *Smoke Signals*, with screenplay by Sherman Alexie, the character Thomas Builds-the-Fire states that Arnold Joseph was imprisoned in the Washington State Penitentiary in Walla Walla "for being an Indian in the twentieth century" (33:39).

6. In contrast to the stereotype of Plains peoples as bloodthirsty warriors is the tradition of counting coup (French for "strike" or "blow"). A warrior who could touch an enemy with a coup stick or lance—in other words, to get close enough to an enemy to kill him but to spare his life—"gained an honor" (Standing Bear 5).

7. Anna Mae Pictou Aquash and Myrtle Poor Bear are two women victimized by the conflict on Pine Ridge. Aquash was an AIM member who died amidst controversy: "A second autopsy revealed that she was executed, killed by a .38 caliber revolver; an FBI autopsy maintains she died of exposure" (Messerschmidt xvi). Myrtle Poor Bear testified against Peltier "under coercion" (xvii).

Works Cited

Alexie, Sherman. *Smoke Signals: A Screen Play*. New York: Hyperion, 1998.

Anzaldúa, Gloria. "'Tlilli Tlipalli': The Path of the Red and Black Ink." *Borderlands: The New Mestiza*. San Francisco: Aunt Lute, 1987.

Brown, Joseph Epes, ed. *The Sacred Pipe: Black Elk's Account of the Seven Rites of the Oglala Sioux*. 1953. New York: Viking Penguin, 1971.

Clark, Ramsey. Preface. *Prison Writings: My Life is My Sun Dance*. By Leonard Peltier. Ed. Harvey Arden. New York: St. Martin's, 1999. xiii–xxii.

Hirsch, Bernard A. "'The Telling Which Continues': Oral Tradition and the Written Word in Leslie Marmon Silko's *Storyteller*." *American Indian Quarterly* 12.1 (1988): 1–26.

Hogan, Joseph C., III. "Guilty Until Proven Innocent: Leonard Peltier and the Sublegal System." *Boston College Law Review* 34.14 (July 1993): 901–35.

Kills Straight, Birgil. "AIM-GCC Profile." *American Indian Movement Grand Governing Council*. March 3, 2005. http://www.aimovement.org/ggc/index.html.

Matthiessen, Peter. *In the Spirit of Crazy Horse*. 1983. New York: Penguin, 1992.

Means, Sherry. "Introduction to the American Indian Movement: 101." *American Indian Movment*. March 3, 2005. http://www.dickshovel.com/aim101.html.

Messerschmidt, James W. *The Trial of Leonard Peltier*. Boston: South End, 1983.

Peltier, Leonard. *Prison Writings: My Life Is My Sun Dance*. Ed. Harvey Arden. New York: St. Martin's, 1999.

Purdy, John. "Crossroads: A Conversation with Sherman Alexie." *Studies in American Indian Literatures* 9.4 (1997): 1–18.

Rich, Elizabeth. "'Remember Wounded Knee': AIM's Use of Metonymy in 21st Century Protest." *College Literature* 313.3 (2004): 70–91.

Sanchez, John, Mary E. Stuckey, and Richard Morris. "Rhetorical Exclusion: The Government's Case Against American Indian Activists, AIM, and Leonard Peltier." *American Indian Culture and Research Journal* 23.2 (1999): 27–52.

Sarris, Greg. *Keeping Slug Woman Alive: A Holistic Approach to American Indian Texts*. Berkeley: U of California P, 1993.

Silko, Leslie Marmon. *Ceremony*. New York: Viking Penguin, 1977.

———. "Language and Literature from a Pueblo Indian Perspective." *Yellow Woman and a Beauty of the Spirit: Essays on Native American Life Today*. New York: Simon and Schuster, 1996. 48–59.

Smith, Paul Chaat, and Robert Allen Warrior. Epilogue. *Like a Hurricane: The Indian Movement from Alcatraz to Wounded Knee.* 1996. New York: New Press, 1990. 269–79.

Standing Bear, Luther. *My People, the Sioux*. 1928. Lincoln and London: U of Nebraska P, 1975.

Wittstock, Laura Waterman, and Elaine J. Salinas. "A Brief History of the American Indian Movement." *American Indian Movement Grand Governing Council*. March 3, 2005. http://www.aimovement.org/ggc/history.html.

3

WRITING, RHETORIC, AND PEDAGOGY

DE-ASSIMILATION AS THE NEED TO TELL

NATIVE AMERICAN WRITERS, BAKHTIN, AND AUTOBIOGRAPHY

✦

Holly L. Baumgartner

NATIVE AMERICAN history is the story and stories of a material oppression that I believe very few people would deny. It is a history of unparalleled genocide—eighty to one hundred million deaths, twenty million in the United States alone.[1] It is a history of violence perpetrated on multiple levels, including personal violence, whereby Natives were tortured, killed outright, torn from parents to be placed in boarding schools and foster homes, put on display at European courts and festivals, and made into spectacle as in the popular Buffalo Bill's Wild West Show in the 1800s (Slotkin 165ff). Even in the 1970s, 42 percent of Native women were sterilized against their will or without their knowledge and used as a high-risk test group by Norplant through the Indian Health Service (Jaimes 326; Talon 66–69; Native American Women's Health Education Resource Center 69). It is also a geographical and cultural violence as in the destruction of Native holy sites, the territorialization and colonization of Native lands, the removal of whole peoples from their homes to federally defined "reserves," the betrayal of political treaties both oral and written, and the mining and stealing of Native resources. This material oppression is often visible in its boundaries: Reservation lands have been whittled down into smaller and smaller parcels encircled by other cultures, and technological and financial boundaries enforce very real limits on what may be accomplished by Native peoples.

However, as many theorists have posited, the boundaries are also linguistic in nature.[2] Native Americans have been dominated through an oppressive use of language by the European invaders and settlers. Sometimes whitewashed terms mask the atrocities in order to make them more palatable, for example in the use of terms like "manifest destiny" and "westward expansionism" for the colonization and remapping of Native lands. Sometimes language oppresses by reducing whole groups of peoples to single entities, such as in the name "Indian" used as a blanket term for many distinct cultures of diverse ethnic heritages and histories. Sometimes language was used to turn people into objects or to dehumanize them, as the "noble savage" imagery so often applied to Native peoples or the depiction or verbal equation of Natives as beasts or animals,[3] a process that continues today in the form of sports team's names or mascots, for example.[4] Perhaps most oppressive, though, was the deliberate ripping away of language from Native peoples by outlawing home tongues or refusing to allow them to be taught or used in Native schools. For example, children brought to the Carlisle Indian School in Pennsylvania during the late 1800s and early 1900s were no longer allowed to speak in their Native languages (Hertzberg 16). The belief was that Native peoples would assimilate more easily and quickly to the dominant culture if they spoke only English. Ultimately, the control of language was an oppressive tool used either to annihilate or assimilate Native Americans.

With the closing of the frontier in 1890, the outright slaughter of Native peoples shifted to a stronger emphasis on assimilation. "The problem of the Indian," it was thought, would disappear if Natives were acculturated and subsumed within the larger culture. Interestingly, the writing of autobiographies by Native Americans began at roughly the same time. (A few autobiographies were written earlier, such as *A Son of the Forest* by William Apess in 1829.) One of the first Natives to write an autobiography in the language of the dominant society was Charles Eastman (Lakota), who was sent to a boarding school and taught the discourse of the dominant culture. Five years later he returned home. He wrote of his experiences as a man trapped between the cultural divide. Eastman's father encouraged him to adapt to the dominant society, while his grandmother pushed him to resist. By necessity, "He became adept at moving between the two worlds" (Eastman xii).

Eastman was educated in medicine at Boston University. Within weeks of his return to Pine Ridge, he was confronted with the Wounded Knee Massacre and the destabilizing knowledge of being a Native doctor surrounded by white soldiers. He devoted his writings to documenting Lakota acculturation and defending Lakota culture. A devout Christian, he declared: "It is my personal belief, after thirty-five years' experience of it, that there is no such thing as 'Christian civilization'. I believe that Christianity and modern civilization are opposed and irreconcilable, and that the spirit of Christianity and of our ancient religion is essentially the same" (158). Eastman used his writing to create a stance for negotiating the conflicts created by the clash between Native traditions and assimilationist teachings. If written language—from treaties, laws, ethnographic studies, maps, anthropological works, textbooks, and other forms of writing—has been oppressive to Native Americans, (especially so since many Native cultures were oral cultures), it has also been a site of rhetorical resistance, with autobiography being one of those rhetorical sites.

To be fully assimilated into the dominant culture is to yield to a monologic voice, what Russian theorist Mikhail Bakhtin calls an "authoritative discourse" ("Discourse" 342). Authoritative discourse "demands that we acknowledge it, that we make it our own" (342). It dictates normative behaviors and demands acquiescence to the status quo. Native Americans living in a country with competing cultures and ideologies that are "opposed and irreconcilable" (Eastman 158) have utilized autobiography to identify and interrogate the authoritative voices controlling assimilationist practices which are an inherent part of lived Native experience today.

Drawing extensively on Brian Swann and Arnold Krupat's anthology *I Tell You Now: Autobiographical Essays by Native American Writers,* in addition to other texts, I introduce each Native American writer with his or her Native nationality in parentheses so as not to reduce individual writers to one national identity.[5] I have also utilized large excerpts from all of the autobiographical selections I chose in order to create a space where Native voices could speak more for themselves rather than me doing the speaking for them. Therefore, I walk a fine line between Native voices and the larger authoritative discourse, in this case, of academe. While many different resistance strategies have been enacted in autobiography, some of the concepts of Mikhail Bakhtin offer a context for a fruitful reading of Native American autobiographical texts. Through Bakhtin's notions of heteroglossia, dialogism, and internally persuasive discourse (as opposed to authoritative discourse), Native American autobiographies may be shown as texts which include an awareness of the multivocality of any writing. This hyperawareness calls into question the univocality of authoritative discourses, undermining and destabilizing them, and ultimately beginning a process of de-assimilation and empowerment, a kind of coming to consciousness.

The acculturation process, especially among speakers of English as a second language and new immigrants, has been studied by many researchers. The stages of that process include euphoria, nostalgia, anomie, and alienation, before the subject becomes acculturated/assimilated.[6] For Native writers, in order to de-assimilate, they may need to enact a countermovement, experiencing or re-experiencing the stages away from acculturation. Linda Hogan (Chickasaw) demonstrates her movement toward liberation, counter-paralleling the stages of acculturation:

> When I began to write, I wrote partly to put this life in order, partly because I was too shy to speak. I was silent and the poems spoke first, I was ignorant and the poems educated me. When I realized that people were going to read the poems, I thought of the best way to use words, how great was my responsibility to transmit words, ideas, and acts by which we could live with liberation, love, self-respect, good humor, and joy. In learning that, I also had to offer up our pain and grief and sorrow, because I know that denial and oppression are the greatest hindrances to liberation and growth. (241)

Thus, autobiography sometimes highlights these stages as part of the de-assimilation process.

However, regardless of where writers stand among the emotional stages described above, an autobiographical interrogation of language and the discourses defining where they are positioned enables the processes of de-assimilation countering the hegemonic quality of acculturation. De-assimilation turns the lethargy of assimilation back into anger and anger into action. Elizabeth Cook-Lynn (Crow Creek Sioux) comments, "That anger is what started me writing. Writing, for me, then, is an act of defiance born of the need to survive" (57). Wendy Rose (Hopi-Miwok) also experienced anger as a turning point and source of inspiration: "I hate it when other people write about my alienation and anger. Even if it's true, I'm not proud of it. It has crippled me, made me sick, made me out of balance. It has also been the source of my poetry" (253). The anger creates a context to begin an interrogation: What is causing the anger? What does it signify? "Being ripped out of my childhood had devastated me, and the devastation began in Oregon. I refused to go to school because my schoolmates mocked my Indianness. I hid away in closets and bit my hands in mute rage. . . . My journals are piled high, each a chunk of my fragmented history," Mary Tallmountain (Koyukon Athabascan) adds (6). Initially, autobiography has a sense of being cathartic, an initial release both physically and metaphorically. As it continues, the action spurred on by writing becomes both a form of empowerment for Native writers as well as a dialogue, meaning that response is implied *of* the reader, a notion I will return to later.

At the same time, writing autobiography is not an easy process for Native peoples. For one, autobiography is not a privileged discourse within the academy; other genres and forms are valued over it. Second, the autobiographical mode has no traditional counterpart among Native cultures. As Brian Swann and Arnold Krupat write in *I Tell You Now*, "the notion of telling the whole of any one individual's life or taking merely personal experience as of particular significance was, in the most literal way, foreign to them, if not also repugnant" (ix). To write in this form is not only to write in a genre often dismissed by dominant society, it is also to step outside of Native cultural tradition just by the decision to engage in its practice. Autobiography, in its form alone, is a deliberate confrontation between writer and tradition. For the most part, Native writers often trace out the conflicts that are experienced personally but are representative of an entire cultural history, a history that also constructs the writer. The movements between personal and cultural are simultaneous, ongoing processes. Sometimes those traces are positive, as in this piece where Joy Harjo (Creek) writes about her father:

> He tries to make sense of this world in which his granddaughter has come to live. And often teases me about my occupation of putting words on paper. I tell him that it is in writing these words down, and entering the world through the structure they make, that has allowed me to see him more clearly, and to speak. And he answers that maybe his prayers, songs, and his belief in them has allowed him to create me. (266)

Those traces may also contain a profound anguish, one that cannot be easily healed, if at all. Haunani-Kay Trask (Hawaiian) explains that "The experience of a legal identity is, as with all identities, both psychological and political. Who we believe ourselves to be is often *not* what the colonial legal system defines us to be" (135). In a sense, much Native autobiographical writing is about negotiating these varying identities. Trask goes on to write that "This disjunction causes a kind of suffering nearly impossible to end without ending the colonial definitions of who we are" (135). Jimmie Durham's (Wolf Clan Cherokee) work also highlights the suffering in these multiply complex roles as well as the split between the psychological and the political suggested by Trask:

> But here is the real thing: I absolutely do not want to communicate anything to you. So, you're probably saying if he doesn't want to communicate, why does he write? Here is the real truth: I absolutely hate this

> country. Not just the government, but the culture, the group of people called Americans. The country. I hate the country. I HATE AMERICA. . . . Why wouldn't I hate this country? Because you are a nice person? Because it makes you feel bad for me to hate this country? You want me to be properly indignant about 'injustices' and still be on the side of you and your friends who are also 'trying to bring about some changes in this country?' Don't ask a white man to walk a mile in your moccasins because he'll probably steal them and the mile, too. Only, just try standing in my shoes for a minute. The fact of the US is destructive to Indian country. . . . Here is what I don't understand: how come so many Indians don't seem to . . . hate this country? Simple—we hate ourselves and each other instead. (Durham 162–63)

For both Trask and Durham, the need to take back definitions of the self is imperative.

To use the word "I" is also a requisite part of the autobiographical mode, but here it often has the shadowed force of "we" behind it. In this sense, Native voice has always contained the knowledge of being multiply voiced, without the "speaking for" that generates a kind of tokenization. Cook-Lynn describes it as a responsibility *to* without a speaking *for*.

> The idea that we can speak for the dispossessed, the weak, the voiceless, is indeed one of the great burdens of contemporary Indian poets today, for it is widely believed that we "speak for our tribes." The frank truth is that I don't know many poets who say, "I speak for my people." It is not only unwise; it is probably impossible and it is very surely arrogant, for We Are Self-Appointed and the self-appointedness of what we do indicates that the responsibility is ours and ours alone.
>
> Therein lies another dichotomy: I claim to be a Dakotah poet by disclaiming that I speak for my people. (58)

At the same time she acknowledges that those poets who compose around the drum, in the traditional ways, tell a different story, "for it remains communal. . . . I have every confidence that they speak in our own language for the tribes" (58). Here, Cook-Lynn is herself defining what kinds of writing will belong, for her, to which discourse community she engages in, an empowering step.

The "I" is interrogated differently by Maurice Kenny (Mohawk), who states:

> So where is this place that I write of? It is the foothills of the Adirondacks, the Lake Ontario summer cabin, . . . it is all of these places and things . . . the persons I have created of wolf or berry, my ancestors . . . my mother, whose own life pain is with me still; my father's dreams and victories; my sisters and their lives; and my first tricycle . . . the "place" is within me and all around—whoever I touch, wherever I travel. It is not the personal "I" but the collective because I wish all peoples to relate to that "I", become that "I" and find their place now that I have mine. (45–46)

Kenny not only constructs the "I" differently, he also gives a poetic definition of Mikhail Bakhtin's notion of heteroglossia.

Bakhtin has written about the heteroglossic nature of language, the polyphony of utterances and texts subject to multiple interpretations. The interaction between speakers, or in this case readers and writers, involves dialogue—both the dialogue of the actual exchange of utterances and the dialogue which is a negotiation of meanings. Heteroglossia is the "social diversity of speech types" (263) as he defines it in "Discourse in the Novel." He writes:

> The novel orchestrates all of its themes, the totality of the world of objects and ideas depicted and expressed in it, by means of the social diversity of speech types [raznorečie] and by the differing individual voices that flourish under such conditions. Authorial speech, the speeches of narrators, inserted genres, the speech of characters are merely those fundamental compositional unities with whose help heteroglossia [raznorečie] can enter the novel; each of them permits a multiplicity of social voices and a wide variety of their links and interrelationships (always more or less dialogized). (263)[w]

Autobiography shares some similarities with the novel: it may be thematic, is a world of objects and ideas, has a narrator, and consciously or unconsciously contains a wide variety of social voices. Similar to Bakhtin's explication of the novel, Native Americans in autobiographical writing often exploit the heteroglossic nature of language as a means of identifying the various socially constructed voices that are linked through assimilation. Paula Gunn Allen (Laguna Pueblo) highlights how an authoritative discourse makes it seem as if there was one normal, acceptable voice, exemplified in the use of her term "people."

> That's where dwell . . . the rich white people who aren't Anglos or Texans but just people, just Americans (not like our white people who aren't people anymore than the Indians or Chicanos are people but rather Anglos, Tejanos, Indians, La Raza, Nativos, whatever.) YOU know, PEOPLE, like are in the magazines and on the radio. YOU know, like in the surveys and the polls. As in "People do this and that" or "People think such and such." People, like live in the America that all the American stuff is developed for and said about and sold to and by. . . . I always knew those sentences didn't mean US, we who lived in confluence. . . . My life is the pause. The space between. The not this, not that, not the other. The place that others go around. . . . It's more a mobius strip than a line. (150–51)

These various voices may never be fully separated or unraveled, but naming them signifies an awareness of the imposed cultural splits which may be so damaging until confronted, and naming may begin the process of de-assimilation, allowing for the potential of a kind of serious play between these voices. An oppressive use of language is to attempt to unify the voices, make them seem as if one voice were possible and "natural." Duane Niatum (Klallam) writes, "But what I am against is a one-dimensional person, or any individual or state that advocates creating such a uniform species of humanity." He clarifies this even more by explaining that he used to live under "the illusion that one could believe in a sense of wholeness in the universe. This illusion sustained my belief in the road I had chosen. And this points to something else I've learned over the years: the need to fight for your values, no matter who attempts to destroy them. We mustn't forget it could be another self" (135–36).

Niatum surfaces some of the many cultural splits Native writers often confront. A writer may be a "crossblood," a genetic mix of Native heritage(s) and non-Native heritage(s). (And maybe we are all crossbloods to some extent.) S/he may be a cultural mix, straddling Native and Western cultures and trying to survive in each or resisting being forced to choose. Jack Forbes (Powhatan-Delaware-Saponi) explains it in this manner:

> Of course, working with the Powhatan-Renape people and with other eastern Indians brought home to me the full impact of colonialism and also the difficulty of being Indian if one is also part African. Being a mixed-blood myself and also a mixture of many tribes, I had long been aware of the significance of being a "half-breed." Back on the east coast,

> however, I became increasingly aware that those of us who looked European and Indian had a hell of an advantage over people who looked Indian and African. I though that the differential treatment was so much white racist bullshit and still do. . . . I really resent white people trying to dissect us and tell us what it is that makes a person Native American. (120–21)

Similarly, s/he may also be confronting the splits between old and new Native cultures, between his or her individual Native culture (for example, Osage, Lakota, Cherokee) and the Pan-Indian consciousness. These are just a few of the splits to be negotiated in addition to professional, academic, age- or gender-related voices, and so on. However, sometimes the negotiation produces positive results, as indicated in the writing of Harjo:

> I walk in and out of many worlds. I used to see being born of this mixed-blood/mixed-vision a curse, and hated myself for it. It was too confusing and destructive when I saw the world through that focus. The only message I got was not belonging anywhere, not to any side. I have since decided that being familiar with more than one world, more than one vision, is a blessing, and know that I make my own choices. (266)

Regardless, the recognition of the cultural splits and voices is first necessary before they can be set loose to play.

Bakhtin also writes that "Heteroglossia . . . *is another's speech in another's language,* serving to express authorial intentions but in a refracted way. Such speech constitutes a special type of *double-voiced discourse*" ("Discourse" 324). The intentions of both character and author are revealed at the same time. In autobiography, the author is also the "character" creating a special kind of double-voiced discourse. When the author is also examining and locating the splits in voice, what I call a meta-heteroglossic writing is created. It is a thinking about voice, how it is composed and why. Gerald Vizenor (Minnesota Chippewa) illustrates double-voiced discourse through a meta-heteroglossic element:

> This is mixedblood autobiographical causerie and narrative. . . . The first and third personas are me.
>
> Gerald Vizenor believes that autobiographies are imaginative histories; a remembrance past the barriers; wild pastimes over the pronouns. Outside the benchmarks the ones to be in written memoirs are neither senti-

> mental nor ideological; mixedbloods loosen the seams in the shrouds of identities. Institutional time, he contends, belies our personal memories, imagination, and consciousness. (101)

Through the interrogations of and the conflicts with the multiple discourses, especially the dominant ones, Native peoples may begin to determine their own positions, where a stance is not the "shroud" of identity. Instead of being held in bondage through language, autobiography offers a liberatory perspective, which does not mean that anyone can be free of the other voices, but that the situatedness of the writer may change in relation to those voices. It is a sort of transformative becoming, as Harjo explains in reference to one of her poems:

> When I began writing the poem, I knew I wanted an actual transformation to be enacted within it. I began with someone's hatred, which was a tangible thing, and wanted to turn it into love by the end of the poem. I was also interested in the process of becoming. I tried to include several states of becoming. The "process of the poem" becoming was one. (269)

Becoming is an integral part of Bakhtin's theory of heteroglossia. "The topic of a speaking person takes on quite another significance in the ordinary ideological workings of our consciousness, in the process of assimilating our consciousness to the ideological world. He goes on to explain that this process is an "ideological becoming" involving "a process of selectively assimilating the words of others" ("Discourse" 341). The key word here is "selectively," which implies a choice, one that has historically been denied to Native peoples.

Kay Halasek, in her book A *Pedagogy of Possibility: Bakhtinian Perspectives on Composition Studies,* further explains Bakhtin's theory of discourse and "the elements of the rhetorical situations in terms of a socially constructed reality and a socially defined individual. Meaning, knowledge, and reality are constructed through language and between ideologically bound individuals within historically situated language spheres" (4). Through autobiography, then, Native writers recognize that their own situatedness is a construction. They have already been defined by the dominant discourse and their interactions with others from the society outside of Native world/s. Any meaning or knowledge they may create for themselves, a different reality than that experienced as Other, as outsider, must begin through language, and hence the turning to autobiography, a chance to *re*construct their lives. Autobiography is especially interesting since many of the essays I have read cannot simply be confined to a person's individual history but are often linked to Native history or the history of a particular Native culture.

Native writers are very conscious of the alternative constructions of their nations' histories as differing from their own experience of those histories. In "Keeping Close to Home: Class and Education," bell hooks writes that holding on to that history as well as the languages involved in that history is vital. "An important strategy for maintaining contact," she writes, "is ongoing acknowledgment of the primacy of one's past, of one's background, affirming the reality that such bonds are not severed automatically solely because one enters a new environment or moves towards a different class experience" (80). This knowledge is echoed in Linda Hogan's writing: "Telling our lives is important, for those who come after us, for those will see our experience as part of their own historical struggle. I think of my work as part of the history of our tribe and as part of the history of colonization everywhere" (233). Many writers link the details of tribal histories in a fluid manner to the events of their own lives, such as in following examples from Jimmie Durham, Jim Barnes (Choctaw), and Diane Glancy (Cherokee). Durham, in reference to the tragic period of 1684–1884, during which his people suffered two smallpox epidemics and forced removal from their homeland, states:

> For us, history is always personal. (I remember the Trail of Tears and Sequoyah's efforts as if I had been there.) History is directly involved with our families and our generations; tied with sacred white cotton string to the sweet and intense memories of our brother or sister is the desperate and intense hope of each generation to change this history. (Durham 159)

Written in a similar vein, Jim Barnes's piece resonates with Durham's as he personalizes the totalizing effects of the monologic voice of "history":

> But I am a child of the past. I live it in my waking dreams. . . . I attacked wagon trains or, on the other side, killed Indians. . . . What's more, and the hell of it all: I see but little hope, rather mainly dissolution of river, of land, and thus of spirit. You can see it on the faces of those who have witnessed, have lived, these civilizing years. (90–91)

Finally, Diane Glancy visualizes herself as walking between two distinct versions of the past, each with its own removals and travails:

> This is often where I struggle. Part of them came across the sea from Europe to Virginia, then west in a wagon . . . where my mother's family settled. The other part of me walked 900 miles on foot during a forced migration of 17,000 Cherokees from the East to Oklahoma. . . . [T]ruly, I have the feeling of being split between two cultures, not fully belonging to either one. (171)

Bakhtin further deepens the significance of heteroglossia with the concept of dialogism, "a world dominated by heteroglossia" (294). Dialogism indicates the fluidity of language. Native writers, and for that matter all writers, are not only writing for themselves, but also situating themselves within a discursive sphere where they are writing from others. The rhetorical context invokes a history, one that is "populated with the intentions of others" (294). Barnes writes, "A writer, whoever he may be, if he believes in art as art, will bring everything to bear upon his art, ethnic or otherwise. The work of Ralph Ellison, N. Scott Momaday, J. Frank Dobie—all are larger than the cultural and geographical boundaries that we might try to fence them with" (94).

Because of the dialogic nature of heteroglossia, and the competition between various discourses, language acts like a contact zone, a site of conflict. Heteroglossia may therefore challenge and interrogate the monologic or official discourses which can be so oppressive, such as religion, science, and academia. The concept is challenging because it reveals language as uncontainable and bearing multiply complex meanings and interpretations that resist closure and static definitions. Code switching is one example of a resistance strategy that plays with the heteroglossic nature of language. Code switching may involve a literal switching between a home tongue and English as one possibility. Cultural theorist Gloria Anzaldúa describes this in an interview with Andrea Lunsford:

> The way I grew up with my family was code-switching. When I am my most emotive self, my home self, stuff will come out in Spanish. When I'm in my head, stuff comes out in English. When I'm dealing with theory, it's all in English, because I didn't take any classes in which theory was taught in Spanish. So the body and the feeling parts of me come out

> in Spanish, and the intellectual, reasoning parts of me come out in English. (63–64)

Code switching also allows writers to "talk back" to dominant discourses as well as foregrounding their own discourses or both or several speech genres. Jimmie Durham writes: "I want us to have an *Eloheh Ga ghasduhn di* at Dhotsua's old Ghadijiya in Goingsnake District, because now it is 1984, exactly one hundred years since the Allotment Act when our first new century of trouble began, and also when the Dhotsue started the Nighthawk and told us that the US government had no power to allot Cherokee land" (157). He describes this as a meditation on his forty-fourth birthday, the average lifespan of a Native man. He weaves together his own personal life history, and the story of the Cherokee, foregrounding the language in a way that emphasizes the personal inside the historical rather than minimizing the Cherokee stance through assimilative language in an oppressive way, the way that certain standard American history textbooks, for example, have presented (or not presented) the view of the Cherokee.

Likewise, Bakhtin rejects the idea of an autonomous self. Halasek affirms that "Any speaker speaks a variety of languages, and in that sense he is . . . polyglossic. But only when the speaker begins to understand the variety and dissonance among languages, and that each language carries its own slant on the world, can he begin to situate himself linguistically (and ideologically) in the world" (8). Carter Revard (Osage) adds, "So like the mockingbird I have more than one song but they are all our songs. It has seemed to me that no one else will sing them unless I do" (80). Autobiography, then, offers the possibility for agency through a conscious situatedness.

In discussing the literary hero, Bakhtin claims the character as one that informs the writer's decisions. Similarly, in autobiographical and other writings the subject of the discourse has agency and is dynamic, a participant not defined through the traditional concept of the subject as passive and more like an object, a thing to be acted upon rather than acting for him/herself. The writer is comprised of the voices of others as is the discourse itself. It carries the history of all that has been said as part of the topic. The writer-as-subject and the audience both must engage with those other voices when engaging the material. Jim Barnes develops this point in greater detail:

> There is no such thing as autobiography or biography. One cannot write one's life, or anyone else's. . . . Poetry works the same way, because for

> each poem there must be a created voice. . . . The best poetry is dominated by speaker and image, image and speaker. The voice is the fiction (the lie) in respect to the poet's life. . . . From the total experience of the poem comes an experience of the speaker, and it is in this combination of fact and lie that Truth stands. If it means something to you, if it affects you, it is a certain truth. (96–97)

In Barnes's piece and many other autobiographies, writers are very aware of the negotiation of meaning that inevitably happens with the audience(s). The actual audience may be very different from the "hoped for" or ideally receptive audience. In *Speech Genres and Other Late Essays*, Bakhtin introduces the concept of the superaddressee, whom Frank Farmer interprets as "a sort of hovering figure that [Bakhtin] identifies as a 'constituent aspect' of every utterance, an invisibly present 'third party beyond the second party who is embodied in the person of the immediate addressee'" (199). Farmer explains that the function of the superaddressee is "to provide speakers with a 'loophole' through which they can flee the oppressions of immediacy" (199). He continues that "we hedge our (speakerly) bets by invoking a third party who will listen to us, who will understand perfectly what we have to say. We do so realizing that we cannot depend on our immediates for the understanding we desire" (200). Farmer states that being misunderstood is less problematic than not being heard at all. For some Native writers, misunderstanding is not only possible but probable, but it is still preferable to not having a chance to speak at all.

The following excerpt from Jimmie Durham shows a clear awareness of who his audience will be. Not many non-Native peoples may "understand" the emotions he conveys here; however, they are sentiments that must be given expression. Paulo Freire has pointed out that "Dialogue cannot be carried out in a climate of hopelessness. If the dialoguers expect nothing to come of their efforts, their encounter will be empty and sterile, bureaucratic and tedious" (80). Implied in the writing of autobiography, in this case Durham's, is the hope that someone *would* understand, not simply empathize or sympathize with his anger. He states:

> The reason I used several voices, or styles, is that I wanted to experiment with mixing different Cherokee speech patterns as a way of showing confusion and the fight for some clarity within that confusion. . . . I wrote the first part of this piece as though I were writing to Indian people, with one half of my brain; with the other half of my brain I was

> writing to the white folks, because who reads all these things? The white folks. (164)

In other cases, the autobiographies reflect a sense of audience that may be an ideal one for understanding, but not necessarily the audience who will read the piece. As Durham asserts, the readers will probably be "white folks," but the formative audience may be intentionally different. Ralph Salisbury (Cherokee) explains: "Sometimes I think I write as some other people say they write, 'to an imagined ideal reader, perhaps someone like my best self,' but I think my essential stance as a writer was formed while sitting with my brothers, my sister, my aunt, my mother . . ." (23). Still other writers invoke a more mystical aspect, where the ideal audience may be the self. Harjo writes:

> . . . looking back I realize the ending must have originated in one of two places. One was a story I heard from a woman who during times of deep emotional troubles would be visited by a woman who looked just like her. She herself would never see her, but anyone passing by her room while she was asleep would see this imaginary woman, standing next to her bed. I always considered the "imaginary" woman as her other self, the denied self who wanted back in. (269)

And perhaps the "denied self wanting back in" is always already implied in Native American writing. To come back in, it, too, would have to be reconstructed as a positively accepted self, and this requires some form of dialogue with the discourses that accentuate the denial. The acceptance may not be possible from those discourses of dominance, but ideally it *could* be.

A last, key Bakhtinian concept is internally persuasive discourse, which involves a "retelling in one's own words" ("Discourse" 341). Bakhtin explains that it is "affirmed through assimilation, tightly interwoven with 'one's own word' ultimately becoming half-ours and half-someone else's." He adds that "Its creativity and productiveness consist precisely in the fact that such a word awakens new and independent words, that it organizes new masses of our words from within . . . it enters into interanimating relationships with new contexts" ("Discourse" 345). Halasek clarifies that in order to interrogate authoritative discourse, internally persuasive discourse must work dialectically with it. It is out of this struggle that human coming-to-consciousness occurs.

Haunani-Kay Trask points out that "the whole area of decolonizing the mind" is a subtle process. "Language, for example, is a critical de-colonizer" (274). In a sense, then, most Native American autobiographical writing involves that dialectical movement between the authoritative and the internally persuasive; it is a site of resistance because it signifies a kind of coming to consciousness, so vital in facilitating de-assimilation. Here Diane Glancy will have the last word, or, as I read it, the beginning word:

> I find that the Indian, as well as poetry, stands between the visible and the invisible worlds, between earth and heaven. The Indian, and poetry to some extent, has been rejected by society and is not at home here. Neither are we at rest in the spiritual world. We are neither here nor there but in the midst of a journey. Part of one, part of the other, revealing neither fully but indicating a struggle for reconciliation on the part of both. (172)

Notes

1. Currently Native demographics are the subject of intense debate. For analysis of the arguments, see Henry F. Dobyns, *Native American Historical Demography: A Critical Bibliography* (Bloomington: Indiana UP, 1976); Russell Thornton, *American Indian Holocaust and Survival: A Population History Since 1492* (Norman: U of Oklahoma P, 1987); and Leo Kuper, *Genocide: Its Political Use in the Twentieth Century* (New Haven: Yale UP, 1981).

2. See, for example, the works of Peter Mason, Tzvetan Todorov, Gerald Vizenor, Stephen Greenblatt, Ward Churchill, and Myra Jehlen, to name a few.

3. See, for example, Larzer Ziff, *Writing in the New Nation: Prose, Print, and Politics in the Early United States* (New Haven: Yale UP, 1991).

4. See, for example, Ward Churchill, *Indians Are Us? Culture and Genocide in Native North America* (Monroe, ME: Common Courage P, 1994).

5. Most of the texts are from Swann and Krupat's *I Tell You Now*, since I feel this book is a fabulous anthology with no intrusiveness on the part of the editors.

6. See Theresa Henning, "The Ethical Excesses of Expressionism: A Response to Critiques of Social Rhetorics," paper presented at the Annual Meeting of the Conference on College Composition and Communication, 1997; Anna Charr Kim, *Composing in a Second Language: A Case Study of a Russian College Student* (IL: National-Louis U, 1995). Émile Durkheim appropriated the term "anomie" for his theory of "anomic suicide." Riaz Hassan, in his article "One Hundred Years of Emile Durkheim's Suicide: A Study in Sociology," *Australian and New Zealand Journal of Psychiatry* 32.2 (April 1998), explains anomie in a manner that resonates here. He describes it as a "result of a sudden and unexpected change in a person's social

position creating a new situation with which he is unable to cope" (169). It is linked to "the strength of an individual's ties to society and the stability of social relations within that society" (168). Colonization, fueled by economic considerations, with its concomitant cultural, religious, and political changes, provided a powerful stage for anomie.

Works Cited

Bakhtin, Mikhail. "Discourse in the Novel." *The Dialogic Imagination: Four Essays by M. M. Bakhtin*. Trans. Caryl Emerson and Michael Holquist. Ed. Michael Holquist. Austin: U of Texan P, 1981. 259–422.

———. *Speech Genres and Other Late Essays*. Trans. Vern W. McGee. Austin: U Texas P, 1986.

Barnes, Jim. "On Native Ground." Swann and Krupat 85–98.

Cook-Lynn, Elizabeth. "You May Consider Speaking About Your Art." Swann and Krupat 55–64.

Durham, Jimmie. "Those Dead Guys for a Hundred Years." Swann and Krupat 155–66.

Eastman, Charles (Ohiyesa). "The Soul of the Indian." 1911. *Masterpieces of American Indian Literature*. Ed. Willis G. Regier. New York: MJF Books, 1993.

Farmer, Frank. "Dialogue and Critique: Bakhtin and the Cultural Studies Classroom." *College Composition and Communication* 49.2 (1998): 186–207.

Forbes, Jack D. "Shouting Back to the Geese." Swann and Krupat 111–26.

Freire, Paulo. *Pedagogy of the Oppressed*. Trans. Myra Bergman Ramos. New York: Continuum, 1970.

Glancy, Diane. "Two Dresses." Swann and Krupat 167–84.

Gunn Allen, Paula. "The Autobiography of a Confluence." Swann and Krupat 141–54.

Halasek, Kay. *A Pedagogy of Possibility: Bakhtinian Perspectives on Composition Studies*. Carbondale: Southern Illinois UP, 1999.

Harjo, Joy. "Ordinary Spirit." Swann and Krupat 263–70.

Hertzberg, Hazel W. *The Search for an American Indian Identity: Modern Pan-Indian Movements*. Syracuse: Syracuse UP, 1971.

Hogan, Linda. "The Two Lives." Swann and Krupat 231–50.

hooks, bell. "Keeping Close to Home: Class and Education." *The Presence of Others*. Ed. Andrea Lunsford and John J. Ruszkiewicz. New York: St. Martin's, 1997. 80–90.

Jaimes, M. Annette, ed. *The State of Native America: Genocide, Colonization, and Resistance*. Boston: South End, 1992.

Kenny, Maurice. "Waiting at the Edge: Words Toward a Life." Swann and Krupat 37–54.

Lunsford, Andrea. "Toward a Mestiza Rhetoric: Gloria Anzaldúa on Composition and Postcoloniality." *Race, Rhetoric, and the Postcolonial.* Ed. Gary A. Olson and Lynn Worsham. Albany: State U New York P, 1999. 43–80.

Native American Women's Health Education Resource Center. "Native American Women Uncover Norplant Abuses." *Ms.* Sept./Oct. 1993: 69.

Niatum, Duane. "Autobiographical Sketch." Swann and Krupat 127–40.

Revard, Carter. "Walking Among the Stars." Swann and Krupat 65–83.

Rose, Wendy. "Neon Scars." Swann and Krupat 251–62.

Salisbury, Ralph. "The Quiet Between Lightning and Thunder." Swann and Krupat 15–36.

Slotkin, Richard. *Gunfighter Nation: The Myth of the Frontier in Twentieth-Century America.* New York: Harper Perennial, 1992.

Swann, Brian, and Arnold Krupat, eds. *I Tell You Now: Autobiographical Essays by Native American Writers.* Lincoln: U of Nebraska P, 1987.

Tallmountain, Mary. "You Can Go Home Again: A Sequence." Swann and Krupat 1–14.

Talon, Jamie. "The Norplant Controversy." *Glamour* April 1995: 66–69.

Trask, Haunani-Kay. *From a Native Daughter: Colonialism and Sovereignty in Hawai'i.* Monroe, ME: Common Courage Press, 1993.

Vizenor, Gerald. "Crows Written on the Poplars: Autocritical Autobiographies." Swann and Krupat 99–109.

INSIDE THE CIRCLE, OUTSIDE THE CIRCLE

THE CONTINUANCE OF NATIVE AMERICAN STORYTELLING AND THE DEVELOPMENT OF RHETORICAL STRATEGIES IN ENGLISH

✦

Karen A. Redfield

> I simply don't think Native American narrators are victims. I think they have and still use storytelling to their own purposes. Far more often than not, those purposes have been obscured by editors, but even in the worst of examples, we should not assume that Native voice and intention have been obliterated.
>
> Kathleen Sands, *"Narrative Resistance"*

> Native Americans began to express their views at least as early as the 1830's in texts published in English, some of which went into several editions. . . . Furthermore, their speeches, delivered in many cities throughout the United States, were attended by large crowds and were subsequently both printed and reviewed in newspapers and journals, as examples of Indian oratory.
>
> Cheryl Walker, *Indian Nation*

I CAME to teach at the Lac Courte Oreilles Ojibwe Community College in January 1997. Along with teaching, I was going to collect student writing samples and conduct interviews with students and staff; this work was the foundation of my PhD dissertation. In addition to that project, I was contributing to the Center for English Learning and Achievement project, specifically in the area of Wisconsin literacy. Although I had never lived through a northern Wisconsin winter, or taught at a tribal college, I was fairly confident that I had packed all the necessities for winter survival and good fieldwork: my almost twenty years of experience as a college composition teacher, both in the United States and in Bolivia; an ethnographic methodology; a contrastive rhetoric paradigm; an open mind, of course; and emergency supplies in case I got snowed in. The first week I was there I was snowed in and the college was closed due to weather, so the supplies did come in handy. In terms of my research, though, I had not packed so well. I was looking for a storytelling template that would support my theory that such a form provided the structure, themes, and tone for many college students' essays. My question was: how could we, as teachers, respect and preserve that form, and still school students in the essayist literacy so crucial to their college success? Fortunately, I was quickly disabused of such narrow formal notions. My storytelling template was, I realized, based on an ethnographic model of preservation, rather than a rhetorical model of dynamic communication. With a clearer mind, I was able to appreciate the variety of English and Ojibwe language communication happening all around me. There is a lively reservation-based public radio station, WOJB, on which it was not unusual to hear a caller to Paul DeMain's "Morning Fire" program speaking Ojibwe on a cell phone. There are also several newspapers: *News From Indian Country, Ojibwe Akiing (Ojibwe Turf),* the *LCO Times* (now the *Chippewa Sun*), and the local Hayward paper, the *Sawyer County Record.* This seemed a great many Indian-centered print media sources for a reservation population of fewer than five thousand people.[1]

An informal survey of my college students suggested that Indian students read more than one newspaper and non-Indian students read only the Hayward paper. Paul DeMain, the managing editor and CEO of *News From Indian Country*, noted that their surveys show that their readers also read "an average of five Native newspapers. One national, one or two regional, and their local tribal publication, at least" (DeMain). He says that non-Native publications are also read, but that they do not tend to be the primary source for of news.

This variety of Native publications in English, with more and more sections using Ojibwe, convinced me that I had wandered into a culturally specific and dynamic rhetorical space. It took another year of research and reflection to become aware of the obvious: I had not come upon a "new" rhetorical space. This is a contemporary space that had developed from all the rhetorical enterprises of the nineteenth century. I define these rhetorical enterprises as exercises in "external" rhetoric: all the rhetorical strategies devised in English to deal with, in various ways and for various reasons, Euro-American colonizers and their rhetoric of nation building. At the end of this essay, I will assert that newspapers, among other examples of Indian publishing, illustrate that rhetoric is again shifting from an external to an internal focus: contemporary Indian rhetoric on reservations, in fiction, journalism, and film, is more concerned with sustaining community and cultural coherence. Much more work can be done in this field, or this space, if you will.

In 1998, I presented papers at both the Conference on College Composition and Communication and the RETAIN conference (Retention in Education for Today's Indian Nations) suggesting those of us who teach Native American literature should design courses that deal specifically and critically with Indian rhetoric written in English. Such a course, to be complete, would need to address some uncomfortable issues such as Indian writers who held fairly strong assimilationist and Christian views in the nineteenth century. Other writers, such as Indian women journalists writing during the Dawes Era, presented "Native cultures as vital parts of American society . . . [attempting] both to legitimate a Native identity and to argue for inclusion as equals in the dominant culture" (Batker 191). For these writers to negotiate a rhetorical path between their Native identity and the white power structure and to argue for the rights and dignity of Native people was complicated and hazardous, to say the least. Many writers lost the respect of their own families and never gained it from their white audiences. It is the attempt to find ways to communicate with non-Native people that I am calling external rhetoric. Some of the samples of writing that survive are school exercises that praise the school's benefactors and exemplify the healthful tonic education could be for Indian people. These letters may be seen as examples of external rhetoric. It is Scott Lyons's contention that, "There is little doubt that acts of deference . . . are intended in some sense to convey the outward impression of conformity with standards sustained by superiors. Beyond this we may not safely go. Each and every act of deference about the attitude behind an act of deference must therefore be based on evidence external to the act itself" (124). In light of this, letters such as those collected in Murray's chapter "Pray Sir, consider a little" (in Jaskoski) are even more poignant, if that is possible.

Indigenous people in the Americas were never silent, even if they were rarely heard by Euro-Americans. Some Indian speakers and writers felt that the key to survival on many levels was to show Euro-Americans how capable of adaptation Indian people were. Yes, they argued, they were intelligent and moral people who could speak to a European or American audience articulately in their own languages and within their own genres. Frederick Douglass employed similar methods in the first edition of *Narrative of the Life of Frederick Douglass, an American Slave.* Like many Indian writers, his tone also changed when he perceived that this method was no longer efficacious. At the beginning of this period of external rhetorical development, American

Indian writers found that "written English was a powerful medium for educating white audiences about the intellectual and creative abilities of Indian people . . . and white injustice to Native peoples" (A. LaVonne Brown Ruoff, "Foreword" in Jaskoski, viii).

There are at least two important reasons to pay closer attention to nineteenth-century written (and oral) texts by Native people in English: one is to marvel at the development of external rhetorical strategies. The other and, for me, most compelling reason is to examine how traditional storytelling continued through this period into the twentieth century. Without the connection of external rhetoric, the jump from traditional stories to contemporary literature and now, film as well, is very long indeed. As Clements has observed:

> Scholars have often noted that the American Indian writers whose work has generated [the current] renaissance represent the continuation of tribal traditions of verbal arts and participate in expressive culture rooted in the spiritual and intellectual contexts of their own communities. Not as much attention, though, has been paid to the ways in which writing by Native Americans in the nineteenth and early twentieth centuries relates to the oral tradition. In fact, many students of this writing, especially autobiographical works, have instead emphasized its parallels to Euroamerican literature. (122)

One such writer of autobiography was the Yankton Sioux writer Zitkala-Sa, also known as Gertrude Bonnin (1876–1938). Her first published work was *Old Indian Legends*, published in 1901, "almost as ethnographic collection of Indian stories and folktales" (Bloom 118). Zitkala-Sa is "hardly considered a major figure within that [Native American literature] tradition, as it is presently being defined" according to some (Okker 124). As Bloom argues, "Nevertheless, she is considered one of the founding voices of the Native American literary tradition" (119). She is also increasingly anthologized in texts for Native American literature courses. If Zitkala-Sa is read from a more historically and politically situated rhetorical position, however, she provides us with a valuable example of external rhetoric. In her Preface to *Old Indian Legends*, Zitkala-Sa asserted that the stories "once told to the little black-haired aborigine had come to belong just as much to the little blue-eyed patriot. The study of Native American storytelling, she claimed, strongly suggests our near kinship to the rest of humanity and points a steady finger toward the great brotherhood of mankind" (Clements 127).

Though "aborigine" may hold negative connotations for some in the United States, it could be seen as a cultural assertion in 1901: we were here first. The finger Zitkala-Sa points at the "great brotherhood of mankind" is "steady"; she has no doubt of the morality of her point of view. And Native American storytelling, far from being simple or primitive, suggests a "near kinship" to humanity. Granted, "near kinship" is a bit too deferential when read now, but the rest of this passage asserts a position that bordered on radicalism.

Her sentimental tale of "The Soft-Hearted Sioux," included in *American Indian Stories* in 1921, was pronounced "morally bad" by a reviewer in the Carlisle school's newspaper *The Red Man and Helper*. It challenged "the very core of educational policy at Carlisle. [It is] a fictional account of the inadequacy of off-reservation schools to prepare Indians to live within their own cultures" (Dexter Fisher qtd. in Bloom 119). The story concerns a young man who has been educated into the white, Christian world, and comes home to find his father near death from illness and starvation. The "educated" young man, with a "soft" heart from looking for Christ, has forgotten how to hunt; his Bible readings do little to help in this area. His father finally begs him to at least kill one of the white man's cattle for food. The young man does, and is caught. His father dies, and the son is to be hung for theft. Awaiting death, the young man wonders who will greet him on the other side. "Will the loving Jesus grant me pardon and give my soul a soothing sleep? or will my warrior father greet me and receive me as his son?" he asks (*American Indian Stories* 124). The story ends without an answer.

The reviewer for the Carlisle newspaper, points out how many people have taken Zitkala-Sa into their hearts and homes, "Yet not a word of gratitude or allusion to such kindness has ever escaped her in any line of anything that she has written for the public" (Fisher qtd. in Bloom 119). Doing this, the reviewer continues, "injures herself and harms the educational work in progress for the race from which she sprang." The reviewer concludes by noting that some Indian people have reached "higher altitudes in literary and professional lines" than Zitkala-Sa has, but among them "we know of no other case of such pronounced morbidness" (Fisher qtd. in Bloom 119).

Zitkala-Sa's fascination with such "unhealthy" matters as disparaging Christianity and white education, and advocating citizenship and suffrage for Indian people are not as evident in her stories as in her journalism and oratory, but it cannot be overlooked. She moved from writing virtual ethnography to critiquing the nationalist and racist rhetorical paradigm of her day. Even in her earlier stories, she asserts that her people and their stories be read with respect.

American Indian Stories, which includes "The Soft-Hearted Sioux" as well as "Impressions of an Indian Childhood" among other autobiographical stories, is a mix of traditional Indian storytelling and standard short story forms. "The Soft-Hearted Sioux" is complete with an exposition, rising action, climax, and resolution. The characters are clearly even if sentimentally drawn (reflecting the taste of the day), and the action takes place in the central location of the Indian community. Zitkala-Sa was educated in white schools in the academic curriculum of the day (as opposed to the work schools). She exhibits her learning of Latin, among other skills, and it is evident that she was astute enough to tell stories so that white people can hear them. She has learned how to incorporate traditional teachings into a new form, making the kind of rhetorical choices necessary for an external rhetoric. The moral of "The Soft-Hearted Sioux," that there is a real danger in losing one's connection to family, culture, spirituality, is consciously not made palatable, though the narrative form was familiar.

In the sections of her own autobiography, Zitkala-Sa is more episodic, despite the linear form of her childhood-to-adulthood narrative. Her stories reminded several of my students of other speakers they had heard or authors they had read. However, Zitkala-Sa had not abandoned storytelling rhetoric completely. At the end of "An Indian Teacher among Indians," the last clearly autobiographical section of *American Indian Stories*, Zitkala-Sa leaves the reader unsure of exactly what will happen next in her life, but not what her feelings are. After suffering the tourists who come to gawk at Indian children in schools, or who have done some small service as teachers, she comments: "In this fashion many have passed idly through the Indian schools during the last decade, afterward to boast of their charity to the North American Indian. But few there are who have paused to question whether real life or long-lasting death lies beneath this semblance of civilization" (99).

To write at all was a political statement. Like many writers of the late nineteenth century, Zitkala-Sa's writings were problematic, from her vacillation between feeling assimilation was inevitable to her denouncement of cultural imperialism in all forms. And yet her work must be seen, as Jaskoski argues for many American Indian writers in English, "as always involved in a dynamic negotiation across many boundaries, barriers, gaps, and silences characterizing the emergent nation. Their understanding speaks to a profound faith in the possibility of language to overcome ignorance and hostility, as well as a remarkable trust, which in the light of history may seem to have been misplaced, in the capacity of their audiences to be persuaded by rational argument and humane principles" (xii).

During this period, many voices were also being raised toward an Indian audience, primarily in the form of newspapers. Littlefield emphasizes that, "As product and process the native press has a long history. . . . The establishment of the first native run press . . . began a press history that continues today" (58). Even scanning very quickly over the publishing landscape of the nineteenth century, we can see the *Cherokee Phoenix* which was written in both Cherokee and English (1824), the *Choctaw Telegraph* (1848), *Copway's American Indian* (1851), and in 1913, the *Society of American Indians Quarterly* (Peyer 257). Some publications, therefore, reflected local tribal needs and interests and others addressed national or inter-tribal audiences. As with other genres, newspapers were not uniform in their philosophies or goals. George Copway, an Ojibwe who became a well-known Christian minister and missionary, reflected the often painful and constant bargaining between cultures in his life and in his writing. He urged "his readers to see him as a text, a personification of Indian progress toward acculturation" (Walker 84). "By appealing to his white readers as fellow Christians, he subtly underscores the equality of Indians with whites, an equality non-Indians often ignored" (Ruoff qtd. in Jaskoski vii). Copway also "[bespoke] the dilemma of the modern Indian caught between a traditional culture which is no longer viable in the old sense and an alien culture which is both destructive and empowering at the same time" (Walker 108). *Copway's American Indian* was "one of the few non-tribal newspapers to be published singlehandedly by an Indian . . . not duplicated in the history of American Indian journalism until 1916, Carlos Montezuma's personal monthly newsletter *Wassaja* (1916–1922)" (Peyer 257).

There are too many journalists, both men and women, both those who wrote for non-Indian publications and those who wrote for or began their own tribal newspapers, to do them any justice here. Again, I would direct you to the work of Jaskoski, Peyer, Walker, and Littlefield, among others. That there were so many people writing in so many different forms, I hope, illustrates my central point that American Indian writers of the nineteenth century were constantly making complex and sophisticated rhetorical choices. They were defining and practicing an external rhetoric on the spot, in the same way that all those who have had to translate between languages and cultures have always done, with the immediacy and fluency that the occasion demanded. It is sadly ironic that in demeaning Hollywood caricatures of American Indians, language is one of the primary targets for ridicule. Valerie Red-Horse, a contemporary actress, writer, director, producer, and MBA, was once told by a casting agent that she spoke too well to get the part of an Indian woman. (Red-Horse's own film *Naturally Native* debuted at the Sundance Film Festival in 1998.)

Language was also one of the first cultural distinctions and comforts excised by boarding school staff. Zitkala-Sa provides an especially painful illustration of this in her description of her own school days in *American Indian Stories.* Children rarely spoke any English when they arrived at boarding school. One of Zitkala-Sa's older classmates attempted to quickly tutor a small group of children in survival English by teaching them the word "no" and exhorting them to use it as a universal answer. One child who was being reprimanded for making a snow angel answered "no" to a teacher's question: "Are you going to obey my word the next time?" After much physical abuse, the young girl finally answered "no" to the right question about falling in the snow again. Zitkala-Sa tells us: "During the first two or three seasons misunderstandings as ridiculous as this one . . . frequently took place, bringing unjustifiable frights and punishments into our little lives" (59).

Learning to communicate in English and adapting traditional rhetorical strategies into useful patterns are linguistic and intellectual accomplishments that have rarely been respected by non-Native rhetorical scholars. From outside to inside: protest, literature, and other contemporary rhetorical strategies, "indigenous media can be understood as part of a powerful new process in the construction of contemporary and future indigenous identities. . . . [I]ndigenous productions are often directed to the mediations and ruptures of times and social relations in ways that point to a cultural future" (Ginsburg 123).

This cultural future includes Native radio and television stations along with print media and films. In the fall of 1999, Canada's 800,000 aboriginal people were able to turn on the Aboriginal Peoples Television Network, broadcasting in English, French, and fifteen aboriginal languages. This will cost subscribers an additional fifteen cents a month ("Aboriginal cable"). Frank Blythe, a founding member of the Native American Public Broadcasting Consortium (NAPBC), estimates that by 1995 there were more than two dozen Native public and commercial radio stations in the United States, an impressive jump from one station in 1971 (in Keith xv). In Australia, Aboriginal people are active in television and film production. In such media production, Ginsburg asserts, "Aboriginal skills at constituting both individual and collective identities through narrative and ceremonial performance are engaged in innovative ways that are simultaneously indigenous and intercultural" (123). In the United States, "Native journalism is a growing field right now, [with] tribal newspapers springing up everywhere," observed Trace DeMeyer, formerly editor of a local Ojibwe newspaper *Ojibwe Akiing* (Ojibwe Turf) and then the editor for the *Pequot Times* before she turned to her own writing projects. Such newspapers provide "a forum for the intellectual discussion of modern issues in our communities. . . . Native societies are not dead societies; they are thriving and need to change as well," noted Paul DeMain, formerly editor of the national newspaper *News From Indian Country*. DeMeyer emphasizes that "Native news from Native writers is essential. . . . Not necessarily that [news] has a Native slant but the Native voice. . . . I have come to realize that news stories are the new storytelling, with triumph or tragedy" (DeMeyer). After reading over tribal (Ojibwe and Oneida) newspapers from Wisconsin for an assignment in my Native American Literature class, Joy Thompson wrote in her journal that a difference she noted between mainstream local papers and the Native press "is that they [tribal papers] recognize the individuals in a more profound way."[2]

Radio and television stations, movies, and newspapers are all forms of contemporary Native communication that exemplifies "internal rhetoric." Indian people are no longer as worried about communicating with "outsiders" as they are about keeping current with Native news and helping stories as well as first languages flourish within the community. The cultural imperatives and rhetorical strategies are now supported by technology and capital; yet the technology has not lost the human connection. As Joy, the student in my class, noted, the Native press recognizes individuals "in a more profound way." For example, following the deaths of Ojibwe activist Walt Bresette and Menominee activist Ingrid Washinawatok, the details of their lives, and in Ingrid's case, the light of her smile, filled pages in *News From Indian Country* and *Ojibwe Akiing*. Both stories received only small mention in Wisconsin's non-Native press, despite the fact that both persons had been active in state environmental and cultural issues.

As Native media grow, there will be less and less need to make stories clear to non-Indian audiences. This is not meant to suggest that Indian sources will become closed, focused only on tribal issues and tribal audiences. It is not wise to live in such isolation. As Camille Lacapa of WOJB radio explains, an important part of their mission "is to reflect credit upon the Ojibwe and other Indian nations and to promote harmony between Indian and non-Indian communities" (qtd. in Keith 79). This stance is not without controversy, however; some tribal members argue that WOJB should focus more on tribal needs and issues. DeMeyer notes that the Native press in Wisconsin addresses issues that affect all state residents, for example a proposed Exxon mine in Crandon, Wisconsin, which opponents believed would irrevocably defile the Sokaogon (Mole Lake) Ojibwes' wild rice beds and water supply and eventually taint water sources for other state residents (DeMeyer).[3]

The Native media are unlikely to ever be completely closed to non-Native audiences, although most Native print media are incorporating more and more first-language sections, which leaves non-Native readers, like the students in my classes, feeling that they are out of the tribal circle. Indian writers, journalists, filmmakers, musicians, and speakers no longer have to be concerned about whether or not non-Indian audiences understand or approve of what they are saying. The concept of audience has shifted back to the tribal community and/or to the broader sense of community captured in the term "Indian country"; in other words, the exigencies now come from internal rather than external rhetoric.

Unlike Zitkala-Sa or George Copway's struggles to retain some dignity and Indian identity within the narrow white definitions of "Indian identity," contemporary "Indigenous media can be understood as part of a powerful new process in the construction of contemporary and future indigenous identities. . . . [I]ndigenous productions are often directed to the mediations of ruptures of times and social relations in ways that point to a cultural future" (Ginsburg 123).

In analyzing the Red Power movement of the late 1960s and early 1970s, Randall A. Lake acknowledges that Indian people "had little success in convincing white society to redress Indian grievances" ("Enacting Red Power" 127). Part of the problem, Lake concluded, was a white refusal to acknowledge or value Indian rhetoric:

> militant Indian rhetoric is more appropriately viewed from a perspective which examines its significance for Indians themselves. . . . [T]he judgments of failure so often leveled against Native American protest rhetoric are problematic because they misanalyze this rhetoric's primary audience. Most Red Power rhetoric is directed at movement members and other Indians for the purpose of gathering the like-minded, and is addressed only secondarily to the white establishment. . . . In brief, AIM may have been judged a failure because its rhetoric is expected to do something which it is not intended to do. ("Enacting Red Power" 128)

Much has changed since 1983, however. There is a growing community of Native scholars and activists, as well as larger cohorts of professionals educated in tribal schools and colleges and working in positions of power. Increases in cultural, political, and economic power also suggest that Native people in general need not pay as much attention to whether or not they are understood by white society. Even Lake is more confident of change in 1991: "The rejuvenation of tribal entities . . . does not constitute final success for Red Power. Yet it is a positive sign of better things to come because it empirically denies the historicist thesis that the time for tribal existence has passed irretrievably. . . . [C]onditions are perpetually ripe for activism and, if today represents a down-turn in the cycle of resistance, inevitably a resurgence will occur" ("Enacting Red Power" 137).

Contemporary resistance, I would argue, is taking a familiar form: internal rhetoric. The activism is reflected by American Indian storytellers, intellectuals, artists, students, and elders, telling their stories in their own languages for their own people. At a recent storytelling festival at the University of Wisconsin-Madison, hosted in part by the American Indian Studies Department, the audience was treated to a feast of languages indigenous to the area we now call Wisconsin: a prayer in Ho-Chunk, a grandmother's translation of a grandson's favorite book into Menominee, a story in Oneida, and stories and jokes in Ojibwe. Most of the evening was translated for the non-Indian audience members, but not all. This in itself is reflects activism and resistance.[4]

We can see activism in such gatherings and in current tribal newspapers from the state. A quick scan of the three newspapers published on the Lac Courte Oreilles Ojibwe reservation in Wisconsin in March of 1999—*News From Indian Country, Ojibwe Akiing,* and the *Chippewa Sun*—gives several hopeful examples of various kinds of activism.

There are many stories about children and their accomplishments, stories of respected elders, of future plans of college students, and the building of new tribal college facilities. There are also stories of local environmental concerns and gaming issues as they relate to the tribe. Words and Web sites are part of this new activism. In other stories (when this chapter was written): then interior secretary Bruce Babbitt was being called on to explain mismanagement as it relates to proposed Wisconsin tribal casino; Minnesota governor Jesse Ventura was being given a lesson in what sovereignty means; DJs in San Diego were ridiculing Indian naming ceremonies and being forced to respond via their Web site to all the e-mails and faxes they received in protest. The same DJs had refused to appear on Native America Calling, a program broadcast over AIROS (the American Indian Radio on Satellite). And, as always, there was a weekly lesson in Ojibwe, as well as the Indian entertainment reviews, information on business and educational opportunities, a section on birthdays, and notices of those who had "walked on" since the last issue. There was even a sports item that my most sports-minded students didn't know about: Kareem Abdul-Jabbar has been working with a high school team on the White Mountain Apache reservation. There were also several stories, primarily in *News From Indian Country*, on issues and current events affecting tribes in several other states, and indigenous stories from all over the world.

Many of these stories may seem no different than those in any small-town American newspaper, an observation many of my students made. But most American small towns and ethnic communities were not under siege for generations, their land, language, spiritual practices, and even children taken away. Most small-town American newspapers do not represent such a triumph of the human spirit or of the tenacity of a rhetorical tradition that was thought to be wiped out or completely assimilated.

Moving Back Inside the Circle

When Kim Blaeser, noted poet and critic, spoke in my Native American Literature class not long ago, a student asked her who the target audience was for her poetry. She answered that it was first and foremost "Indian people who know the things I know." Although Blaeser believes that her work is accessible and meaningful to non-Indian audiences, it is one of her priorities to "become a voice for [Indian] people who may not be writers" (Blaeser, Lecture). It is this sense of audience and the rhetorical practices that carry it out that I suggest make up a return to "internal rhetoric" as the first concern of many Native writers.

Thomas King has said that when he reads a section in *Medicine River* in which Joyce Blue Horn asks Will, the narrator, if he can really take a picture of her whole family, a Native audience laughs (Rooke 64). When Joyce Blue Horn says, "I got a big family" the impact is lost on Will, who has recently returned to the community. Native audiences laugh, King says, because they are not surprised that Joyce is counting fifty or so people among her "immediate family." Self-described Ojibwe grandmother and storyteller Anne M. Dunn often uses names and place in her collection of cultural and autobiographical stories entitled *Grandmother's Gift* that mean little to anyone outside of her community, and yet the book is the second she has published. Thomson Highway's play *The Rez Sisters*, nominated for the Governor General's Award in Canada, has several passages in Cree and Ojibwe, most translated into English, but not all. Louise Erdrich's novel *The Antelope Wife* begins with an untranslated dedication in Ojibwe.

The rhetorical form that is the most "internal," it could be argued, is parody. In order to get the joke, one must understand the context, the particulars, and the nuances of what is being parodied. For the purposes of this discussion, Shelley Niro's (Mohawk) 1998 film parody *Honey Moccasin* best illustrates the vitality of several forms of contemporary American Indian rhetorical practices and venues.[5] Set on the fictional Grand Pine Reservation, the film follows the search for a thief who stole a powwow outfit, and the rivalry between two bars, The Smokin' Moccasin and The Inukshuk Café. Along the way, the viewer is treated to a reservation cable access show, less-than-objective reporters, a fashion show of powwow outfits made of car tires and breakfast cereal, and the transformation of bar owner Honey Moccasin into a supersleuth via a surrealistic sequence in which she turns into Wonder Woman and Pocahontas first. Honey's daughter Mabel, a film school student, literally acts as a historic witness in a performance piece that involves slides of tragic historical events being projected onto a teepee built around her; only Mable's face is visible. The slides are juxtaposed with Mabel's rendition of "Fever."

In coming back to the reservation, Mabel and her cousin Zachary John (who has been stealing and dressing up in the powwow outfits) reflect the respected homing plot and the belief that art can provide both healing and redemption. However, the parody prevails. The film serves as an "irreverent reappropriation of familiar narrative strategies [which serve] as a provocative spring-board for an investigation of authenticity, cultural identity, and the articulation of modern Native American experience in cinematic language and pop culture" (Women Make Movies).

Despite an almost complete semester of reading various genres of contemporary American Indian writing, and a good bit of preparation, students are often perplexed after they have seen *Honey Moccasin*. They feel that they didn't "get the joke." Some feel that they had a comfortable sense of what Indian writers and filmmakers are going to say, and the film unhinges them a bit. If we are lucky, we end the semester with a lively discussion about how identity is constructed by one's self and by others and the rights of an artist to choose her own narrative stance and forms, even if they are not comfortable for an "external," primarily non-Indian student audience. Such a parody could not have been written by Zitkala-Sa, but I would argue that this parody could not have been written without her.

In instances of humor and language, in issues of form and theme, in focus and in details of name and place, and in moral teachings, American Indian rhetoric has "migrated home." As Blaeser explained to my class, she titled her anthology of Ojibwe short stories *Stories Migrating Home* because migration signifies both going and coming, an image that also means a movement between internal and external rhetoric.

In "Rhetoric: Its Function and Scope" Bryant defines rhetoric in this way: "First of all and primarily . . . to be the *rationale of informative and suasory discourse*. All its other meanings are partial or morally colored derivatives from that primary meaning. . . . Rhetoric aims at what is *worth* doing, what is worth trying. It is concerned with *values*" [original emphasis] (271, 285). I conclude with Bryant's definition of rhetoric because it gets at the heart of what American Indian rhetoricians, orally and in print (and now in film), in first languages and English, have based their rhetoric on for generations: values. As Walker has noted, Indian writers began to express "their views at least as early as the 1830's in texts published in English" (8). This proves a strong sense of rhetorical agency and cultural identity. I agree with Sands: "I simply don't think Native American narrators are victims. I think they have and still use storytelling to their own purposes" (12).

Why should non-Indian researchers and teachers be concerned with American Indian rhetoric? For three main reasons: first, so that teachers can facilitate success for Indian students in college (and other) classrooms by utilizing principles of contrastive rhetoric. Second, because American Indian communities and American writing in all genres are dynamic contemporary sites of rhetoric; we can learn much about the power and practice of rhetoric by studying with American Indian storytellers, writers, and scholars. And third, it is time. We are all living in a contact zone, and the healthy future of this country depends on mutual understanding among all the nations and communities within our borders. We have been given, in Oneida poet Roberta Hill Whiteman's words, "the gift of words / to bring us comfort and care." Let us finally begin to respect the use of this gift as it has been used by Indian rhetoricians in the continuance of storytelling and the development of rhetorical strategies in English.

Notes

I offer *miigwetch* to Agnes Fleming for the opportunity to learn and to teach at the Lac Courte Oreilles Ojibwe Community College, and to all the kind and generous students and colleagues at the college. And a special *miigwetch* to Maddy Moose, a skilled Ojibwe teacher, who always said that all good and useful work is grounded in the community and in our own heart.

1. I am choosing to use "American Indian" instead of "Native American" in most cases for several reasons, among which are: that most of my friends in Wisconsin refer to themselves as Indian people; that the University of Wisconsin–Madison has named its Native Studies department "American Indian Studies"; that *Tribal College* states that it is the journal of American Indian higher education; and that the RETAIN conference acronym stands for "retention in education for today's American Indian nations." I realize that naming is a personal and sensitive issue; I mean no offense to anyone. I also use the terms "Native people" and "indigenous people," more in accordance with what is used in Canada.

2. The quotation from my Madison Area Technical College student is used with her permission.

3. The Sokaogon Ojibwe bought this land in 2004; there will be no mining.

4. For a deeper analysis of Ojibwe storytelling, consult J. Randolph Valentine's work "Amik Anicinaabewigoban: Rhetorical Structures in Albert Mowatt's Telling of an Algonquin Tale," *Memoir 13, Algonquin and Iroquoian Linguistics* (Winnipeg: University of Manitoba, 1966).

5. Thanks to Melanie Herzog, artist and art professor at Edgewood College, who introduced me to the film *Honey Moccasin*.

Works Cited

Batker, Carol. "Overcoming All Obstacles: The Assimilation Debate in Native American Women's Journalism of the Dawes Era." *Early Native American Writing*. Ed. Helen Jaskoski. Cambridge: Cambridge UP, 1996. 190–203.

Blaeser, Kimberly M. Lecture on Native American poetry. Madison Area Technical College, Madison, Wisconsin. April 12, 1999.

———. *Stories Migrating Home*. Bemidji, MN: Loonfeather Press, 1999.

Bloom, Harold, ed. *Native American Women Writers*. Philadelphia: Chelsea House, 1998.

Bryant, Donald C. "Rhetoric: Its Function and Scope." *Professing the New Rhetorics*. Ed. Theresa Enos and Stuart C. Brown. Englewood Cliffs, NJ: Prentice Hall (Blair Press), 1994. 267–97.

Clements, William M. "This Voluminous Unwritten Book of Ours: Early Native Writers and the Oral Tradition." *Early Native American Writing*. Ed. Helen Jaskoski. Cambridge: Cambridge UP, 1996. 122–35.

Cruikshank, Julie. *Life Lived Like a Story: Life Stories of Three Yukon Native Elders*. Lincoln: U of Nebraska P, 1990.

DeMain, Paul. Personal interview. March 25, 1999.

DeMeyer, Trace. Personal interview. March 25, 1999.

Erdrich, Louise. *The Antelope Wife*. NewYork: HarperPerennial, 1999.

Ginsburg, Faye. "Production Values: Indigenous Media and the Rhetoric of Self-Determination." *Rhetorics of Self-Making*. Ed. Debbora Battaglia. Berkeley: U of California P, 1995. 121–38.

Jaskoski, Helen, ed. *Early Native American Writing*. Cambridge: Cambridge UP, 1996.

Keith, Michael C. *Signals in the Air: Native Broadcasting in America*. Westport, CT: Praeger, 1995.

Lake, Randall A. "Between Myth and History: Enacting Time in Native American Protest Rhetoric." *Quarterly Journal of Speech* 77.2 (1991): 123–51.

———. "Enacting Red Power: The Consumatory Function in Native American Protest Rhetoric." *Quarterly Journal of Speech* 69.2 (1983): 127–42.

Littlefield, Daniel F., Jr. "The American Native Press and American Indian Studies." *Wicazo Sa Review* 2.2 (1986): 51–58.

Lyons, Scott. "Crying for Revision: Postmodern Indians and Rhetorics of Tradition." *Making and Unmaking the Prospects for Rhetoric: Selected Papers from the 1996 Rhetoric Society of America Conference*. Ed. Theresa Enos. Mahwah, NJ: Lawrence Erlbaum, 1997. 123–32.

Okker, Patricia. "Zitkala-Sa." *Native American Women Writers*. Ed. Harold Bloom. Philadelphia: Chelsea House, 1998.

Peyer, Bernd C. *The Tutored Mind: Indian Missionary-Writers in Antebellum America*. Amherst: U of Massachusetts P, 1997.

Redfield, Karen A. "Opening the Composition Classroom to Storytelling: Respecting Native American Students' Use of Rhetorical Strategies." *Perspectives on Written Argument*. Ed. Deborah P. Berrill. Cresskill, NJ: Hampton Press, 1996. 241–56.

Rooke, Constance. "Interview with Tom King." *World Literature Written in English* 30.2 (1990): 62–76.

Sands, Kathleen M. "Narrative Resistance: Native American Collaborative Autobiography." *Studies in American Indian Literatures* 10.1 (1998): 1–18.

Walker, Cheryl. *Indian Nation: Native American Literature and Nineteenth Century Nationalisms*. Durham: Duke UP, 1997.

Whiteman, Roberta Hill. *Philadelphia Flowers*. Duluth, MN: Holy Cow! Press, 1996.

Women Make Movies. *Honey Moccasin*. http://www.wmm.com/catalog/pages/c451.htm (accessed October, 10, 2003).

Zitkala-Sa. *American Indian Stories*. 1921. Lincoln: U of Nebraska P, 1985.

4

A THEORY OF RHETORIC, A RHETORIC OF THEORY

CRITICAL TRICKSTERS

RACE, THEORY, AND *OLD INDIAN LEGENDS*

✦

Robin DeRosa

THIS project grew out of my essay, "Assimilated Positions: Storytelling and Silence in Zitkala-Sa's *Old Indian Legends*." In the paper, I used a postmodern approach to the text, which I neither fully defined nor problematized. When I was asked by one reader to step up to the plate, so to speak, and justify my use of theory in the paper, I realized I had only a slight philosophy in place about what it might mean to rely heavily on contemporary literary theory in an essay dealing with a work by a Native American author. My rote postmodern answers (that theory itself isn't racialized, and that the particular historical context of *Old Indian Legends*—or of postmodernism, for that matter—was irrelevant) didn't seem right, since my essay was implicitly concerned with how theory is generated, with history, and with context. I decided to revisit my approach to *Old Indian Legends*, and to tease out the problems and promises that a variety of theoretical approaches might offer a non–Native American literary critic concerned with resisting a system of textual appropriation within the discipline of (and I highlight the name) English. In this paper, I will move through the work of some of the key critics involved in the debate about the relationship of theory to race. Drawing on the diverging and converging points that they offer, I will attempt to develop an approach to *Old Indian Legends* that is explicit in its methodologies, true to the historical context of the collection, and critical of racist categorizations of the assimilated Native American. Because my revised reading of *Old Indian Legends*, which I include as the final portion of this essay, relies so heavily on the *conversation* between the critics I will cite (and not on a pick-and-choose, seamless synthesis of their work), I will need to begin by asking how these critics talk to one another, how they enter the ongoing dialogue about race and theory.

One of the most famous essays critiquing the use of theory in the academy, especially as it is used to approach texts by people of color, is "The Race for Theory" by Barbara Christian. At the crux of Christian's argument is a simply stated but not easily answered question: "For whom are we doing what we are doing when we do literary criticism?" ("Race for Theory" 343). Christian is primarily concerned with the way theory tends to remove texts from the realm of practice, and the way that contemporary theory (which isn't fully defined as a particular collection of critics in the essay) emphasizes the "how" of literature, marking the "what" as irrelevant. This directly contributes to theory's culpability in the reinscription of a dominant white canon, and the exclusion of "new" and/or "undiscovered" texts by people of color. She describes how the apparently neutral terms employed by contemporary literary theory, such as "text" and "discourse" (both of which she employs in her essay, but not without red flags), originate from the Latin, and recall specific literary critical and cultural histories that excluded creative writers (and critics) of color. The fact that one's use of theory currently has professional consequences and may inform decisions of hiring, tenure, and academic reputation leads Christian to assert that it cannot be ignored, but should not be blindly employed without critique. Christian claims that theory is often prescriptive and is often grafted onto a body of work because of the theorist's own desire or will, *not* because it has been generated by the body of work itself; however, she does not suggest that all theory is always a colonizing gesture. "People of color have always theorized," she writes, "but in forms quite different from the Western form of abstract logic" ("Race for Theory" 336). She discusses narrative theorizing, language play, riddles, and proverbs, asserting that theory generated from within a particular tradition can not only be useful, but can as well be a necessary means of literary and bodily survival. Christian, then, is not "against theory," but is instead against several pitfalls of "doing theory." First, she cautions against exteriorly generated theory being applied willy-nilly to any text at hand. Second, she critiques the idea of the "disembodied texts," pointing out how deconstruction and other contemporary modes of interpretation remove practice from theory. Third, she admonishes critics for using particularly complicated diction that originates not from some neutral wellspring of language, but from particular white Western philosophical movements with specific political relationships to racism. Each of these points flows toward a larger, more positively articulated remedy to these problems. The goal, according to my reading of Christian, is not to *not do* theory, but to do it in such a way that it remains firmly attached to the context surrounding the text at hand.

In her essay on Tony Morrison's *Beloved,* which was redeveloped in collaboration with Helene Moglen for a conference at Santa Cruz, Christian argues more directly with theorists who try to fix various texts within a stable, unchanging critical system. The essay was delivered with some trepidation, as the introduction to *Female Subjects in Black and White* explains, since the conference was comprised of a partly "hostile" audience of (partly) white, post-structural feminists and an equally upset group of African American scholars concerned with the survival and explication of previously ignored African American texts.[1] With a very divided group in front of her, Christian critiqued the critical turn toward "Afrocentricism," arguing that it "is generated from narrow nationalist Western thinking, that it is akin to Eurocentricism, which it apparently opposes but also mimics." She continued, "Many contemporary forms of Afrocentricism undercut the very concept they intend to propose—that there are different interpretations of history and different narratives, depending on where one is positioned. . . . The perspective I am proposing is one that acknowledges the existence of an African cosmology, examines how that cosmology has been consistently denigrated in the West, and explores its appropriateness for texts that are clearly derived from it" ("Fixing Methodologies" 365).

Christian explains how any theory that is generated from without, even "well-intentioned" theory, can have an effect opposite that intended, fixing works in stasis, rather than allowing them to be set free by their contexts. She also reiterates that theory itself is historically generated and must examine its own methodologies even as it applies them to "other" works. What I find so inspiring about the conference at Santa Cruz and the essays collected in *Female Subjects in Black and White* is that they reflect an attempt to enter a politically charged arena. They show that buried within the vehement differences of approach is a genuine belief that there is something to be learned *from* theory, and there is something to be learned *about* it.

Tey Diana Rebolledo echoes Christian's underlying question about purpose in her essay, "The Politics of Poetics: Or, What Am I, a Critic, Doing in This Text Anyhow?" Admonished by some editors for including complete works by other writers in her own criticism, Rebolledo speaks out about her choice to work actively against critical tendencies to "appropriate" work by Chicana/o writers, her choice to "reproduce" rather than "re-appropriate" whole texts (349). She nearly quotes Christian directly in her advice that to avoid colonizing gestures, critics must "let the literature speak for itself," developing their theories from what the literature is saying, rather than vice versa (350). Like Christian, Rebolledo is wary of contemporary theories that kill off the author in order to make room for the reader's personal responses to the text. Rebolledo argues that textual interpretation is a merger of authorial intent, the text itself, and the (separate) interpretation of those two aspects by the reader. Rebolledo brings "interpretation" into Christian's arena, allowing for the autonomy of the critic while refusing to allow that autonomy to overtake and/or control the meaning of the author's work. This seems crucial to me if we are to consider Christian's essays in relation to racist, canonical, and/or "offensive" texts. Surely we, as critics, do not want to obscure the historical contexts that relate such texts to the political distribution of power in the world, but at the same time, we might not feel comfortable being complicit in such readings. In other words, Rebolledo offers us the possibility of naming that which has been historically responsible for oppression while at the same time offering the possibility of resistance to such inscription. In this sense, there might be room for imaginative criticism—for non-dominant readings of texts that point to subtext, anxiety, silent spaces, and possibility—and more importantly, this room would be within a larger room of historical context and cultural specificity. Rebolledo provokes me to ask whether the critic's role must be purely that of a sensitive archeologist or historian, or if it might also be that of a poet, an activist, and an agent. I would reiterate here that Rebolledo subordinates the interpretive aspects of reading to the discovery of authorial context and the examination of what is literally present in the text, but I do not think this subordination is meant to be limiting, but only to ensure that the point from which the critic departs is true to the tenor of the text.

Among other critics who have been influential in the critique of the uses of theory in approaching non-Western texts, three critics—Karen Oakes, Elaine A. Jahner, and Aijaz Ahmad—add useful new insights to the debate. In "Theoretical Reservations and a Seneca Tale," Oakes argues against Gerald Vizenor in favor of social science insights and cultural context to avoid the kind of "misreading" that Vizenor seems to celebrate. Like Christian, Oakes notes, through a quotation from Paul Lauter, that the use of some theoretical language, such as that most often employed by postmodernists, is not very different from that of the "Latin scrawls of physicians to pharmacists: to keep the unwashed out of the game" (Lauter, quoted in Oakes 147). While Oakes does take issue with what she sees as postmodernism's tendency to disconnect the "word from the world," or theory from any real practice, she does clarify that her goal "is not to vilify or discard a particular approach, but instead to point to the uses to which it is put" (138, 148). Oakes is less concerned with the historical origins of various theories than she is with the way such theories impact the academy and the world beyond. Christian might argue, as would I, that this impact is intentional and insidiously connected to the ways in which it grew up in the university, but Oakes leaves open the possibility that theory can be appropriated for productive and sensitive use with texts by and about people of color. By laying her emphasis on the use of theory, rather than on the nature of theory, Oakes deemphasizes the existence of theory as what Henry Gates Jr. might call a "thing," and instead suggests that it is a *process* that can change its shape according to its context, much like the literary traditions that she discusses.

Aijaz Ahmad, in his compelling examination of theory's relationship to class, nation, and literature, takes a more traditionally Marxist approach to the discussion of cultural specificity. Arguing that theory has displaced the activist culture from which he claims it sprang and replaced it with a so-called textual culture, Ahmad suggests one possible analysis for how post-structuralism (in particular) rose to a kind of power within the academy. He cites the monolithic defining of nationalism (which shifts from an "unconditional celebration" to a "contemptuous dismissal") as a precursor to radical theory that is "pitched self-consciously against . . . well-known Marxist premises" (41). His development of this idea is worth quoting at some length:

> An obvious consequence of repudiating Marxism was that one now sought to make sense of the world of colonies and empires much less in terms of classes, much more in terms of nations and countries and races, and thought of imperialism itself not as a hierarchically structured system of global capitalism but as a relation, of governance and occupation, between richer and poorer countries, West and non-West. (41)

According to Ahmad, this shift from material conditions to *ideas* as that which defines culture attaches all "visionary hopes," as he calls them, to ideologies of decolonization. He critiques the idea that ideologies, independent of class reality, can materially alter the conditions of imperialism, as opposed to simply reinscribing a capitalist, imperialistic structure. Interestingly, Ahmad figures post-structuralism as a theory born out of Marxism and the critique of Marxism, but which is always in denial of its own past. Ahmad provokes us to ask what the relationship is between ideologies and material conditions, between criticism and activism, and between post-structuralism and Marxism. Though his work clearly sets up these dichotomies and shows the very real ways that these categories are often at odds with each other, he also suggests that the dichotomies are in some ways false, and that the binaries are perhaps not as rigid as we often maintain.

Elaine A. Jahner is also concerned with how theory has emerged in the academy. In "Metalanguages," she suggests that theory has the potential to satisfy what she calls a desire for "scholarly tidiness" (155). She echoes the professional concerns raised by Christian by positing theory not as that which ultimately enlightens one's approach to a particular text, but as that which meets the needs of scholars looking for a niche within the university walls. Jahner is also aware of the fact that criticism is "always thoroughly implicated in philosophical traditions whose relationships to the native literatures of this content are what we question, not what we want to assume as the origin of our descriptive categories" (155). But Jahner, more so than Christian, feels that now is the time for culturally specific modes of analysis to merge with other kinds of specifically *literary* modes of analysis: "The most helpful research is that which presents and criticizes the notion of the subject as a linguistic and hermeneutic category, thus permitting a consideration of the subject that subsumes other crucial categories—such as race—keeping all analysis firmly based within the acknowledged (and therefore explicit) critical assumptions of a given social and historical configuration" (184). This self-consciousness on the part of the critic connects with a knowledge of the text's own historical moment to posit a new kind of theory that is neither aloofly disconnected from the real world, nor insistent on an anti-literary scientism. Jahner suggests that N. Scott Momaday and other Native American writers and critics have begun to generate such an approach to theory, an approach that collapses the most apparently fixed of binaries: the theory/practice divide.

Before taking a look at cultural specificity as a useful mode of literary analysis, I would like to consider some of the criticism that has emerged in response to critiques of theory in general, and post-structuralism in particular. A variety of writers have suggested that post-structuralism should not be rejected for application to texts by people of color; some have argued that post-structuralism is in fact the most useful and liberating theory currently articulated for discussing how Native American texts, for example, *mean.*

Gerald Vizenor suggests that postmodernism is a uniquely Native American theory: "The postmodern opened in tribal imagination; oral cultures have never been without a postmodern condition that enlivens stories and ceremonies, or without trickster signatures and discourse on narrative chance—a comic utterance and adventure to be heard or read" (x). For Vizenor, tribal literature, oral in origin, is, *even in its printed form,* always a "pose in a language game" (x). Oral cultures, he claims, carry with them a conception of language that is inherently less structural than the origins of Western print culture; the "pose" implies that the postmodern printed word is "not a source of aesthetic presence or historical modernism" (x).

In a recent story, Vizenor creates young Native American children learning to read English by having words printed on leaves and then hidden in the snow by their mother to be retrieved and made into a sentence. For Vizenor, this way of taking in a language highlights his perception of a distinctly Native American, orally generated relationship between concrete sound and visual representation, as opposed to an anthropological or colonialist *abstract* language.[2] This *postmodern* condition highlights printed language's separation of word from the thing it describes, but also gestures toward a unification of the signified with its signifier. Vizenor refuses to situate postmodernism in a white Western philosophical tradition and instead suggests that contemporary theory can be regenerated through distinctly Native American literary (including oral) traditions. He looks to postmodernism as an important *literary* alternative to social scientific analytical methodologies: "Social science theories constrain tribal landscapes to institutional values, representationalism and the politics of academic determination" (Vizenor 5). Echoing Jahner, Vizenor suggests that postmodernism is almost an anti-theory, which, unlike other modes of classification, has as its main tenet a recognition of the inescapable cultural impetus to fix and label. This being said, however, Vizenor's postmodernism is also a revelation of how this impetus can be undermined by its own examination. For Vizenor, postmodernism is a communal, comic, and playful game that is aligned with a Native American worldview and that, through its playfulness, ultimately gestures toward the way we have come to understand the real.

If we imagine for a moment what some of the critics we examined above, who had substantial critiques of contemporary theory in its application to texts by people of color, might have to say about Vizenor's celebration of a postmodern Native American literary tradition, we might suggest that they would ask him how postmodernism's refuting of all historical fact and social scientific discoveries might impact the real lives of contemporary Native Americans. In other words, what happens to the practice if we do accept Vizenor's theory? Jane Tompkins, in "'Indians': Textualism, Morality, and the Problem of History," attempts to answer just such a question. Tompkins talks about her preparation for teaching a course in colonial American literature; as she plunges into her research, she discovers that "some of the conflicting accounts [of what happened during the period] were not simply contradictory, they were completely incommensurable." "I found myself," she continues, "in an epistemological quandary, not only unable to decide among conflicting versions of events but also unable to believe that any such decision could, in principle, be made" (61). Though her postmodern background tells her on one level that truth cannot be discovered, her conscience suggests to her that, given the atrocities that the Native American suffered at the hands of the colonists, she simply must arrive at some kind of judgment. "If studying history couldn't put us in touch with actual events and their causes," she asks, "then what was to prevent such atrocities from happening again?" (61).

Tompkins arrives at a method that aims to ameliorate her fear of fixing or cementing "truth" (nearly every author I have examined shares this fear) while at the same time it works to address the issue of what Tompkins calls "morality." "My problem," she states, "presupposed that I couldn't judge because I didn't know what the facts were" (74). But she suggests that her moral conscience was, in fact, already judging the colonists' actions, and that her intellectual methodologies were working overtime to try to justify her feelings. She suggests that her post-structural premise that "all facts are theory dependent" is as situated in a particular historical moment (namely in contemporary literary theory) as any writer's from the colonial period. She continues:

> The level at which my indecision came into play was a function of particular beliefs I held. I was never in a position of epistemological indeterminacy, I was never *en abyme*. The accounts that all accounts are perspectival seemed to give me a superior standpoint from which to view all the versions of "what happened," and to regard with sympathetic condescension any person so old-fashioned and benighted as to believe that there was really some way for arriving at the truth. (75)

Ultimately, Tompkins is critiquing the way that the idea that all facts are only facts-within-a-perspective tends to evacuate statements of their very content. But, she says, "and it is a crucial but—all this is true only if you believe that there is an alternative" (76). She believes this "disappearing effect" only occurs when one believes that somewhere, somehow, there are "true facts" outside of the perspectival system. If one believes instead that perspective itself *is* fact, then there is no "just" or "only" about perspective. Despite her critique of postmodernism, which, I think, is actually a critique of how postmodernism has been misunderstood or misused, Tompkins ultimately suggests that the "real" that can be discussed through a postmodern lens is a "real" that has everything to do with "practice."[3]

While Vizenor and Tompkins attempt to refigure postmodernism to fit the challenges presented by Native American texts and narratives on race and ethnicity, Michael Awkward is more concerned with refuting Barbara Christian's seminal work critiquing theory. Most notably, Awkward suggests that Christian's assertion that potentially radical African American critics who use (or even create) contemporary theory have been unfortunately co-opted by the professionalism of contemporary theory is an "attack on their personal integrity and recent work" ("Race for Theory" 336, Awkward 362). He continues: "She apparently cannot even conceive of the possibility that these critics *choose* to employ theory because they believe it offers provocative means of discussing the texts of nonhegemonic groups, that theory is viewed by them as useful in the critical analysis of the literary products of 'the other'" (Awkward 362). Awkward is alluding to a tendency in Christian that he sees as disturbing: that race becomes a "pass" that predicts or permits particular kinds of literary inquiry. Of course, this is partly Christian's point, that cultural specificity must be welcomed into literary analysis in order to prevent the abuses of theory that she describes. But Awkward wonders (in a gesture that perhaps goes too far in an attack relating specifically to Christian) whether there isn't a limiting maneuver in the attachment of race to *kinds* of theory. Awkward argues that despite the origins of particular kinds of literary theory, and despite the androcentric uses to which it has been put, that many theorists of color (including himself) have found it useful in many ways. In particular, he mentions Henry Louis Gates Jr., Hortense Spillers, Houston Baker, and Mary Helen Washington. He concludes his essay with a quotation from Gates about the translation of literary theory into the "black idiom," an idea that we will turn to now as well. I find Awkward's essay useful in asking the large, complicated question of what it means if we racialize theory itself.

"This is the challenge of the critic of black literature," writes Gates in *Figures in Black*, "not to shy away from literary theory; rather, to translate it into the black idiom, *renaming* principles of criticism where appropriate, but especially *naming* indigenous black principles of criticism and applying these to explicate our own texts" (*Figures in Black* xxi, original emphasis). For Gates, it is a moral imperative to use any tools available that enable the critic "to explain the complex workings of the language of a text" (*Figures in Black* xxi). Gates, like Awkward, is unwilling to refute contemporary literary theory's potential as it might apply to works by people of color, but even more significantly, he is interested in how the history of theory has been (over)written by an exclusionary, white literary critical voice. Gates suggests that "signification," a theoretical term supposedly developed by Ferdinand de Saussure, is in fact a two-centuries-old tradition connected to the black vernacular. In his examination of the "signifying monkey" in slavery stories and songs as well as in jazz, Gates suggests that the development of the concept of a trope in general (and parody, more specifically) was actually systematized through a uniquely African American history. Gates asks us to question our assumptions that contemporary theory in all of its dimensions is necessarily a white-only endeavor and firmly demonstrates how, as Christian noted, "people of color have always theorized" ("Race for Theory" 336). Gates wants to take language itself, that which has occasionally been vilified as too disconnected—within theory—from the concerns of the physical world, and place it into a decidedly concrete, culturally specific heritage.

In "Talkin' That Talk," Gates states that for him, race is not "a thing." "If we believe that races exist as things, as categories of being already 'there,'" he writes, "we cannot escape the danger of generalizing about observed differences between human beings as if these differences were consistent and determined, a priori" (402). But Gates takes issue with Tzvetan Todorov's assertion that race doesn't exist, claiming instead that tropes, traditions, and histories are fundamental in understanding how "race" itself gets its meaning as a figure for something that has *no essential* existence (which I would argue is dramatically different than claiming that something simply does not exist). While Todorov calls Gates self-contradictory when Gates refutes essentialism but still advocates for a literary theory indigenous to African American literatures, Gates suggests that these two positions do not, in fact, form a paradox. Gates is interested in how language and what Vizenor might call "language games" ultimately form certain patterns and methodologies that can be applied to the specific traditions that generate them. This approach might very well be called both postmodern and culturally specific.

Despite certain pointed contradictions, these varied discussions tend to work together rather than against each other. There doesn't seem to be a progression, or some kind of linear movement from one critique to another, but instead a multiplicity of voices arise together, creating a debate that is marked less by a binary set of oppositions than it is by a kind of dialogic (or multilogic) conversation. If there is one commonality that emerges in nearly every critic we have thus far discussed, it is the issue of cultural specificity and its relationship to theory. Henry Louis Gates Jr., Aijaz Ahmad, and

Karen Oakes spoke convincingly on this topic, and with their frameworks in mind, I would like to turn now to critics addressing the issue more directly, and with more of an eye toward Native American textual concerns.

Perhaps no critic of Native American literatures has been so prolific and so heeded on the issue of cultural specificity as Paula Gunn Allen. In "'Border' Studies: The Intersection of Gender and Color," Allen advocates for removing the criticism of Native American literatures from the binary of oppression, and instead situating it into a uniquely and fully Native American context. She does not wish to erase the very real oppression that Native communities have faced since European "settlement," but she wants to suggest that there is much more to Native American work than resistance or assimilation to or subversion of the so-called dominant white paradigm. She calls postmodernism a "self-referencing, nearly psychotic death dance" where "meaning is largely a trick of the mind" ("'Border' Studies" 307). We might imagine Tompkins responding with a redefinition of the "real" as that which is both concrete and produced by figures of language, but even if there is a potentially overdetermined refuting of postmodern theory in Allen's work, there is also a celebrating of the kind of language-based approach to race and theory advocated by Gates in *The Signifying Monkey.* Like Christian, Allen is interested in how contemporary theory has negatively classified and excluded writers of color, and like Gates, she is interested in how such theory can be resisted in favor of a more culturally specific set of reading tools. What I am resisting here is a kind of simple dichotomy that places Christian and Allen *against* theory and *against* critics such as Gates. Within their work, each of these critics responds positively to the others, situating themselves against certain arguments and aligning themselves with certain other arguments.

Thinking back to Awkward's reading of Christian, we might ask ourselves what we make of Allen's statement that "the idea of expending life force in oppression and resistance strikes most Indians, even today, as distinctly weird" ("'Border' Studies" 310). The problem inherent in such a statement is that it classifies Native Americans in such a way that would undoubtedly not apply to many people for whom it pretends to speak.[4] But this is not carelessness or ignorance on Allen's part. She has, in fact, pointed to one of the stickiest points about cultural specificity. Can a theory, even when generated from within, as Allen so clearly does, ever pretend to speak directly to a particular literature, or is the degree of context, specificity, and disclaimers necessary for such an undertaking simply infinite? Must we go back to Christian and assert that all theory somehow reduces and classifies, or can we advocate for a cultural specificity that is always already incomplete, and yet still effective, useful, and enlightening? We must ask ourselves how or if Allen's advice "to begin anew" in reconstructing the canon will change the problems inherent in the very idea of canonicity. What I take from Allen is a recognition that certain academic tendencies to group, theorize, and understand might be filled with critical pitfalls, but that this does not mean that all attempts to understand a culture from within are necessarily always useless.

In "Expanding the Canon of American Realism," Elizabeth Ammons responds directly to this question, raised for her in part by Allen's work. In her discussion of how cultural specificity and its always-present limitations of knowledge affect the role of "teacher," Ammons writes, "We *won't* know everything. Our authority as professors will change. . . . The question is how to teach what we cannot know, either through experience or training, everything cannot be the complete authority" ("Expanding the Canon" 104).[5] Ammons makes explicit the problem inherent in Allen's classifying of Native American levels of comfort with protest and her belief in an essential difference of culture. But Ammons makes the problem explicit while simultaneously refusing to solve it. This strikes me as particularly productive, for it attends to the ways in which theory—*all* theory, according to Christian and others—has an innate tendency to reify that which it most wishes to liberate. But at the same time, it suggests that this tendency can be controlled and highlighted in such a way as to minimize its insidiousness. In addition, cultural specificity can relieve postmodernism's habit of "mistaking the menu for the meal" and can pay attention to how history functions as a context for a theory that both frees literature from the clutches of one right reading and binds it to its own literary and cultural tradition (Allen, "'Border' Studies" 312). In this way, "context doesn't distort the document" at hand, connected as it is to historical fact (Allen, *Studies in American Indian Literature* x). But as Tompkins and Ammons encourage us to remember, "fact" is always related to our own critical positions, and we must make the limits of our positions known—not to limit us, but to free us.

Two works have been instrumental in the debate over how these questions have impacted Native American literary criticism: Greg Sarris's *Keeping Slugwoman Alive* and Paula Gunn Allen's *Spider Woman's Granddaughters*. The first is a wonderfully enjoyable study of Native American storytelling based loosely on Sarris's friendship with Mabel McKay, a Cache Creek Pomo basket weaver and medicine woman. Sarris considers McKay's specific example as a jumping-off point for a discussion of cultural specificity. McKay's baskets are often displayed in museums and in university galleries as "autonomous pieces of art" (Sarris 55). Sarris argues that the context of the baskets is displaced when they are produced for the exhibition value. McKay herself has much to say on how her baskets are appropriated by the institutions that show them: "Whatever I say—whatever I talk about the basket—the white man just turns around and does his own way anyway" (qtd. in Sarris 51). "You think about your basket," McKay tells Sarris of a gift basket she gives him. "This ceremony feeds it, keeps it going" (qtd. in Sarris 61). McKay and Sarris suggest that context is not only important in order to avoid what Allen calls textual "distortion," but also to give meaning to texts. Sarris distinguishes between an anthropological artifact, which is situated into a fixed, true historical spot, and a contextualized work, which is always (and only) meaningful through a dynamic cultural interaction. This brilliant and simple distinction, which, as Sarris notes, is a new interpretation of Bakhtin's theory of heteroglossia (the multitude of voices), urges critics to consider context not only because it avoids the trap of a simplistic colonizer/colonized binary, but also because it invests the text at hand with significance that can *only* be seen by considering how the text interacts with its author, its culture, and its audience. This does not seem to me to remove creativity or agency from the critic, but instead it seems to deepen the critical scope threefold, giving every reader more textual information to consider.

Paula Gunn Allen's book *Spider Woman's Granddaughters* is an anthology of traditional Native American tales and contemporary writing, all by Native American women. In her introduction, Allen performs a process similar to Gates's development of the signifying monkey. She begins to outline some of the specificities of the Native American aesthetic with the goal of generating a set of lenses through which the literature can be approached by all readers (including self-professed literary critics). Like Vizenor, she is interested in asking how the oral tradition distinguishes Native American culture from a "modern Western tradition," and she suggests that Western prohibitions against mixing (miscegenation, class mixing, homosexuality, mixing levels of diction or spiritual beliefs) is nothing like the less divisive and more communal Native American worldview. She also suggests that the WASP literary ethos, which privileges both an individual hero engaged in an ultimately resolvable conflict and the Aristotelian unities, is not applicable to Native American stories that instead tend to privilege a non-individualistic, non-conflict-centered common understanding derived from ritual tradition shared by an entire tribe (*Spider Woman's Granddaughters* 5).[6] It is crucial to our discussion here that these remarks are placed by Allen at the beginning of her edition, thus acting (as they are titled) as an introduction. Allen challenges her readers to move through the anthology with a new theory in place, applying a culturally specific literary tradition to the included works.

In the interest of always highlighting the difficulties that each of these critics confronts, I would like briefly to mention two scholars who critique some of the issues involved with a culturally specific literary analysis. In comments on the *American Indian Quarterly's* special issue on writing about American Indians, Devon Mihesuah "reminds readers" that "there is no one Indian voice," but reminds readers, too, that it is crucial to continue to ask, "Where are the Indian voices?" (92–93). Mihesuah is interested in this idea of "voice" as something that is not bound to the body of any identifiable Indian person, but that is instead a collective of sometimes competing voices that together make a tradition. She warns strongly, however, against a definition of "race" or "culture" that cements identity into something readily *identifiable*. "In an attempt to establish a voice devoid of non-Indian influence," she writes, "some Indian graduate students push the concept of essentialism, an idea that may have some merit but that it also dangerous" (103). Though I wonder why such a tendency is restricted to graduate students, Mihesuah recognizes how the academy has pushed nonwhite scholars toward a survivalist essentializing of racial identity, but she encourages Indians to resist such tendencies, as they ultimately strengthen the very racist practices that made them appealing in the first place. Mihesuah, like Gates, suggests that racial identity can be perceived as a tradition, as a set of tropes, and as a rhetorical structure that have concrete, physical effects on literature, the academy, and critical perspective.

In *The Voice in the Margin: Native American Literature and the Canon*, Arnold Krupat suggests "evocation" rather than "representation" as what literary critics should try to do to cultures they approach (11). He vehemently denies that evoking a cultural context requires a genetic tie to the culture one is studying. He condemns (non-Indian) theorists who manufacture a remote Native American bloodline in order to add credibility to their work. Krupat suggests that essential perceptual lenses do not exist, but instead advocates for an anti-essential approach to race and ethnicity. This does not, according to Krupat, deny the reality of cultural specificity. In fact, Krupat's major point is that texts must be examined from the point of view of their contexts, and that theorists must "speak with our ears open" so as not to occlude the reality of what the text reflects (*The Voice in the Margin* 17). Both Mihesuah and Krupat hope to redefine cultural specificity as that which is dynamic, polyphonous, anti-essential, and yet very, very real. Just as Elizabeth Ammons asks of the supposedly universal term "American Realism," "Whose reality?" and "Whose America?" Mihesuah and Krupat, along with many other critics, encourage us to take our terms to task, not taking for granted that either "race" or "theory" is apolitical, monolithic, or self-evident ("Expanding the Canon" 95).

In reading many critics' discussions of the Native American trickster figure(s), I became aware of some obvious parallels between what literary criticism has to say about tricksters and what it has to say about the relationship of theory to race. I think trickster might offer critics an interesting metaphor within which we might define our roles in the texts we study, as well as a relevant context for working with "assimilation period" texts by Native American authors.

The so-called assimilation period, loosely dated from the 1880s to 1934, saw an increase in the US government's articulation of its anxiety about the Native American presence in the country. The BIA schools that Zitkala-Sa so movingly chronicles in *American Indian Stories* actively aimed to assimilate Native Americans, robbing them of their tribal and family connections, their languages, their appearances, and their cultures. Custer's defeat by the Sioux and the Cheyenne at Little Big Horn in 1876 and the increase throughout the 1880s of the Ghost Dance, a nonviolent ceremony of resistance that sought to protect Native Americans from white violence, created an air of fear among many white Americans and the US government. In 1890, the massacre at Wounded Knee left hundreds of Native Americans dead when US troops invaded a Ghost Dance ceremony. Legislation made it a crime for Native Americans to "speak their own languages, to practice traditional religious rituals, or to wear traditional dress or their hair at a male warrior length" (Brown 127). The Dawes Act (or General Allotment Act) in 1887 provoked the loss of two-thirds of Native American land to white settlement, and Paula Gunn Allen notes that a subtext of the Dawes Act's white greed was the forcing of Native Americans into nuclear households, the transplanting of a communal tribal culture into a "civilized" European domestic pattern (*Spider Woman's Granddaughters* 10).

Trickster, of course, is a figure familiar to Native American (oral) literatures long before the nineteenth century. Iktomi, the trickster in *Old Indian Legends,* is a Lakota figure who "frequently change[s] forms, don[s] disguises, break[s] cultural taboos and natural laws" (J. Smith 46). Iktomi, as Jeanne Smith tells us in "'A Second Tongue': The Trickster's Voice in the Works of Zitkala-Sa," is an integral part of Lakota tradition, and tales including Iktomi appear in nearly every collection of Lakota legends. The trickster in general, and Iktomi in particular, is used in Native American tradition as both a hero and a scapegoat. Though he is often cited as the namer of all creatures and the inventor of language and culture, trickster remains an outsider, and as such, Smith notes, has the capability of both saving *and* destroying that culture (47). Given the (all too brief) history I sketched above, we can see how trickster might embody both the particular Native American culture still alive and well in tribal America *and* the threat posed by assimilationist governmental practices that daily encroached on Native American culture. Smith suggests that Zitkala-Sa uses Iktomi to write "from the gap between tradition and assimilation," and I would suggest that this is the kind of "borderland" to which Allen refers (J. Smith 57).[7] Not a figure of either a pure Native American culture or an assimilated or polarized biculturalism, trickster occupies a borderland position that partakes of both cultures without being fixed in either. Elizabeth Ammons posits this as a relation of both/and rather than either/or: "Embodied in trickster and trickster energy is a principle of human rebellion and resistance that exists both within a protagonist/antagonist framework *and* within a totally different context, one in which the disruly—the transgressive—is accepted as part of the community's life. . . . [T]he dynamic is one of interaction rather than dominance and submission" (*Tricksterism in Turn-of-the-Century American Literature* ix).

We might extend these definitions of trickster to include a kind of "trickster criticism" or a criticism that challenges its own internal structures from inside those structures, even as it strengthens those structures from outside of them. To clarify that tricky statement: trickster criticism might work from a culturally specific context, situating the considered text within its own literary tradition while at the same time it questions its own position in relationship to the culture it attempts to define. The goal here is not, of course, simply to play some semantic game whereby I adeptly mash each of the critical positions I've described in this essay into one seamless "theory," but instead to view theory, like trickster, as a dialogic or multiplicitous *process*, which can accommodate contradiction without dissolving itself into an abyss of nothingness. According to Gerald Vizenor, "trickster" is as much an attempt to reach *beyond* the word as it is a reveling in the omnipotence of the word (192). We might see theory in much the same light. We use it not simply to revel in our rhetorical prowess, but instead to gesture toward the practices that our very critiques create. If we conceive of the work we do inside texts as both an act of disruption and an act of community building, we might begin to build a theory that is both tied to cultural specificity and that always agitates the very terms we employ to talk about culture itself. This contradiction is inherent in trickster and in trickster criticism and does not spin out into (only) a language game. The proliferation of the contradiction, I think, keeps us centrally focused on Rebolledo's question (What am I doing in this text anyway?), a question that it is theory's function to answer and re-answer through its application.

"Trickster criticism," while perhaps born as a term in this essay, is nothing new. In fact, as an individual writer, I may actually *not* be able to put this theory into action at all in this essay. But if I think of this approach as one born out of conversation between a multiplicity of diverging and converging opinions, I can resist the tendency to let theory pigeonhole the work I study. Building off the groundwork I have laid regarding the tenor of the assimilation period in America and the trope of the trickster figure in Lakota and Native American myth, I will turn now to Zitkala-Sa's *Old Indian Legends* with the aim of reworking some of my initial ideas about the book within a framework of trickster criticism. As I noted, such criticism necessarily relies both on the cultural specificity of the work's context, and on the destabilizing of universalisms that might lock the text into a fixed position. The reading I offer, which is informed by postmodernism, Native American literary traditions and trickster legends, and various critical responses to the use of theory in addressing texts by people of color, will attempt to investigate its own investments, as does Jane Tompkins in her essay, in order to avoid some kind of a "meta-position" that might suggest an outside stance or distance from the politics of the text's historical moment or of contemporary critical discourse.

In this next section, I will explore how two consecutive stories from *Old Indian Legends*, "The Tree-Bound" and "Shooting of the Red Eagle," self-consciously comment on their own construction as English retellings of Sioux legends. The many doublings and repetitions in the stories work to establish colonialism not as that which erases a Native culture, but as that which alters an original (or pre-colonial) culture and is, in turn, altered by that original. As anthropologist Julie Cruikshank notes, the instability of origins that postmodernism has attributed to "late twentieth-century uncertainties" has in fact been theorized by Native storytellers as "springing from the structure of colonial practices that took root more than a century ago" (3). Like Vizenor, Cruikshank questions literary history, offering critics the opportunity to resituate the terms of theory into frameworks other than those of a white, Western tradition, indeed to note how specific traditions themselves develop terms that are sometimes quite like—and sometimes quite unlike—terms from different traditions. Zitkala-Sa herself articulates this instability of origins and describes her position as a kind of translator.

"In both Dakotas," she writes, "I have often listened to the same story told over again by a new story-teller. While I recognized such a legend without the least difficulty, I found the renderings varying much in little incidents" (v–vi).[8] Here, Zitkala-Sa establishes a theory of repetition and difference that will become central to the themes in the legends themselves: repetition both does and does not alter the original that it repeats. The shifts in the "little incidents," which seem inconsequential as she describes them here, will turn out to be crucial in "The Tree-Bound" and "Shooting of the Red Eagle," as repetition draws attention to the way that retelling also remakes meaning. "Generally," Zitkala-Sa writes about the multiple versions of the legends, "one [story] helped the other in restoring some lost link in the original character of the tale" (vi). The "original" is not some external fact, but a state produced through the merging of varied translations. In other words, originality in this paradigm is not defined as something entirely new, but as a shared pool of sometimes competing versions of stories. This kind of originality patently rejects the kind of rugged individualism that Elizabeth Ammons describes as characteristic of (white, Western) literary realism at the turn of the century. In fact, to redefine originality (or theory) as that which is a mix of a multiplicity of voices is to refigure dramatically the very center of the realist tradition and the very center of certain racist, anthropological, and literary worldviews.

Zitkala-Sa concludes her preface by suggesting that truth "lies in the eye of the beholder," and that "sincerity of belief, though it were based upon mere optical illusion, demands a little respect" (vi). These definitions of truth, originality, and repetition, derived from a Native American worldview, emerge in her retelling of the legends not only with regard to the Native oral tradition, but also with regard to Zitkala-Sa's own relationship to the use of English and to the translation of these legends from the Sioux language into America's "second tongue," as she refers to English in her preface. "English itself" writes literary critic Martha J. Cutter, "leaves [Zitkala-Sa] no place from which to speak with force and power" (40). Cutter believes that the assimilationism of the period necessarily mandates that all Native Americans who speak English are unresistant, co-opted, and not autonomous. It is my contention that such a maneuver, which I believe parallels Christian's maneuver in claiming all postmodern (female) critics of color are necessarily "co-opted," ignores the critical difference that emerges in certain kinds of repetitions and translations. I would like to ask how the retelling in English of these "Old Indian Legends" might be a repetition that both reinscribes *and* reconfigures imperialism in turn-of-the-century America. Cherokee elder Sarah Hutchison has said, "I knew a mockingbird that made the sound of a rotating sprinkler. I went out many times in the night to turn it off—and it wasn't on" (131). Like the effect of the mockingbird who impersonates the sprinkler, might there ultimately be a confusion between original and copy that contests the apparent simplicity of the assimilationist philosophy?

In his introduction to *On the Translation of Native American Literatures,* Brian Swann, quoting William Powers, asserts that because of the large number of (culturally insensitive) white translators and the number of translations produced by Native Americans trained in "white man's schools," a good deal "of what passes today for Indian culture and religion has been fabricated by the white man" (xvii). Clearly, the history of translation of Native American texts, which Zitkala-Sa self-consciously enters in her preface, is deeply vexed and imprinted with a colonial dynamic. But must we believe that because Zitkala-Sa was indeed educated in an assimilationist boarding school that she unwittingly (re)produces a translation that is, in some essential way, "white?" For readers of *American Indian Stories,* it seems ludicrous to believe this, since Zitkala-Sa's autobiographical writings demonstrate resistance, anger, and deep understanding of the political, cultural, and bodily violence inherent in assimilation. In "On the Translation of Native American Song and Story: A Theorized History," Arnold Krupat suggests that while perfect or fully "correct" translation of Native American oral literatures is impossible, there are three characteristics that make for a better attempt: "command . . . a basic philological *control* of the language of the original; detailed knowledge of the culture of the original, an ethnographic control; some developed sense of the strategies of literary expression both oral and textual in general" (24).

What strikes me in these three conditions, in particular in the first two, is the diction that Krupat chooses ("command," "control"). Where is the Native American translator here? Though Swann suggests that some of the earliest translations to English of Native American oral texts were most likely written by Native Americans, Krupat approaches translation as the job of an outsider, who comes to the text ready to dominate and tame. Krupat unwittingly reproduces the kind of atmosphere that, in fairness, much of his article critiques. There is no doubt that Zitkala-Sa is aware that despite the facts of the matter, the translation of Native American oral texts was, at the turn of the century (and possibly even today), a largely white, European endeavor that was deeply scarred by the tenor of colonialism. Given such a context, I believe it is imperative that we "open our ears" (as Krupat previously suggested) to hear how Zitkala-Sa reshapes the very face of translation, challenging the assumption that her English voice is necessarily whitewashed, and resisting the colonialist vision of translation as a controlling or commanding endeavor. Instead, I'd suggest a less binary approach based on the idea of community and multiplicity so much a part of the Native American texts themselves. In *Smoothing the Ground: Essays on Native American Oral Literatures,* Kenneth Lincoln offers a summary of such an approach: "When more than one language and culture and space/time lie at either end of this multiple and metaphorical process, the translator must look two ways, at least, at once: to carry over, as much as possible, the experiential integrity of the original, and to *re*generate the spirit of the source in a new verbal performance" (10). The "reciprocal" process that Lincoln describes, though still mired in opposites ("two," "either end"), alludes to a more polyphonous approach to translation. Lincoln continues on, describing the relationship of such a process to tribal ethic; but still, in both of Swann's collections, very few translators and/or critics speak from the Native American point of view. Turning now to the inner working of *Old Indian Legends,* we must keep in mind the covert charges of assimilationism levied by history at the Native American translator; we must ask how Zitkala-Sa uses English to enter into a dialogue with Native American culture, rather than to wield a monologue against it like a sword.

From the very beginning of "The Tree-Bound," we are made aware that the text itself is self-conscious about its status as a translated text, a liminal text that is both Native and English simultaneously. We are told, "Again and again sang a . . . birdie—'Koda Ni Dakota! . . . Koda Ni Dakota!' which was 'Friend, you're a Dakota! Friend, you're a Dakota!'" (77). The text seems to point out that it is not actually a story told in English, but is a story told in the Sioux language that translates itself as it is told. The text continues to translate itself, interpreting the meaning of the birdcall: "Perchance the birdie meant the avenger with the magic arrow, for there . . . he strode" (77). This suggests that repetition and interpretation are parallel actions, or varying degrees of the same technique. The avenger, who plays a key role in both stories, enters into the legend just as a text (the birdie's song) is directly interpreted, in a sense a symbol of the process of interpretation itself. The first place where this metaphor is explicitly reinforced is when the avenger kills the string of buffalo with his single arrow. His arrow is so directly released, it can penetrate each of the heads, one after the other. The arrow is a metaphor for the story itself, released from a single mouth (which has the same shape as the bow), but penetrating many different ears. What is striking about this metaphor is that it suggests that the story, or the arrow, remains unchanged and pure from one target to the next. The arrow here represents a pure meaning that is not altered by repetition or interpretation; the buffalo fall dead as the arrow strikes them, ending the chain of meaning and resisting the pull of discourse to proliferate. The avenger then, enters the story as a symbol for that which transforms the unstable discursive process into a stable artifact.

Zitkala-Sa's avenger is a version of a traditional Dakota hero. Jeanne Smith, quoting Julian Rice, explains that in traditional tellings, the avenger, called "Blood Clot Boy," is born of a drop of blood falling from a piece of buffalo meat; the blood is all that Badger can beg from Bear, who has, perhaps like the white man, come from far away and usurped Badger's home. "From this clot," writes Smith, "grows the first human, who takes back the usurped hut for the badger and sends the bear away" (50). In the traditional story, Smith notes, Blood Clot Boy becomes a village hero by making the buffalo population thrive. Zitkala-Sa, clearly acquainted with this traditional tale, introduces the avenger in a similar story ("The Badger and the Bear"), but alters her use of the avenger figure in slight but crucial ways. In Zitkala-Sa's retelling, it seems significant that the beasts that he so easily killed are the very beasts whose own death wounds gave him life. As the buffalo are felled by his arrow, we might imagine the bloodied grassland giving rise to an infinite number of new avengers. In a metaphorical sense, the avenger is part of a closed system, responsible for his own birth over and over again. The repetition of the scene flourishes at three levels, as the string of buffalo falls and the avenger's own creation myth replays itself. But at the same time, the repetitive cycles seem to preserve the mythical intactness of the origin; each buffalo falls exactly as the one before, and when we imagine each rebirth of the avenger, we must imagine it exactly as we heard in the original story. The avenger and his arrow, then, suggest a kind of discursive system that relies heavily on the figure of an "original," which uses death to end the proliferation of meaning, which uses birth as a symbol of pure repetition, and which admits no relativism or relationships into its own meaning-making process. Thirdly, however, Zitkala-Sa inverts Blood Clot Boy's relationship to the buffalo; in the original myth, Blood Clot Boy gives (metaphoric) birth to the buffalo herds, and in Zitkala-Sa's version, the buffalo give a similar symbolic birth to the avenger. Of course, both myths posit the blood clot as the genesis of the very myth itself, but after that initial birth, the slight alteration of the original suggests that Zitkala-Sa's retelling is both just like and just unlike the previous versions. In addition, by rekilling the buffalo and thus enacting the avenger's birth over and over, Zitkala-Sa suggests that the avenger can multiply himself, proliferating a stable Native American culture in the face of assimilationist forces.

Iktomi, the trickster figure in these two stories and in much of *Old Indian Legends*, has a markedly different relationship to meaning-making than the avenger. Iktomi hides, ready to ambush the avenger when he passes by. As he waits, he mimics the excitement of the messengers. In a marvel of the quote-within-the-quote, the text reads: "'"He is coming!" said the people,' muttered Iktomi" (84). Iktomi is presented from the beginning as a repeater, filled with the words of other people. But unlike the avenger, whose repetitions preserved a distinct original, Iktomi significantly changes the meaning of his repetition without changing the words themselves. While the messengers were clearly excited by the avenger's approach, Iktomi is poking fun at their awe of the man when he mimics their words. Just after this repetition, we are told that the bird sings his familiar refrain ("Koda Ni Dakota! Friend, you're a Dakota!") as Iktomi covers his mouth, laughing at both the bird and the avenger. Iktomi, by covering his mouth, seems to imply that he will stop the chain of repetitions that surround the section. But immediately, that gesture is revealed to be empty, as Iktomi launches into an invective against the bird and the avenger himself, describing how a bird will be shot and the avenger will be yoked to the tree bark. Iktomi is constantly using words to describe what will happen next. The past and future are, for Iktomi and certain other Native American tricksters, discursively created.

In contrast, the avenger's silence is notable throughout the two stories. Importantly, the avenger never once speaks except when he is in the tree. He only smiles when Iktomi first addresses him and does not talk until he "began to scale the tree" (86). I would argue that this text preserves certain spaces within its own landscape where English does not reach. Just as the bird's call gets translated, implying that there is an original Native text enclosed within the translated English work, the avenger's silent gestures allow him to escape the text's English translation. When he is released from the tree by the young woman, we are told that he "waved his hand . . . before her face. This was a sign of gratitude used when words failed to interpret strong emotion" (89). The girl, for her part, is "too shy for words" (89). Even Iktomi, when he is disguised as the avenger, realizes that he has to be "wordless" and "silent" (94). Of course, Iktomi fails at his attempts to stay quiet, but the avenger is successful except when he is up—or within—the tree.

The tree then functions as a translating device, making the avenger accessible to the English-speaking reader, and to English-speaking Iktomi. The avenger-tree moans, recalling the moans of the telegraph pole that Zitkala-Sa describes in "School Days." Like the pole, which was "planted by white men" (*American Indian Stories* 48), the tree is a symbol of the natural as it has been translated into English. The tree speaks in clear English, as the avenger never did before. The point is not so much that the tree—and the avenger—have been co-opted by an English voice, but that incarceration is equated with a loss of the text's Native space. When the avenger is released and he gestures in gratitude to his silent savior, he reclaims his resistance to the text's colonizing efforts. Even the narrative of the text cannot gain access to his thankful emotions, which are quantified and expressed only by being labeled inexpressible.

Given the reading I have set forth thus far, it seems as if the text works to contain, erase, and/or preserve a kind of pure Native space, uncontaminated by the poison of English and its signifying powers. But this would imply that somehow Native languages are uncomplicated by colonialism, and Native cultures reducible to a transparent set of signs. Interestingly, this aligns with the simple tone and style of *Old Indian Legends*; in addition, if we accept this reading, we might suggest that it highlights the silencing effects of assimilation on Native voices. Though I believe this is one plausible interpretation of the stories, I would also argue (perhaps paradoxically) that Zitkala-Sa inverts these paradigms and reveals them to be ironic. Some critics allow Iktomi to exist as a simple figure for white colonialism and its duplicitous tricks, as Margaret Lukens has argued; others, such as Dorothea Susag, have suggested that he is an equally as simple figure for Native avoidance of assimilation. I would like to suggest that he inhabits the position of the assimilated Native, but that this assimilation is redefined as resistant, repetitious, and parodic. In this sense, then, Zitkala-Sa actually questions the pure Native discourse, suggesting that the avenger's meta-discursivity is an impossibility on a multicultural, multilingual continent. Perhaps Elaine Jahner recalls just this questioning when she suggests that any metalanguage tends to fix and classify in problematic ways (155). In addition, Zitkala-Sa provokes us to consider the very concept of "biculturality," and how such a term inscribes a white Western either/or dichotomy onto a more multiplicitous Native American framework. If we think of Zitkala-Sa's own biculturality not as a DuBoisian double voice or as a simple assimilationist or colonial tendency, but instead as a borderland of polyphony, dynamism, and unified difference, we might release her from the translator's dilemma set forth by

Swann and others that automatically presumes her efforts in English to be a result of a less Indian (or non-Indian) assimilated position.

Consider, for example, the end of the "Shooting of the Red Eagle"; we are told that the avenger "won the beautiful Indian princess who never tired of telling to her children the story of the big red eagle" (99). The stories we have just read, then, are told as much by the avenger's wife as they are by Zitkala-Sa herself. On the one hand, we are told that the Indian princess is one of two daughters whom the chief puts up as prizes for the successful eagle killer, and on the other hand, we know that the young silent savior-woman returns to the village at the end of "The Tree-Bound" carrying "her story" about the avenger to the people (89). Thus, the ends of both stories concern the telling of those stories by a young woman; even if the chief's daughters and the savior-woman are meant to be distinct, the text certainly suggests a parallel, even implying perhaps that the savior-woman is one of the daughters. In any case, both the daughters and the savior-woman are silent characters who never speak throughout the course of the stories but who each ultimately become storytellers. The silent Native who becomes the teller of the very stories we've just heard is a doubled figure: both unassimilated and resistant *and* in control of the English translations of her story. Extending this reading, we might ask how the avenger's unpolluted signifying space suffers as a result of the story's structure as a whole. As much as he controls his meanings through the narrative, he is always destined to be told and retold as the hero of his own legend. This maneuver seems highly resistant to me, rather than some kind of capitulation. Colonialism becomes a back-and-forth gesture, where power can fluctuate across an axis rather than be permanently assigned to a "dominant" group. Thus, the failure of the avenger to escape the text's signifying power is also the success of Iktomi to revel in it. This is, of course, precisely *not* a discourse of "margin," "center," "dominant," "assimilated." Instead, like Allen, Zitkala-Sa suggests that such a reductive paradigm reinscribes oppressive politics. She chooses to use her stories to offer a new, less polarized way of thinking about power, a "theory" that is a precursor to some of the discussion offered by the critics I discussed above.

Though Iktomi ends up publicly humiliated for his trickstering in these legends, I think it is possible—even imperative—to recognize the triumphs of this figure in these tales. Iktomi is able to move back and forth between the silenced Native text and the articulated English version, inhabiting both sides of the dichotomy, ultimately collapsing the distinction between them. "Some people talk Iktomi language," one popular Sioux trickster tale goes,

"They are right and they are wrong" (Erdoes and Ortiz 94). When Iktomi casts his spell on the avenger at the tree, he mumbles inaudibly before his voice gradually rises to a whisper and finally a loud chant: "Grow fast, grow fast to the bark of the tree" (87). The bark encloses the avenger, who begins to plead in common English. Iktomi has the power to take that which resists discourse and make it signify. When he takes aim at the eagle, he misses the mark, demonstrating that his meaning proliferates beyond his control, that his words don't fly direct. At the same time, he can successfully disguise himself, playing at being "wordless, like a bashful Indian maid" (94). Here, he is equated with the avenger, the chief's daughters, and the shy savior-woman. He *plays* at being *authentically* Native, undermining the purity of such categories that separate one culture from another. The parody involved in a trickster tale, according to Barbara Babcock, "[suggests] that any particular ordering of experience may be arbitrary and subjective" (181). Iktomi's echoing of the avenger confuses rather than reinforces the supremacy of the avenger figure. Iktomi is trapped in signifying English, but this is not so different than the avenger, who is also destined to figure as the hero of the story forever and ever. Though it seems as if the avenger comes out on top, I would argue that Iktomi is actually the sole figure in the tales who is able to escape the text's colonialism. While the avenger and his straight-shooting arrow are ultimately undermined by the way the story works to embed them in the self-conscious retelling of the piece, keeping them alive in a never-ending repetition of births like the blood clot births, Iktomi finds a true escape from the text as he is "chased away beyond the outer limits of the camp ground" (98). Iktomi's escape occurs when he is replaced by the real avenger, who shows up at the camp. The disguised Iktomi, as a double or repetition, is supplanted by the "original."

We must ask ourselves, I think, what kind of a victory it is for the avenger, the supposedly authentic, unassimilated Native, to wind up captive to the story's retelling. Perhaps the killing of the (red) eagle is less a static sign for the death of white colonialism than it is a complex symbol that also encompasses a death of the "red" or Native presence itself. This is not at all to imply a self-loathing on the part of Zitkala-Sa; instead, I mean to note how the cultures converge and lose distinction in a way which violently challenges the assimilationist notions of erasure or resistance. In discussing Zitkala-Sa's college speech contest, which she won while orating under a degrading "squaw" banner, Sidonie Smith argues that she "destabilized 'race' as a defining categorization of human potential" (S. Smith 133). I would suggest that she does that here, as well, though not without simultaneously foregrounding race, culture, and language issues as central to the stories' meanings. While I support the reading of these stories that argues that the adamantly Native avenger has his revenge upon the threat of white imperialism, I also acknowledge a competing reading, which sees the *assimilated* Iktomi position as fundamentally resistant, flexible, cagey, and savvy about its own relationship to the text that colonizes (or fails to fully colonize) it.

The title page of *Old Indian Legends* states that the stories are "retold by Zitkala-Sa" (iii). On the facing page, a picture of the avenger waving to the silent savior-woman appears with this familiar caption from the story: "This was a sign of gratitude used when words failed to interpret strong emotion" (ii). The juxtaposition of the repetitive storytelling with the silent gesture highlights Zitkala-Sa's interest in asking how silence and English translation are linked in these versions of the legends. Is the text a simple celebration of Native silence and resistance in the face of increasing political pressure to articulate an assimilated identity? Perhaps it is also a statement about how texts themselves relate to the imperial project, and about how they can be manipulated by those whom they "colonize." In fact, though Iktomi mimics the avenger in these two stories, we are left unsure of the precise origin of the "original" himself (which blood clot boy is he, after all?). If we consider assimilation to be not a simple matter of erasure or overtaking, we can begin to make parallels about Zitkala-Sa's own use of English to tell her Sioux tales. The use of the colonizer's tools by the colonized not only suggests a kind of resistance, but also suggests that the position of power is itself dramatically unstable, able to be inhabited by those who supposedly, by definition, are excluded from its space. Zitkala-Sa and Iktomi are both a kind of trickster in these tales, playing at a literary fluency and finally refiguring the very definition of "fluent" itself.

Of course, I am suggesting that I, too, have played "trickster" in these tales, that I have used a theory-in-motion to work—from within Zitkala-Sa's context—against racist assumptions about the assimilated Native American position both in the stories and just outside of them in the real life of Zitkala-Sa, the author. I am aware, however, that trickster criticism necessarily misses the mark. Indeed, like the teacher who must cede authority to the very forces of a multicultural, multivocal classroom, trickster critics must bury in all of their theory a celebration of the failure of all systems of classification. This is not equivalent to a throwing up of hands, or to any kind of abyss at the core of textual explication. Instead, what I am suggesting is that precision is not the goal of the trickster critic. It is precisely in the conversations between Christian and Awkward, Gates, Vizenor, and Allen; between reader and text; between author and text; and between history and historicity that we come to an understanding of what is true based not on a stable, credible nature of things, but on a tenuous, changing polyphony of cultural contexts. It was my goal in this essay not to provide a model that might be adopted (or adapted) for use with other works, but to model how we can *do* theory (not use it) in a way that reflects all of the dynamics and diversity of the works we read.

Notes

1. The introduction also states that many of the African American nonparticipants in attendance were there not so much because they had interest in the theme of the conference ("Psychoanalysis in African American Contexts: Feminist Reconfigurations") but because "they were interested in seeing so many black women scholars in the flesh" (Abel, Christian, and Moglen 4).

2. For more on the difference between Native American and colonial perceptions of language, see Gerald Vizenor's interview in *Winged Words* (Coltelli 159).

3. The position Tompkins outlines is, as she describes it, "a version of neopragmatism" (Tompkins 76). For an exposition, she points her readers toward *Against Theory: Literary Studies and the New Pragmatism,* ed. W. J. T. Mitchell.

4. For the second year in a row, Native Americans have protested in Plymouth on Thanksgiving, renaming the holiday a "day of mourning." Since King Philip's Wars, Native Americans have been actively fighting colonization, and despite a communal worldview, many Native Americans would probably refute such a statement as Allen's.

5. Here, Ammons draws on an untitled paper given by Renato Rosaldo at the MLA conference in New York in 1992.

6. For more on how Eurocentric "master codes" differ from Native American tropes and traditions, see Elizabeth Ammons's introduction to *Tricksterism in Turn-of-the-Century American Literature.*

7. I also borrow heavily here from themes sketched out in Gloria Anzaldúa's *Borderlands/La frontera.*

8. All page numbers without an author's name refer to *Old Indian Legends.*

Works Cited

Abel, Elizabeth, Barbara Christian, and Helene Moglen, eds. *Female Subjects in Black and White.* Berkeley: U of California P, 1997.

Ahmad, Aijaz. *In Theory: Classes, Nations, Literatures.* London: Verso, 1992.

Allen, Paula Gunn. "'Border' Studies: The Intersection of Gender and Color." *Introduction to Scholarship in Modern Languages and Literatures.* Ed. Joseph Gibaldi. NY: MLA, 1992. 303–19.

——, ed. *Spider Woman's Granddaughters: Traditional Tales and Contemporary Writing by Native American Women.* Boston: Beacon 1989.

——, ed. *Studies in American Indian Literature: Critical Essays and Course Designs.* NY: MLA, 1983.

Ammons, Elizabeth. "Expanding the Canon of American Realism." *American Realism and Naturalism.* Ed. Donald Pizer. Cambridge: Cambridge UP, 1995. 95–114.

——. Introduction. *Tricksterism in Turn-of-the-Century American Literature: A Multicultural Perspective.* Ed. Elizabeth Ammons and Annette White-Parks. Hanover: UP of New England, 1994. vii–xiii.

Anzaldúa, Gloria. *Borderlands/La frontera: The New Mestiza.* San Francisco: Aunt Lute, 1987.

Awkward, Michael. "Appropriative Gestures: Theory and Afro-American Literary Criticism." *Within the Circle: An Anthology of African American Literary Criticism from the Harlem Renaissance to the Present.* Ed. Angelyn Mitchell. Durham: Duke UP, 1994. 360–67.

Babcock, Barbara. "A Tolerated Margin of Mess: The Trickster and His Tales Reconsidered." *Critical Essays on Native American Literature.* Ed. Andrew Wiget. Boston: G. K. Hall, 1985. 153–85.

Brown, Alanna K. "Mourning Dove, Trickster Energy, and Assimilation-Period Native Texts." *Tricksterism in Turn-of-the-Century American Literature: A Multicultural Perspective.* Ed. Elizabeth Ammons and Annette White-Parks. Hanover: UP of New England, 1994. 126–36.

Christian, Barbara. "Fixing Methodologies: *Beloved.*" *Female Subjects in Black and White.* Ed. Elizabeth Abel, Barbara Christian, and Helene Moglen. Berkeley: U of California P, 1997. 363–70.

——. "The Race for Theory." *Making Face, Making Soul=Haciendo Caras: Creative and Critical Perspectives by Feminists of Color.* Ed. Gloria Anzaldúa. San Francisco: Aunt Lute, 1990. 335–45.

Coltelli, Laura. *Winged Words: American Indian Writers Speak.* Lincoln: U of Nebraska P, 1990.

Cruikshank, Julie. *The Social Life of Stories: Narrative and Knowledge in the Yukon Territory.* Lincoln: U of Nebraska P, 1998.

Cutter, Martha J. "Zitkala-Sa's Autobiographical Writings: The Problems of a Canonical Search for Language and Identity." *MELUS* 19.1 (1994): 31–46.

Erdoes, Richard, and Alfonso Ortiz, eds. *American Indian Trickster Tales.* New York: Viking, 1998.

Gates, Henry Louis, Jr. *Figures in Black: Words, Signs, and the "Racial" Self.* New York: Oxford UP, 1987.

——. "Talkin' That Talk." *"Race," Writing, and Difference.* Ed. Henry Louis Gates Jr. Chicago: U of Chicago P, 1985. 402–09.

Hutchison, Sarah. "The Power of Story." *Surviving in Two Worlds: Contemporary Native American Voices.* Ed. Jay Leibold. Austin: U of Texas P, 1997. 122–31.

Jahner, Elaine A. "Metalanguages." *Narrative Chance: Postmodern Discourse on Native American Indian Literatures*. Ed. Gerald Vizenor. Norman: U of Oklahoma P, 1989. 155–85.

Krupat, Arnold. "On the Translation of Native American Song and Story: A Theorized History." *On the Translation of Native American Literatures*. Ed. Brian Swann. Washington: Smithsonian Institution P, 1992. 3–32.

——. *The Voice in the Margin: Native American Literature and the Canon*. Berkeley: U of California P, 1989.

Lincoln, Kenneth. "Native American Literatures." *Smoothing the Ground: Essays on Native American Oral Literature*. Ed. Brian Swann. Berkeley: U of California P, 1983. 3–38.

Lukens, Margaret A. "The American Indian Story of Zitkala-Sa." *In Her Own Voice: Nineteenth-Century American Women Essayists*. Ed. Sherry Lee Linkon. New York: Garland, 1997. 141–55.

Mihesuah, Devon A. "Voices, Interpretations, and the 'New Indian History.'" *American Indian Quarterly* 20.1 (1996): 91–108.

Mitchell, W. J. T., ed. *Against Theory: Literary Studies and the New Pragmatism*. Chicago: U of Chicago P, 1985.

Oakes, Karen. "Theoretical Reservations and a Seneca Tale." *Tricksterism in Turn-of-the-Century American Literature: A Multicultural Perspective*. Ed. Elizabeth Ammons and Annette White-Parks. Hanover: UP of New England, 1994. 137–57.

Rebolledo, Tey Diana. "The Politics of Poetics: Or, What Am I, a Critic, Doing in This Text Anyhow?" *Making Face, Making Soul=Haciendo Caras: Creative and Critical Perspectives by Feminists of Color*. Ed. Gloria Anzaldúa. San Francisco: Aunt Lute, 1990. 346–55.

Sarris, Greg. *Keeping Slugwoman Alive: A Holistic Approach to American Indian Texts*. Berkeley: U of California P, 1993.

Smith, Jeanne. "'A Second Tongue': The Trickster's Voice in the Works of Zitkala-Sa." *Tricksterism in Turn-of-the-Century American Literature: A Multicultural Perspective*. Ed. Elizabeth Ammons and Annette White-Parks. Hanover: UP of New England, 1994.

Smith, Sidonie. "Cheesecake, Nymphs, and 'We the People': Un/National Subjects about 1900." *Prose Studies* 17.1 (1994): 120–40.

Swann, Brian. Introduction. *On the Translation of Native American Literatures*. Ed. Brian Swann. Washington: Smithsonian Institution P, 1992. xiii–xx.

Tompkins, Jane. "'Indians': Textualism, Morality, and the Problem of History." *"Race," Writing, and Difference*. Ed. Henry Louis Gates Jr. Chicago: U of Chicago P, 1985. 59–77.

Vizenor, Gerald, ed. *Narrative Chance: Postmodern Discourse on Native American Indian Literatures*. Norman: U of Oklahoma P, 1989.

Zitkala-Sa. *American Indian Stories*. Lincoln: U of Nebraska P, 1985.

———. *Old Indian Legends*. Lincoln: U of Nebraska P, 1985.

COMMUNICATING HISTORY

JAMES WELCH'S *KILLING CUSTER* AND THE CULTURAL TRANSLATION OF THE BATTLE OF THE LITTLE BIGHORN

✦

Anthony G. Murphy

IN 1990, Blackfeet poet and novelist James Welch was asked by filmmaker Paul Stekler to join with him in co-writing a screenplay for a documentary on the Battle of the Little Bighorn, also known as Custer's Last Stand. Welch agreed, and in 1992 the film, called *Last Stand at Little Bighorn*, was broadcast as a successful, highly rated part of the PBS *American Experience* series. The documentary project led to a contract for Welch to write a more detailed account of the battle, which appeared in 1994 as *Killing Custer: The Battle of the Little Bighorn and the Fate of the Plains Indians*. Embarking on this historical project, Welch admitted feeling "more than a little trepidation," especially as he asked himself, "What can one say about the battle that hasn't been said before?" (Welch 20–21). Welch answers his question with another: "So what's special about this book?" and answers, "Maybe nothing" (22). He further explains that *Killing Custer* "certainly will not provide any startling revelations from a historical or military standpoint" (22). This assertion, in the prologue of the text, has garnered Welch some harsh criticism from other scholars of the Battle of the Little Bighorn, particularly Gregory Michno in *Lakota Noon: The Indian Narrative of Custer's Defeat*. Michno calls into question Welch's credibility as a historian by labeling him a "self-acknowledged fiction writer and poet," and wonders what the point of a new work on the Battle of the Little Bighorn might be if it indeed lacks "startling revelations from a historical and military standpoint" (x). Michno does rightly point out the logical fallacy that while Welch's work purports to "tell the Indians' side of the story" (Welch 20), there is a great deal of dependence upon "secondary white source material" (Michno x) that Welch himself claims has been "carefully distorted throughout the years to justify the invasion and subjugation of the indigenous people" (Welch 46). I think, however, that by focusing on the factual veracity of *Killing Custer,* Michno misses the point of Welch's project. Welch's early acknowledgement that he is a fiction writer and a poet sets the stage for what is a very personal text, the project of which is to connect the battle and its contexts to contemporary Indigenous America. Welch has written a cultural translation of an event that has not only achieved the status of myth in American culture but was also a watershed moment in the history of Indian-white relations in America. Through his cultural translation of Custer's Last Stand within contemporary contexts, Welch communicates a revised, empowering history for today's American Indians.

The difficulties that surround contemporary ideas of history arise largely from the idea of assigning truth-value to historical accounts. The *Oxford English Dictionary* (*OED*) makes this problem clear from the outset with its first definition of history as "A relation of incidents (in early use, either true or imaginary; later only of those professedly true); a narrative, tale, story." The truth-value of history is given decidedly more credibility when it is further defined as "A written narrative constituting a continuous methodical record, in order of time," "the formal record of the past," or as "the branch of knowledge which deals with past events." Despite the veracity implied by weighty phrases like "formal record" and "branch of knowledge," it is difficult to ignore the *OED*'s opening definition of history as first either true or imaginary, and later as only professedly true.

Postmodern discourses of history make it virtually impossible to assign truth-value to the historical past. In "The Question of Narrative in Contemporary Historical Theory," Hayden White describes the historical narrative as a "simulacrum of the structure and processes of real events" (3). The contingency of historical truth-value becomes more apparent when White points out that "The story told in the [historical] narrative is a 'mimesis' of the story lived in some region of historical reality, and insofar as it is an accurate imitation it is to be considered a truthful account thereof" (3). The closest that White gets to any sort of truth-value of history is through the chronicle, a "set of events simply listed in the chronological order of their original occurrence" (19), which merely "describe[s] a situation" (2). While the chronicle shares chronology as a code between itself and narrative historical discourse, narrative historical discourse "utilizes other codes as well and produces a meaning quite different from that of any chronicle" (19).

Paul Ricoeur points to the historian as one source of the "other codes" that impact upon the meaning found in narrative historical discourse, explaining that the "[particular historian] retains from the past only what, in [their] estimation, should not be forgotten, what is memorable in the strict sense" (295). Ricoeur feels that what is worth retaining are "the values which governed the actions of individuals, the life of institutions, the struggles of the past" (295). Ricoeur makes historical truth-value contingent on the historian, which Roland Barthes supports through the idea that "historical discourse is essentially a product of ideology" (Barthes 153). The construction of the subject of the historian through ideology brings with it more codes that reveal meaning. The community of which the historian is a part, and which is also partially constructed through ideology, also affects the historical discourse.

For Irish critic Donnchadh O'Corrain, history is "constructed," and communities "define their present identity and political awareness by choosing their past . . . from a wide range of symbols" (25). This past is not, however, static, as it is chosen "from many possible pasts and the choice is conditional in that it is constantly reaffirmed, . . . adjusted, or radically revised to meet the consciously changing needs of the community as a living organism" (O'Corrain 25). While O'Corrain paints a view of the constructedness of history that might serve to affirm cultural identity for Native American communities, the potential danger of constructed histories is articulated by historian Eric Hobsbawm, who warns "I used to think that the profession of history, unlike that of, say, nuclear physics, could at least do no harm. Now I know it can" (qtd. in Hall 65). Hobsbawm's concerns are grounded in the belief that history "is the raw material for nationalist or ethnic or fundamentalist ideologies. . . . The past is an essential element, perhaps the essential element in these ideologies. If there is no suitable past, it can always be invented" (qtd. in Hall 65). Postmodern historiography's emphasis on the constructedness of history and on issues such as the ideological contingency of historical truth-value affects powerfully the cultural production of still colonized cultures like those of Native America. The historical truth-value of a revisionist historical text such as Welch's account of the Battle of the Little Bighorn is made contentious not only by postmodernism's belief in what has been referred to as the "impossibility of retrieving truth" (Brydon 142), but also by postcolonial notions of authenticity.[1]

In *Killing Custer,* as well as the film documentary that preceded the book, one of the most important tasks for Welch was to "tell the Indians' side of the story . . . to give the Sioux, the Cheyennes, and Custer's much-maligned Crow and Arikara scouts a voice" (20). This idea of being able to speak for heterogeneous groups of Native Americans opens itself up to questions and criticism from within postcolonial theory. In postcolonial criticism, the critique of authenticity arises out of "some decolonising states arguing for a recuperation of authentic pre-colonial conditions and customs" (Ashcroft et al., *Key Concepts* 21). Acknowledging that Native America is still colonized, ideas of authenticity need to be examined in light of Native American historiography, which, while not necessarily articulating the desire for recuperation of precolonial conditions and customs, does seek to rewrite the record of the precolonized and colonized past. While not necessarily denying that "Markers of cultural difference may well be perceived as authentic cultural signifiers," the question asked as a kind of cautionary note by postcolonial critics is whether or not "claim[s] to authenticity . . . imply that these cultures are not subject to change" (Ashcroft et al., *Key Concepts* 21). Adding another level to the earlier mentioned "tension with the imperial power," Gareth Griffiths implicates the imperial center in the critique of authenticity. While acknowledging the legitimacy of "the claim of Aboriginal peoples . . . to restitution of their traditional lands and sacred places, or to the voices and practices of their traditional cultures," Griffiths cautions that "What I am concerned with is the impact of the representation of that claim when it is mediated through a discourse of the authentic adopted and promulgated by the dominant discourse which 'speaks' the indigene within a construction whose legitimacy is grounded not in their practice but in our desire" (Griffiths 83).

The paradox outlined above by Griffiths underlies the issues of authenticity that affect the reading of Welch's revisionist history. Griffiths's essay, quoted above, is provocatively titled "The Myth of Authenticity," and this destabilization of the authentic, in combination with the postmodern historiographic impossibility of retrieving historical truth, is a cause for concern for indigenous scholars. Arif Dirlik lays the charge that "The denial of authenticity to cultural claims beyond localized constructions is accompanied by the denial to the past of any authority to authenticate the present" (2). Concentrating on issues of power that he feels Griffiths overlooks in "The Myth of Authenticity," Dirlik posits the danger, using Disney as an example, that "postmodern/postcolonial denials of historical or cultural truths render the past or other cultures more readily available for commodification and exploitation by abolishing the possibility of distinguishing one invention from another" (8). Dirlik challenges and further problematizes the postcolonial skepticism of cultural authenticity as "ahistorical cultural essentialism," saying that "indigenous voices are quite open to change; what they insist on is not cultural purity or persistence, but the preservation of a particular historical trajectory of their own" (18). Using the "indigenist ideology" (or "indigenism") of Ward Churchill,[2] Dirlik constructs a historicism that acknowledges the colonial past not to restore a precolonial ideal, but instead to "draw upon the past to create a new future" (19). Instead of adherence to a precolonial cultural identity, there is an ongoing negotiation with the changes that colonialism has wrought upon the indigenous culture. These negotiations are at the heart of indigenism as described by Churchill, which seems similar to Griffiths's description of the aboriginal writer "grounding his identity in essentialist difference as a political strategy." Dirlik's use of indigenism is not far removed from postcolonialism's qualified acknowledgement that, "In some respects, cultural essentialism, which is theoretically questionable, may be adopted as a strategic political position in the struggle against imperial power" (Ashcroft et al., *Key Concepts* 21).[3] Dirlik considers the past as a "project" that has the potential to be productive in positive ways for indigenous cultures (24). He concludes by allowing for the postmodern denial of historical truth, while simultaneously leaving open the possibility for indigenous writers like James Welch to make productive forays into this destabilized historicism:

> If the past is constructed, it is constructed at all times, and ties to the past require an ongoing dialogue between present and past constructions, except in linear conceptions of history where the past, once past, is irrelevant except as an abstract moral or political lesson. The repudiation of linear temporality in indigenous ideology suggests that the past is never really past, but offers "stories" that may be required to resolve problems of the present, even as they are changed to meet present needs. (Dirlik 24)

Dirlik's conceptions of past as project and as dialogue between past and present constructions of history provide a way in which to understand what James Welch has undertaken in his history of the Battle of the Little Bighorn. Welch's project is a reexamination of Custer's Last Stand from the point of view of the Native Americans who were involved in the conflict (17). To appropriate another strategy, this time from Edward Said, *Killing Custer* presents a "contrapuntal reading" of a historical event, but also, in the spirit of Dirlik's "dialogue between past and present," enacts a "cultural translation" of that event. Contrapuntal readings provide a "counterpoint to the text [or in this case the inscription of a historical moment by the imperial center], thus enabling the emergence of colonial implications that might otherwise remain hidden" (Ashcroft et al., *Key Concepts* 55–56). Because the history of Custer's Last Stand has become mythologized in American culture from the privileged perspective of the American imperial center, the category of cultural translation is particularly appropriate for understanding a revisionist history of the event.

The concept of cultural translation builds from theories of linguistic translation.[4] As the phrase implies, cultural translation moves beyond literal translation in the linguistic sense of the word, to encompass ideas of "dialogue," both in Dirlik's sense of dialogue between past and present, as well as the project of a dialogue between indigenous culture and that of the imperial center. For Krupat, the cultural translator "does not immediately assume that unusual difficulty in conveying the sense of an alien discourse denotes a fault in the latter, but instead critically examines the normal state of his or her own [discourse]" (Krupat, *Turn* 35). For a text to be read as a cultural translation, Krupat feels that it should demonstrate both alternate strategies to the readings of the dominant culture and indigenous perspectives (*Turn* 38). Cultural translation as "project" acts as a link between indigenist historicism and postcolonial notions of hybridity, where indigenism acknowledges the colonial past as it seeks an indigenous cultural identity, while also acknowledging the "transformative cultural, linguistic and political impacts of the colonizer" (Ashcroft et al., *Key Concepts* 119).

Cultural translation works well with Homi Bhabha's theory of a hybridized "third space of enunciation" that, while acknowledging the "hierarchical nature of the imperial process," at the same time "stresses [the] interdependence and the mutual construction of [the] subjectivities" of the colonizer/colonized (Ashcroft et al., *Key Concepts* 118). Robert Young points out that Bhabha's notion of hybridity allows for seeing the mutual construction of colonizing and colonized subjects as "an active moment of challenge and resistence against a dominant colonial power . . . depriving the imposed imperialist culture, not only of the authority that it has for so long imposed politically, often through violence, but even of its own claims to authenticity" (23).

Welch's *Killing Custer* fulfills the mission of hybrid indigenous literatures to "weave constantly and creatively between what is native, and the culture of the invader; to cross registers and undermine fixed points of view" (Boehmer 230). Not only communicating between past and present, Welch's historical text also communicates between the two cultures of Native and white America. While Welch's celebrity as a poet and novelist and the revisionist nature of the work would bring a Native American readership to the text, the readership (as well as the audience of the documentary that preceded it) would likely be largely white, garnered through the film's appearance on PBS and the book's original publication through mainstream publisher W. W. Norton (and subsequent paperback release by Penguin Books). In the interests of this communication between cultures, Welch navigates the interdisciplinary ground of postmodern historiography and postcolonial and indigenist theory to communicate a recontextualized history of the Battle of the Little Bighorn to both white and Native audiences, not just as a catalyst for the end of a traditional way of life for the Plains Indians, but also to show how the repercussions of this epoch-making event have affected the lives and culture of Native America to the present day.

Welch generally operates through a series of temporal shifts between historical events, contemporary contexts, and his own research efforts. Along with its division into ten chapters, the work is also divided chronologically into three larger sections. The first of these sections deals with earlier historical contexts that led up to the Battle of the Little Bighorn, while the second concentrates on the more specific temporal setting of the battle itself. The third section contains not only a chronicle of the post-battle events that saw the end of the way of life of the Plains Indians, but also contextualizes these events within the twentieth century and contemporary Native America. As well, this section includes Welch's narrative of his involvement in the making of Paul Stekler's documentary.

The first chapter of the text serves as an example of the temporal shifts that take place throughout, as well as exemplifying the kind of cultural translation that occurs in the work. The chapter describes the Marias River Massacre, which took place on January 23, 1870, more than six years prior to the Battle of the Little Bighorn. In a tragic case of acknowledged and ignored mistaken identity, the US Army killed 173 members of the Blackfeet band of Heavy Runner, a chief who had, just days earlier, signed a peace accord with the United States government. The chapter moves from 1870 to 1985 and Welch's efforts to rectify the disappearance of the massacre from "public consciousness" by finding the site, which was also lost from the historical record, and includes descriptions of the site and Welch's personal observations and commentary. There is also another temporal shift to the present of the book's writing and the mention of other strategies for reclaiming Native American history, such as Blackfeet educators beginning field trips for their students to the site of the massacre. The temporal shifts, especially the movement between and interconnectedness of the nineteenth century and the present, exemplify Welch's fulfillment of Dirlik's construction of indigenous historicism, where "the point of departure . . . is the present, and its goal is not to restore a bygone past, but to draw upon the past to create a new future" (19).

Along with an active resistance to the kind of temporal faithfulness typical of the linear chronology of the historical chronicle, Welch subverts the dominant history of Custer's Last Stand by focusing on Indian testimony of the events of and surrounding the Battle of the Little Bighorn. Through the strategic essentialism of "giving the [heterogeneous groups of] Indians a voice," Welch provides a distinctly "indigenous perspective" that Krupat feels is necessary to cultural translation. The use of accounts by the Indian participants in the battle as credible testimony is a relatively recent phenomenon; this testimony has previously been "dismissed as unreliable by historians" (Welch 162). Welch's work, especially the middle chapters on the battle itself, depends heavily upon the testimony of Indian participants and their ancestors.

The best example of the controversy surrounding the Indian testimony is found in one of Custer's Crow scouts, named Curly. Curly was released by the Seventh Cavalry from duty along with the rest of the Crow scouts just prior to the end of the battle. He ended up watching the battle with field glasses from a ridge about a mile and a half east of the site, and was, in Welch's words "the last man on the army side to see Custer and the Seventh Cavalry alive" (21). Curly survived to be interviewed several times after the battle, but was "branded a liar and a publicity-seeker" because of "discrepancies" between the interviews (Welch 21, 162). Welch attributes these discrepancies to the incompetence of translators, the "leading" of witnesses to the story that the interviewer wanted to hear, and Curly's willingness to be "agreeable" (21).

Welch includes the following explanation from Robert Utley, which not only discusses the problems involved in linguistic translation but also speaks to Krupat's notion of cultural translation: "Indian testimony is difficult to use. It is personal, episodic, and maddeningly detached from time and space, or sequence and topography. It also suffers from a language barrier often aggravated by incompetent interpreters, from the cultural gulf between questioner and respondent, and from assumptions of the interviewer not always in accord with reality" (qtd. in Welch 164). While Utley's positing of a potential "reality" above reaffirms the problematic nature of historiographic reality in postmodern/postcolonial discourses, it is more important to my discussion to note his explanation of the problems surrounding the indigenous witness testimony, particularly that of Curley. Utley, pointing to new evidence culled from new studies of the battle site, feels that interviewers of Indian participants in the battle approached the interviews with preconceived "erroneous assumptions," and then "bent the responses to fit those erroneous assumptions" (Welch 164).

Other claims by Curley that have been invalidated are that he stayed with Custer up until the last half hour of the Last Stand (as opposed to leaving with the other scouts when they were released earlier by Custer), and that Custer led troops down to the Little Bighorn River that separated the soldiers from the Native encampment and was the first to fall (Welch 164–65). Indian testimony as well as new archaeological evidence show that Custer came nowhere near the river as he and his troops moved north through coulees to "Last Stand Hill," which itself was some distance from the river (Welch 151, 165).

Showing the potential of cultural translation for communication between the imperial center and colonized indigenous peoples, Welch demonstrates that recent research from the fields of history and archaeology includes fresh perspectives on the battle that corroborate Indian witness testimony. In 1983, a grass fire burned the Little Bighorn battlefield bare. A year later, archaeologist Richard Fox, "using a grid system, metal detectors, and controlled excavation," was able to "track the development and conclusion of the battle, including tracing shell and bullet patterns as the fight progressed" (169). John Gray's 1991 work *Custer's Last Campaign* depends on topographic and time and motion studies to reconstruct the events that took place. Not only does Gray's research, according to Robert Utley, "[make] sense of Curley's testimony" (164), but Welch uses this new information, in a demonstration of the subversive and resistant possibilities of a hybrid historiography that combines the testimony of Indian participants in the battle with the findings of Fox and Gray's archaeological and technological methodologies.[5]

This hybrid historiography also serves to undermine the assumptions of historical authenticity long held by the imperial center of American society that has until now attempted to maintain hegemonic control over the Custer Myth. This control has been exerted in various ways with one of the more overt being the exclusion of certain historical information from the bookshop at the visitor center at the Custer Battlefield Monument, which is run by the Custer Battlefield Historical and Museum Association. One of the books not sold at the visitor center is Dee Brown's *Bury My Heart at Wounded Knee*, which Welch characterizes as "Perhaps the first book to [incorporate

Indian testimony] in a popular way" (47). The Custer Battlefield Historical and Museum Association, however, found the book to be "subjective and too slanted in favor of the Indians" and thus kept it from their shelves (Welch 47).

The mythologized Last Stand includes a heroic portrayal of the Seventh Cavalry fighting "a controlled action against the Indians," and Welch explains further that "According to many historians and buffs, [the soldiers] set up skirmish lines, retreated in order, obeyed their officers' commands, conducted the best fight possible under the circumstances" (169). Conversely, Indian testimony, which is now being corroborated by the recent research of Fox and Gray, has always maintained that "Custer's troops panicked almost immediately when the Indians attacked in force. They bunched together in helpless clusters, shooting wildly in all directions until their guns were empty. Then many took off running, making it easy for the horseback Indians to pursue and kill them" (Welch 169).

The most controversial Indian testimony, which has long been disavowed by Custer historians, has contended that many Seventh Cavalry soldiers killed themselves and each other in less than "honourable" fashion. Warriors from diverse tribes, such Wooden Leg (Cheyenne), Turtle Rib (Minneconjou Sioux), and Foolish Elk (Oglala Sioux), all provided testimony of this phenomenon. Wooden Leg witnessed large skirmish groups of cavalry soldiers killing each other, while both Turtle Rib and Foolish Elk witnessed the same incident, in which a soldier "break[s] away on a fast horse . . . gallop[s] away from the battle," and while pulling away from his pursuers, takes out his pistol and shoots himself in the head (171). These revelations brought to light by Indian testimony have long been denied by historians and "Custer Buffs," and not only serve to problematize any ideas of historical authenticity that the American imperial center might attach to the version of the past it holds to be true, but also serve to educate the American mainstream society as to the colonizing roles that society has played throughout their history. Of course, any claim to authenticity on the part of Indian witness testimony is suspect in light of the problems with linguistic translation. Welch, although acknowledging (via Robert Utley, above) the problems of translation in regard to Indian testimony, does not devote space in *Killing Custer* to the authentication of the sources of Indian testimony. Thus, before the reader can deem the testimony credible or incredible, they are obliged to check Welch's sources and try to access the credibility of the translator/translation, which as critics like Walter Benjamin and Gayatri Spivak attest is itself a highly problematic task.

Another alternative strategy of Welch's cultural translation that resists and subverts the more traditional chronicling of the Battle of the Little Bighorn is the linking of the battle forward in time to the contemporary problems of Native Americans. Repeatedly in the book Welch shifts to a highly personal narrative mode to discuss a variety of different subjects, all pertaining to Native America and linking back to the Little Bighorn. He recounts a number of visits to the Custer National Battlefield Monument; the first, in 1974, included a run-in with a park warden who issued a stern reprimand for the sacrilege of eating a sandwich too near the monument (95–96). Welch's personal narratives reveal the colonization of twentieth-century Native America through stories such as Welch's mother's boarding school experience at the Haskell Indian school in Lawrence, Kansas. The boarding schools, in Welch's words, were an effort to "cut [that] generation off from their traditional upbringing" (227).

Out of Welch's narratives of the filming of the documentary comes the story of a chance dinner with Native American activist Russell Means. Welch uses this chance encounter to tie a narrative thread that connects the Wounded Knee Massacre of 1890 to the 1973 takeover of the hamlet of Wounded Knee by AIM (American Indian Movement) leaders Means and Dennis Banks, as well as a large group of AIM members. In this way, Wounded Knee serves double duty in the assertion of an indigenous cultural identity, not only as the site of the last massacre that sealed the fate of the Plains Indians, but also as a contemporary site of resistance to the colonizer. Welch mentions Russell Means not only in the context of the Wounded Knee protest of 1973, but also the 1992 Sun Dance held by Means and other activists at Medicine Tail Coulee near the Little Bighorn battlefield site. The Sun Dance was held as "a counter-demonstration to the anniversary of the battle" and to "the five hundredth anniversary of Columbus' journey to the New World" (Welch 105). In the same way that Welch takes the reader past the iconography of the Custer Myth to see the complexity of the Seventh Cavalry general, so too does the reader see a more complex Russell Means than the media's representation of the resistance leader. By linking past and present in these ways, Welch demonstrates that despite the end of the Plains Indians' way of life that was precipitated by the Battle of the Little Bighorn, active resistance to the colonizer continues to the present day.

Native American writer and scholar Gerald Vizenor, depending on postmodern theorist Jean-François Lyotard, says that "Native American histories and literatures, oral and written, are imagined from "wisps of narratives" that, according to Lyotard, are "stories that one tells, that one hears, that one acts out; the people does not exist as a subject but as a mass of millions of insignificant and serious little stories that sometimes let themselves be collected together to constitute big stories and sometimes disperse into digressive elements" (Vizenor 3).

The "big story" that is told through the connection of the narrative "wisps" or threads in *Killing Custer* is a collective story about the colonization of Native America and the ongoing resistance of the indigenous population. Welch's "narrative wisps" comprise a twentieth-century contextualization of the Battle of the Little Bighorn and related epochal events like the Wounded Knee Massacre that connects to Dirlik's point that "The repudiation of linear temporality in indigenous ideology suggests that the past is never really past, but offers "stories" that may be required to resolve problems of the present, even as they are changed to answer present needs" (24).

The alternative strategies necessary for cultural translation have, in Welch's case, been largely historiographic. Krupat, however, also posited "indigenous perspectives" as one of the criteria for cultural translation. The very notion of an indigenous perspective not only seems to demand an opposing non-indigenous perspective, but also requires due caution over the potential for harmful essentialisms that might arise. However, to again invoke the postcolonial idea of "strategic essentialism," *Killing Custer* demonstrates that opposing cultural conceptions of land were at the heart of the conflict between Plains Indians and white settlers and soldiers. If the mission of cultural translation is for the parties involved to have to examine their own cultures as they translate the "other" culture, then the juxtaposition of worldviews presents a crucial moment for intercultural communication and the mutual understanding that is possible from cultural translation. In the context of the Battle of the Little Bighorn, the opposition between Western European and North American Aboriginal cultural conceptions of land is focused in the Black Hills of South Dakota. Welch sees this cultural difference as a foundational cause of the demise of the Plains Indians' way of life, and as leading to the Battle of the Little Bighorn. The Laramie Treaty of 1868 gave the Indians involved "all of South Dakota west of the Missouri River, including the Black Hills," for what was to be called "the Great Sioux Reservation" (68–69). Despite the treaty, which Welch emphasizes was "broken immediately and repeatedly," in 1874 Custer led an expedition into the Black Hills in order to substantiate rumors that gold could be found there. Gold was discovered, and "within a year, there were fifteen thousand miners in the Black Hills" (84). Welch presents evidence that Custer was complicit with the United States' government-sanctioned ecological imperialism in the Black Hills, and that his complicity led to an intense hatred for him on the part of Plains Indians. Custer, despite being a Civil War hero and achieving national fame (even before his death), apparently was always looking for ways to become wealthy. This desire led him to many questionable business schemes that would have allowed him to profit from the very land he was driving the Indians from and the colonial practices in which he took part as a cavalry officer. These schemes included selling stock in his name for a bogus Colorado silver mine, stagecoach companies, and the presidency of a company that would try to sell "questionable" horseshoes to his own United States Army (Welch 217). At the time of the publication of *Killing Custer*, the United States government had still refused to either return the Black Hills to the Sioux under the terms of the Laramie Treaty or to offer an acceptable settlement (68).

The Western European cultural conception of land was based at the time of colonization on the concept of *terra nullius* or "empty lands," which means that while the land may be inhabited by an indigenous population, it is not being productively occupied. Peter Knudtson and David Suzuki, in *Wisdom of the Elders*, characterize the Western European worldview as "spiritually detached," where land is "lifeless" and "inert, a two-dimensional physical surface (if we exclude a third dimension, which grants rights of access to urban high-rises above or to mineral or water rights below)—to be surveyed, subdivided, and zoned" (121). In the United States, Manifest Destiny provided a "God-given" right to push ever westward in search of new territories for white settlers to occupy and for railways to traverse. The worldview of the Sioux and Cheyenne, however, included the belief that lands like the Black Hills were sacred and could not be sold. The Black Hills were believed to be the place where the Sioux and Cheyenne people originated, and Welch describes the hills as "the centre of their universe, a source of strength and reassurance, especially since the whites came onto the northern plains" (82). Welch's words here sound similar to the following "definition of the sanctity of geographic space" from historian J. Donald Hughes: "Sacred space is a place where human beings . . . experience a sense of connectedness to the universe. There, in some special way, spirit is present to them" (Knudtson and Suzuki 123).

Risking another instance of strategic essentialism, it is possible to say generally that North American Aboriginal people share a belief in their interconnectedness with the universe and all its creations that is not shared by the Western worldview. In an article entitled "The Sacred Hoop," Paula Gunn Allen, coming from the worldview of the Plains Indian peoples, explains that "The notion that nature is somewhere over there while humanity is over here or that a great hierarchical ladder of being exists on which ground and trees occupy a very low rung, animals a slightly higher one, and man (never woman)—especially 'civilised man'—a very high one indeed is antithetical to tribal thought" (246). Allen further explains that "The American Indian sees all creatures as . . . necessary parts of an ordered, balanced, and living whole" (246). Establishing the commonality of this belief system among Native peoples early in the text, Welch refers, as an aside to finding the Marias River Massacre site, to the sacredness of Chief Mountain (in the Rockies) as a site of vision quests to his own people, the Blackfeet (39). This affirmation of the land's sacredness and the human interconnectedness to the land in Native American spirituality occurs repeatedly in the text. The description of the Lakota Sioux Sun Dance ceremony of June 1876 that opens chapter 2 contains many references to sacred connections to the land, including first and foremost the site of the Sun Dance, the Deer Medicine Rocks, which are "a grouping of tall standing boulders etched with prehistoric carvings along the Rosebud River in Montana," and which are sacred to both the Lakotas and the Cheyennes (48). Central to the Sun Dance is the tree-pole around which the dancer dances. The ritual preparation of this tree is intimately connected to the Native worldview as it is painted with colors that represent the four horizontal directions (48). The Sun Dance site was always circular, reflecting the notion of the "sacred hoop," which Welch describes as "encompass[ing] all life— [the Indians'], the animals', the trees', the stones'" (131). Other Sun Dance rituals, such as prayer, reflect the Native interconnectedness to nature. The sacred pipe is filled "with grains of tobacco representing six directions, including sky and Grandmother Earth, all the fliers and four-leggeds, each time invoking their help to make the ceremony correct and to take pity" (48–49). The Sun Dance of 1876 was especially important as Sitting Bull danced his way to a vision foretelling the attack and victory that was to come at the Little Bighorn (51).

From the historical setting of the 1876 Sun Dance, Welch also connects an enduring Native worldview in more contemporary settings. The section on boarding schools shows the lengths to which the imperial center can go in attempting to erase the culture of the colonized. These schools, by separating Native children from their families, sought to cut a generation of Indians off from their "upbringing . . . beliefs and lifeways" (227). When preparing for the PBS documentary, Welch meets Cheyenne elder Ted Rising Sun, who embodies a hybrid spirituality that encompasses both Native spirituality and Western European religious beliefs. Rising Sun is not only a traditional elder in his Cheyenne community but is also a Mennonite

Church deacon on the reservation (209). The filming of a crucial scene for the documentary led to a firsthand experience with Native spirituality tied to nature. Filming a night scene at the battleground, a violent prairie storm arose with lightning, thunder, and rain. Director Paul Stekler and the crew were becoming increasingly concerned with the closeness of the lightning strikes, when crew member Roy Big Crane (Salish) burned sweet grass in a protective circle around the crew (278). The references to Native spirituality in Welch's text can be read as culturally translative counterpoints to references to 1880 Indian agent reports that mention that "[Indian] morals, *from a Christian, or civilized standpoint,* are as bad as need be, but from their own standpoint are perhaps not as bad as might be expected" (emphasis added) (Welch 230). Or this quotation from Custer's own *My Life on the Plains,* in which he characterizes the Indian as "the representative of a race whose origin is, and promise to be, a subject forever wrapped in mystery: a race incapable of being judged by the rules or laws applicable to any other known race of men" (Welch 130).

James Welch's *Killing Custer* raises the question of how colonized indigenous peoples claim or reclaim their past amidst the historical instability of the postmodern age. In his cultural translation of the Battle of the Little Bighorn, Welch navigates across a potentially rocky terrain that encompasses postmodern historiography, postcolonial theory, and indigenous ideology. By implementing the alternate strategies and supplying the indigenous perspectives necessary for cultural translation, one of the mythologized cornerstones of American history is revised, creating a mode of anticolonial resistance that educates while it subverts the assumptions of the imperial center. The need for works of cultural translation that help shift the points of view of opposing cultures is perhaps best demonstrated when Cheyenne tribal elders Ted Rising Sun and Bill Tall Bull reveal a telling difference in what is mythologized in each culture involved in a historical conflict like the Battle of the Little Bighorn. Rather than "bask in the memory that once their people were victorious in battle," Cheyenne and Lakota elders instead choose to reify for their people the tragic memory of massacres of their people and events like the assassination of Crazy Horse (285). Welch's personal narratives add a powerful and valuable element of autobiography to the history, so that he is not only telling the side of the story of the Indians involved at the Little Bighorn, but also builds from that epoch-making event to tell the story of his generation of Native Americans living in the contemporary United States. By employing strategies of cultural translation, Welch communicates not only with his own people, but with white America as well, and in this way the text becomes a place where hybridity can exist, in Homi Bhabha's redemptive sense as an empowering space in which cultural difference may operate.

Notes

1. Any claim to postcoloniality for North American Aboriginal peoples is answerable to the justifiable counterclaim that Aboriginal people remain colonized to this day. In *The Turn to the Native: Studies in Criticism and Culture* (1996), Arnold Krupat describes the situation for Native Americans as "domestic imperialism or internal colonialism," and as "politically sustained subalternity" (30). Despite the validity of this counterclaim, an argument may be made for the postcoloniality of those peoples still under the imperial power of the colonizer. To make this argument I want to pilfer a strategy from Krupat, in whose work useful definitions are strategically redeployed for what he calls the "particular modality" of the relationship between Native American literature and "the postcolonial literatures of the world" (32). First, I will redeploy the definition of "post-colonial" from *The Empire Writes Back,* where the term is defined as covering "all the culture affected by the imperial process from the moment of colonisation to the present day" (Ashcroft et al. 2). Such a definition allows for the inclusion of cultures like those of Native America, which are still suffering "domestic imperialism." Although he acknowledges that the status of "post" has yet to be achieved for colonized Native North America, Krupat applies to Native literature a broader theoretical sense of the postcolonial. Krupat borrows again from *The Empire Writes Back,* the authors of which describe postcolonial literatures as having "emerged in their present from out of the experience of colonization and asserted themselves by foregrounding the tension with the imperial power, and by emphasizing their differences from the assumptions of the imperial centre" (2). This broad sense of the postcolonial must be qualified somewhat in light of the question whether or not Native American writers such as James Welch have yet "emerge[d] . . . out of the experience of colonization." The tension with the imperial power that is foregrounded in *Killing Custer* resonates in the difficulties that postmodern and postcolonial conceptions of history pose for the articulating of a Native American cultural identity by writers such as James Welch.

2. Ward Churchill defines himself as "indigenist" in the following manner:

> I am one who not only takes the rights of indigenous peoples as the highest priority of my political life, but who draws upon the traditions—the bodies of knowledge and corresponding codes of values—evolved over many thousands of years by native peoples the world over. This is the basis upon which I not only advance critiques of, but conceptualize alternatives to the present social, political, economic and philosophical

> status quo. In turn, this gives shape not only to the sorts of goals and objectives I pursue, but the kinds of strategy and tactics I advocate, the variety of struggles I tend to support, the nature of the alliances I'm inclined to enter into, and so on. (403)

3. In an interview with Ellen Rooney, Spivak defines "strategic essentialism" in a very activist sense as "strategic use of a positivist essentialism in a scrupulously visible political interest" (Spivak 3).

4. In *The Turn to the Native,* Krupat builds his notion of "cultural translation" from Rudolph Pannwitz, cited in Walter Benjamin's "The Task of the Translator": "Our translators have far greater reverence for the usage of their own language than for the spirit of the foreign works. . . . The basic error of the translator is that he preserves the state in which his own language happens to be instead of allowing his language to be powerfully affected by the foreign tongue" (Krupat 35).

5. My use of the term "hybrid historiography" is adopted from Raymond DeMallie's description of the Brule Sioux winter counts as a "hybrid document," which, as Arnold Krupat explains, "employs traditional mnemonic devices important to cultures who preserved and transmitted knowledge orally while 'appropriating the numerical chronology,' as well as some of the alphabetic writing of the whites" (Krupat, "America's Histories" 131).

Works Cited

Allen, Paula Gunn. "The Sacred Hoop: A Contemporary Perspective." *The Ecocriticism Reader: Landmarks in Literary Ecology*. Ed. Cheryll Glotfelty and Harold Fromm. Athens: U of Georgia P, 1996. 241–63.

Ashcroft, Bill, Gareth Griffiths, and Helen Tiffin. *The Empire Writes Back: Theory and Practice in Post-Colonial Literatures*. London: Routledge, 1989.

———. *Key Concepts in Post-Colonial Studies*. London: Routledge, 1998.

Barthes, Roland. "Historical Discourse." *Structuralism: A Reader*. Ed. Michael Lane. London: Jonathan Cape, 1970. 145–55.

Boehmer, Ellke. *Colonial and Postcolonial Literature: Migrant Metaphors*. Oxford: Oxford UP, 1995.

Brydon, Diane. "The White Inuit Speaks: Contamination as Literary Strategy." *The Post-Colonial Studies Reader*. Ed. Bill Ashcroft, Gareth Griffiths, and Helen Tiffin. London: Routledge, 1995. 136–42.

Churchill, Ward. *Struggle for the Land: Indigenous Resistance to Genocide, Ecocide, and Expropriation in Contemporary North America*. Monroe, ME: Common Courage Press, 1993.

Dirlik, Arif. "The Past as Legacy and Project: Postcolonial Criticism in the Perspective of Indigenous Historicism." *American Indian Culture and Research Journal* 20.2 (1996): 1–31.

Griffiths, Gareth. "The Myth of Authenticity." *De-Scribing Empire: Post-colonialism and Textuality*. Ed. Chris Tiffin and Alan Lawson. London: Routledge, 1994. 70–85.

Hall, Catherine. "Histories, Empires and the Post-Colonial Moment." *The Post-Colonial Question: Common Skies Divided Horizons*. Ed. Ian Chambers and Lidia Curti. London: Routledge, 1996. 65–77.

Knudtson, Peter, and David Suzuki. *Wisdom of the Elders*. Toronto: Stoddart, 1992.

Krupat, Arnold. "America's Histories." *American Literary History* 10.1 (1998): 124–46.

———. *The Turn to the Native: Studies in Criticism and Culture*. Lincoln: U of Nebraska P, 1996.

Michno, Gregory. *Lakota Noon: The Indian Narrative of Custer's Defeat*. Missoula: Mountain Press, 1997.

O'Corrain, Donnchadh. "Legend as Critic." *The Writer as Witness: Literature as Historical Evidence*. Ed. Tom Dunne. Cork: Cork UP, 1987.

Ricoeur, Paul. "The Narrative Function." *Hermeneutics and the Human Sciences: Essays on Language, Action, and Interpretation*. Ed. John B. Thompson. Cambridge: Cambridge UP, 1981. 274–96.

Spivak, Gayatri Chakravorty. "In a Word: Interview." *Outside in the Teaching Machine*. New York: Routledge, 1993.

Vizenor, Gerald. "A Postmodern Introduction." *Narrative Chance: Postmodern Discourse on Native American Indian Literatures*. Ed. Gerald Vizenor. 1989. Norman: U of Oklahoma P, 1993. 3–16.

Welch, James. *Killing Custer: The Battle of the Little Bighorn and the Fate of the Plains Indians*. 1994. New York: Penguin, 1995.

White, Hayden. "The Question of Narrative in Contemporary Historical Theory." *History and Theory: Studies in the Philosophy of History* 23.1 (1984): 1–33.

Young, Robert. *Colonial Desire: Hybridity in Theory, Culture and Race*. London: Routledge, 1995.

THE WORD MADE VISIBLE

LESLIE MARMON SILKO'S *ALMANAC OF THE DEAD*

✦

Ellen L. Arnold

> To those far-off Maya, writing was of divine origin: it was the gift of Itzamna, the great creator divinity the word made visible.
>
> Michael Coe, *Breaking the Maya Code*

Seeing Double

LESLIE MARMON SILKO comments in her introduction to *Yellow Woman and a Beauty of the Spirit* (1996) that she is interested in "the written word as a picture of the spoken word" (14). As I have argued elsewhere in relation to Silko's first novel *Ceremony* (1977), Silko's concern with the visualization of narrative in both image and written text is part of an ongoing project in her work to close the gap between signifier and signified, to recontextualize printed language and reconnect the written word with the dynamic, multisensory, multidimensional experience of orality.[1] Silko's second novel, *Almanac of the Dead* (1991), continues this project, working overtly to subvert the objectivist paradigm that Walter Ong argues is an aspect of literate consciousness, a paradigm that equates consciousness itself with visual activity and fixes knowledge in two-dimensional space. In contrast to the oppositional positioning of orality and literacy associated with Ong's work, however, Silko's work seeks not to "simulate" the oral or valorize the oral over the written, as many critics have maintained, but to explore the potentialities of the relationships between the oral and the written.[2] *Almanac of the Dead* draws heavily on the preconquest written literatures of the Americas to make a link through orality from the literacy of today to that of an earlier time, and thus to reground the act of seeing, the practice of reading, and the production of knowledge in sensory, experiential fields.

All of Silko's writing is, to use her image in *Yellow Woman and a Beauty of the Spirit,* "structured like a spider's web," with the earth as the center and "[h]uman identity, imagination and storytelling" radiating out from that center like the strands of the web (*Yellow* 21). The web metaphor is central to Silko's conceptualization of the way her writing expresses Pueblo language use.[3] As the threads crisscross one another, says Silko, "the structure emerges as it is made" and "you must simply listen and trust, as the Pueblo people do, that meaning will be made" (49). This process weaves highly complex structures of meaning in Silko's writing, as her texts move across multiple narratives, discourse fields, levels of meaning, epistemologies, perspectives, and fields of vision, asking the reader to become a "multiplicity of readers" (Langen 7) negotiating a multiplicity of stories.[4] Powerful resonances among and across these multiple strands—aural and visual, word and image, myth and history, linear and cyclical time, abstract and experiential—create an emergent reality that encompasses and interrelates (but does not merge) apparent dualisms, including the literacy/orality split. Thus, the intratextual, intertextual, and paratextual[5] resonances between the narrative text of *Almanac of the Dead* and the visual images that are structurally and thematically central to it—the ancient pictographic almanacs of the Mayans and Aztecs and their contemporary parallels in the imaging technologies of mapping, photography, television, and computers—encourage the reader to "see" differently in both text and world.

Silko and many of her critics have commented on the integral importance of the photographs in her autobiographical collection *Storyteller* (1981) to the project of the book. "The photographs . . . have a special relationship to the stories," Silko notes; "The photographs are here because they are part of many of the stories and because many of the stories can be traced in the photographs" (*Storyteller* 1). Toby Langen argues that the presence of the photographs in the text and the fact that their titles are listed in the back of the book force readers to slow their pace as they search for the photographs' relation to the text, thus "invit[ing] a more 'oral' tempo into our reading" (9). Linda Krumholtz demonstrates how the juxtaposition of photograph with story enables the reader to "reread" the photographs (for example, the picture of the Laguna scouts for the U.S. Army that follows "A Geronimo Story") in a manner that reverses the power relationships in the history they represent. In her self-published book *Sacred Water* (1993) and "An Essay on Rocks" in *Yellow Woman,* Silko experiments further with the integration of text and image, allowing the photograph to "form a part of the field of vision for the reading of the text and thereby become part of the reader's experience of the text," especially as a way to connect story and identity with place through the subliminal interplay of photograph and word (*Yellow* 169). *Almanac of the Dead* contains no photographs, but descriptions of photographs and visual imagery are fundamental to the text, and push readers to study the visual in imagination, to read the visual into the written word, and thus to locate themselves sensorially within the landscape of the story. Moreover, the reader must learn to read both image and landscape for the "words" that are written there. Landscape, Silko says, like dreams, has the power to "seize" powerful emotions and deep instincts and "translate them into images—visual, aural, tactile" (*Yellow* 38). The "glyphs" written in rock and wood, revealed in photographs, tell stories that must be read in relationship to the total environment, with the body and the spirit; they ask the same "focus of . . . prayer and concentration" with which the ancient people marked the rock faces of canyon walls with sacred pictographs and petroglyphs (*Yellow* 29, 175).[6] Silko's own "glyphic" designs for the novel—the map that appears on the inside front and back covers of the hardback edition, the drawings that mark the title page and interior textual divisions—frame the narrative text and ask the reader to enter it with this broader visual, experiential, and spiritual focus.[7]

In *Yellow Woman*, Silko recalls the beginnings of *Almanac* in a roll of black and white film she took in the arroyo behind her house, a series of seemingly unrelated images—a black sedan parked in a wash, a spider's web, a pile of rocks—which when printed and viewed together told a story that became central to the novel (23). In the photographs, Silko explains, the black sedan took on a sinister cast, the spider's web became the shadowy outline of a shallow grave, and a narrative of kidnapping and murder emerged from them. Thus from the representations of objects fixed on the surface of the photographic paper, through their extensions into space and narrative time and their resonances with each other and the emotions and consciousness of the photographer, emerged a fuller, different reality from the one Silko saw initially. Silko implies in her writing that printed text, like photographs, freezes the dynamic flow of life, making it available to abstraction and analysis, and may be similarly recontextualized. Indeed, the process of abstraction may potentiate the reader/viewer's ability to see the larger story—the way each word or image participates in a network of stories—and thus to recognize consciously how the written word may participate in the living dynamism of the world much like the oral/aural word.

The development of *Almanac of the Dead* was also closely tied to the appearance of a giant stone snake at the mouth of the Jackpile uranium mine in Laguna in 1980, an event Silko and other Laguna people consider to be an omen of great spiritual significance.[8] Silko interprets the stone figure as the return of Ma ah shra true ee, the serpent messenger from the Fourth World of Laguna tradition who once inhabited Ka'waik, the lake for which Laguna Pueblo was named.

> But neighbors got jealous.
> They came one night and broke open the lake
> so all the water was lost.
> The giant snake
> went away after that,

Silko reports (*Yellow* 127). "In a way," she says, "I had to write this novel in order to figure out for myself the meaning of the giant stone snake" (*Yellow* 144). In 1986, stalled in her writing, she painted a mural of a giant snake on the wall of the Tucson building in which she worked (reproduced in a black and white photograph in *Yellow Woman,* 150–51).[9] A similar line drawing appears on the title page of *Almanac* and at the top of the Five Hundred Year Map that precedes the text of the novel, reinforcing the recurring textual imagery of snakes, each with its own story, that weaves *Almanac* together: Ma ah shra true ee; Quetzalcoatl, the plumed serpent of the Aztecs; Damballah, the gentle snake spirit of West Africa; the snakes painted in Silko's fictional Almanac of the Dead, the snakes Zeta communes with, the snakes of Menardo's dreams; and intertextually, the yellow spotted snake that brings Tayo the message from the underworld that "the world [is] alive" (*Ceremony* 221), the rattlesnakes Silko talks with in her own backyard, the rubber snakes she photographed in her rain pond for *Sacred Water*. As travelers to and from the worlds below, the snakes are embodiments of interconnection and manifestations of the prophecy that the Almanac of the Dead carries in its calendar of days, so that the novel itself becomes the message of Ma ah shra true ee. Similarly, the graphic spider that appears on the title page and at the opening of each of the novel's six main parts links *Almanac* to *Ceremony* and Pueblo mythic history, reminding us that, although she is not named in the text, it is the voice of Grandmother Spider, the heart of earth, that these messages carry.

The Almanac of the novel's title refers to an invented fifth Mayan codex; like the four actual Mayan codices that survived the destruction of the invading Spanish and Portuguese in the early 1500s and now reside in Dresden, Madrid, Paris, and Mexico City, the fictional Almanac of the Dead consists of fragments of hieroglyphic and phonetic narrative and calendrical records on ancient parchment and skins, painted by the calendar priest-scribes who mediated between Mayan royalty and their gods and ancestor spirits.[10] The Mayans charted the cycles of Venus, eclipses, and other astronomical events with great accuracy and reckoned time by a complex intermeshing of two independent calendars: a 365-day solar calendar, consisting of eighteen named months of twenty numbered days each, with an unlucky period of five unnamed days falling at the end; and the 260-day sacred almanac, which names each of its days with a name and number determined by rotating through a sequence of twenty god names coupled with a number one through thirteen.[11] Each day had a personality and a complex of specific attributes; in Silko's words, "These days and years were all alive, and all these days would return again" (*Almanac* 247). The Calendar Round (solar calendar) operates on a continuous cycle of fifty-two *tun*s (years), while the Long Count of the almanacs, constructed in elaborate cycles of twenty and thirteen, is based on a 7200-day *katun* (each divided into twenty 360-day *tun*s), of which there are thirteen. When all thirteen *katun*s have run their course (roughly 256 years), the great wheel of time is complete and history begins to repeat itself (Bierhorst 270). Highly trained calendar priests or daykeepers among the Mayans (and later the Aztecs) used the almanacs to determine auspicious days for ritual, planting, and other activities, to invoke the gods and spirits, and to divine the future. Silko's Almanac correctly gives 11 Ahau as the *katun* predicted by the actual almanacs for the return of Quetzalcoatl and the "coincidental" date of Cortes's arrival in Mesoamerica (*Almanac* 575). The current *katun* will end in 2012 (Coe 62), a date some popular apocalyptic movements have adopted as the beginning of a period of violent change.[12] As Freidel, Schele, and Parker point out, these complex interlocking calendars allow "linear time to unfold in a cyclic structure," so that time "appears to move in a straight line within ever larger circles of time" (63). Such an interrelationship of linear and cyclical time is suggested visually by the figure—the line of spiraling waves—that appears on *Almanac*'s title page. Bierhorst also observes that the Mayans spatialized temporal concepts, assigning each of the "year-bearers," the first day of each year, to one of the four world-directions and its associated color; thus, the calendar cycle also performs a counterclockwise circle passing through the directions and the colors east/red, north/white, west/black, and south/yellow (270).[13]

Almanac of the Dead was deeply influenced by Silko's interests in archeoastronomy and popular science[14] and especially by the Mayan calendar and its expression in the "rich visual languages" of the Mayan and Aztec codices, or screenfold books (*Yellow* 21). "What interested me," she comments, " . . . was their notion of time; they believed time was a living being that had a personality, a sort of identity. Time was alive and might pass, but time did not die" (136). Silko relates this experience of time to Einstein's theory of the curvature of space-time, and to the views of the Laguna people she grew up with of time visualized as "round—like a tortilla" (136), with specific moments and locations which are never lost. She explains, "There are no future times or past times; there are always all the times, which differ slightly, as the locations on the tortilla differ slightly" (137). In the structural and thematic interplay of the oral, the written, and the visual in *Almanac*, Silko evokes the thought-world of the ancient almanacs, which employed both hieroglyphic/pictographic and phonetic writing to record a similar sense of space/time in which all time is always present, made visible in the written records of its intricate cycles, and what Dennis Tedlock terms a "mythistory" (64) in which mythic and historical narratives are understood to be part of a coherent whole.[15] As Murray Jardine points out (citing Ong, Havelock, and others), pictographic writing retains much of the phenomenological sound-dimension of words. Since pictographs represent words with pictures of concrete things or events, "the meaning of the word can only be understood by fairly direct reference to its existential context, which in turn means that words will still tend to be understood as events rather than signs or referents" (9). In designing the novel as an almanac, Silko clearly wishes to evoke this kind of textual merger of the oral and literate. The writing in the screenfolds must be read like paintings, she says; "the colors and lines and figures within give the reader the clue of how to read" (*Yellow* 156). *Almanac of the Dead* must be similarly read, for color and shape, for the "aspects of the divine world" (*Yellow* 157) alive in its images.

As *Ceremony* both narrates and performs a healing ceremony, *Almanac of the Dead* both narrates the history of an almanac and functions as an almanac, a calendar of days. The fragments of the Almanac of the Dead interspersed throughout the complex narrative web of the novel form a text within the text which tells "the people" (and its readers) "who they were and where they had come from" (*Almanac* 246) and "the days yet to come" (137). In contrast to the continuous text of *Ceremony*, *Almanac* is broken into short sections to resemble the fragments of the original codices (*Yellow* 140). As the story of the Almanac moves through the novel, it acquires the stories of those whose lives it touches, assimilating them into itself until the entire novel becomes the Almanac, and its characters, the days. The Almanac (like the historical codices) predicts days of fire and flood, earthquakes and swarming insects, and the return of the great serpent who will signal the coming end of alien rule and the restoration of the land to its rightful inheritors. Simultaneously, these events unfold in the narratives, gathering in a "tidal wave" (*Almanac* 518) rolling toward revolution (which, again, is suggested by the wave-like graphic on the title page). The novel culminates on the edge of chaos, on the verge of the collapse of Euro-American domination and the resurgence of indigenous peoples prophesied by the Mayans and many other indigenous apocalyptic traditions as well, including the Aztec, Hopi, Laguna, and Lakota Ghost Dance traditions invoked throughout the novel. However, as Linda Hogan points out, the Mayan understanding of time as cyclic, of history as repeating itself, differs from modern Western notions of history as a straight line leading to an apocalyptic end (*Dwellings* 93). By layering these apocalyptic narratives within these cultures' creation stories of repeated destruction and emergence through concentric worlds to the present world, Silko enfolds her apocalypse within an understanding of the ongoing process of creation that is both ancient and modern, mythic and scientific.

The creation and emergence stories that inform *Almanac of the Dead* share the understanding of a continually developing cosmos, passing through multiple cycles of creation, degeneration (usually a failure on the part of humans or protohumans to acknowledge the gods or to respect and return the gifts of the natural world), and purification through destruction that opens the way to rebirth and reemergence into a new world. In Mayan, Aztec, and Laguna mythistories, the world we presently inhabit is the Fifth; for traditional Hopis and Navajos, this is the Fourth World. For each, the previous world ended in flood. In the traditions of the Hopis and many of the Pueblos, including the Lagunas, emergence occurred at a specific place through an opening in the earth called *sipapu*, which is reproduced in the center of each ceremonial kiva. In ethnographic accounts, emergence from the underworld is often represented in linear, even hierarchical terms, as if each world were left behind for a "better" one; however, visualized within the larger perspective of a concentric or hemispheric unfolding of creation, the "underworld," the worlds "below," can be understood to be "within" this one as well, as our current world is present within those to come (see, for example, Williamson). As the Mayan calendar interrelates linear and cyclical time, these myths of ongoing creation also enfold historical development within the patterns of mythic timelessness. Such a vision of concentric unfolding and cyclic emergences to new worlds might be imagined as chaotic shifts to new levels of complexity and consciousness.

Native scholar Elizabeth Cook-Lynn criticizes Silko's vision of "a continent stolen, bathed in blood, its Natives buried in poverty" and her failure to prophesy a future in which "we continue as tribal people who maintain the legacies of the past and a sense of optimism" (73–74). Yet, Silko makes it clear that she intends her vision to be a hopeful one; for her, the disappearance of "things European" is a "spiritual process" (*Yellow* 125), and the retaking of the land, a metaphorical reconnection and resacralization of human relationship to the natural world. Silko's prediction of a revolution in consciousness has much in common with the popular vision of a "paradigm shift" from a worldview dominated by objectivism, mechanism, and consumerism, toward a paradigm of interconnectivity and wholeness; but for Silko this shift is not an epistemological break with the past so much as it is the emergence of a new epistemology which encompasses both paradigms. And as it describes this shift, the novel also enacts it, moving the reader toward a restructuring of consciousness, pushing the reading process, at the interface of the reader and the text, toward the creation of something new.

Emily Hicks describes the "double vision" of the "border text," which records the interference patterns produced between two cultures in the interaction of referential codes (xxix). However, the double vision created in the experience of reading across apparently contradictory paradigms and epistemologies holds the potential not just to record those interactions, but to shift them to a new complexity of understanding that is "post" or beyond dualisms. This "post-ness" or "beyondness" must be understood, within the frame of a visual/kinesthetic sense of the concentric unfolding of creation, to enfold (but not necessarily erase) the dualisms that it exceeds. The practice of seeing double, like *Almanac of the Dead* itself, inhabits an interdimensionality where seeing/reading are both visual—grounded in the concrete world of sensory experience—and visionary—capable of accessing other realms of experience where larger interrelationships are visible. Within this space we can see objectively, from the outside at a distance, and at the same time perceive from within our embeddedness in the larger field in which our seeing participates with the seen, in which subject and object are mutually creating.

Re-si(gh)ting the Boundaries/Refocusing the Text

Almanac's single large illustration, the Five Hundred Year Map, highlights the novel's resemblance to the Mayan and Aztec screenfold books, which could be opened out to enable visualization of large portions of the narrative at once (*Yellow* 156). Like the original codices, the map tracks both historical and mythic events, linear and cyclical time. And like the rich precontact maps structured on the four quarters of the world that Gordon Brotherston surveys in his *Book of the Fourth World,* which "trace process and formation, like histories, setting politics into cosmogony," Silko's map also reflects a "deeper notion of geography" that moves across multiple levels of significance (Brotherston 82, 87). The map visually depicts Silko's stated purpose for the novel: "I wanted to shape time inside my *Almanac.* I wanted to use narrative to shift the reader's experience of time and the meaning of history" (*Yellow* 140). The map distills and visually connects the multiple narratives of the massive novel, linking the movement and interactions of the characters and events inextricably to place and framing them by blocks of text that situate those characters and events within the five hundred years of history that shape them and the future they contain. It collapses space and time, encouraging the reader to visualize the written text spatially. By spatializing time and including in the cast of characters Geronimo, the First Black Indians, and an ancient spirit messenger, the map perforates the border between the living and the dead, allowing history to become an animate force in the novel. Thus both the map and the novel create not so much a mythic timelessness (as many have termed the space/time of *Ceremony*), as a "timefullness," in which all times are present at once.[16]

The map also visually counters the east-west movement of Manifest Destiny and the settling of the North American continent with north-to-south and south-to-north movement, a strategy of anticolonial resistance that Arnold Krupat terms "anti-imperial translation" (*Turn* 51). In this emphasis on north-south movement, Silko brings to life patterns of movement characteristic of this area of the continent before the arrival of the European invaders: the traditional migration stories of the Laguna, who came south from the land of the Anasazi on the Colorado Plateau, and of the Aztecs, who also migrated south (and still prophesy a return to their mythical home Aztlan in the North); the historical trade routes between Mesoamerica and the Southwest; and the more recent migrations of the Yaqui north into Arizona to escape persecution in Mexico. These lines of motion converge on Tucson and relocate the center of the continent to the area of the current US-Mexico border, recreating an older "nation" defined not by artificial boundaries—lines drawn on a map—but by shared histories, mythic traditions, and languages (the Uto-Aztecan language group, which Silko notes in *Yellow Woman* still extends as far north as Taos Pueblo and as far south as Mexico City [122]). While the national border separating the United States and Mexico is drawn in a straight, heavy line across the map, the large-print title MEXICO pushes up against that line as if to claim it and the unnamed country above it. The map also textually announces the novel's intent to remap those shared histories to include the hidden atrocities committed by the European invaders against America's indigenous peoples and those peoples' unrecounted acts of defiance and resistance, which will eventually culminate in the "disappearance of all things European" and "the return of all tribal lands." At the same time, text and arrows point off the page and into the world, toward the "East Coast," "South to Cartagena and Buenos Aires," and "North to Alaska," implicating both continents in the unfolding of the map's lines of influence, which move out from as well as toward the center that is Tucson. Thus the map echoes *Ceremony*'s "homing-in" (Bevis) or centripetal emphasis (Owens 172) within a centrifugal pattern that expands to encompass the hemisphere, five hundred years of history, and the future as well, reflecting the structure of the novel itself, in which events and images are unfolding, exploding, and flying apart, while simultaneously connecting and converging.

If Silko disrupts binary categorizations of oral and written in *Ceremony* by suffusing the written word with the phenomenology of orality, in *Almanac* she complicates this relationship by circling back (or perhaps more accurately, *around*) to draw on the graphic texts of Mesoamerica, the first written literatures of the Americas. In an essay in *Yellow Woman,* Silko notes that "Books have been the focus of the struggle for the control of the Americas from the start," beginning with the destruction of the great libraries of the Americas in 1540 by Bishop Landa (165); "Europeans were anxious to be rid of all evidence that Native American cultures were intellectually equal to European culture," she adds (21). Gordon Brotherston notes that this practice continues into the present, reflected in the Eurocentric bias that "celebrates the Semitic-Greek alphabet . . . as a turning point in human achievement" and ignores the history of writing in the Americas, or conversely "forgets" indigenous graphic practices in the interest of an imagined "uncontaminated orality," as Brotherston suggests Lévi-Strauss did in his desire to characterize "the New World as some preferable other" (45, 42).

Almanac of the Dead confronts this historical amnesia and at the same time subverts Euro-American attempts to fix and imprison the living texts of the surviving original codices as artifacts. Silko's fifth almanac, smuggled north by children fleeing enslavement and eventually passed through the old Yaqui woman Yoeme to her twin granddaughters, Lecha and Zeta Cazador, reenacts the material history of the original Mayan almanacs. As it travels, the Almanac of the Dead evolves and changes: parts are lost, eaten, or sold as artifacts; it accumulates Aztec additions, Latin and Spanish retellings, drawings of snakes, and an assortment of notes, translations, clippings, and stories, including portions of "farmer's almanacs" and accounts from Yoeme's own life. As Lecha and Seese transcribe the text and notes into a computer, the Almanac also acquires fragments of Lecha's diaries, recording her efforts as a television psychic to divine the location of the lost or murdered, and an account of Seese's dream of her kidnapped and murdered baby—the first inclusion by a non-Native. Thus, the power of the Almanac metaphorically leaves the hands of the Mayan priestly and royal elite and is passed on to "the people"—the displaced, the mixed blood, and even some Euro-Americans. As it is translated into computer language, the Almanac also appropriates modern technology and the potential to reach exponentially vaster audiences. Unlike the four extant Mayan codices, confined to museums and untranslatable until recently, or the later documents like the *Popol Vuh* or *Books of Chilam Balam,* whose originals have been lost and are available only in the alien language of the European invaders (all now reduced to objects of academic study and commentary), this almanac remains alive and moving; like the living oral traditions of native North America, it grows, changes, and expands to meet the needs of the people and the times, and in the process, it gradually permeates the world the invaders have made.

As Silko situates her novel in the intersections of oral and written traditions by simulating the Mayan almanacs, she also positions her text in the intersections of multiple national and tribal myths and histories. To enact textually the reindigenization of the Americas that the Five Hundred Year Map prophesies, she suffuses the novel with references, images, and stories that blend (and often encompass) Euro-American with/in Native American traditions and perspectives, in ways that reflect both similarities and differences among them. For example, by giving the name Yoeme—the word by which contemporary Yaqui people refer to themselves—to the twins' grandmother, Silko invokes the broad mythic history of the Yaqui. According to Larry Evers and Felipe Molina's book *Yaqui Deer Songs,* the oral narratives of the Yaqui record an old split that occurred in response to a prophecy of the coming of the Europeans between the Surem, the "enchanted people" who went away "to preserve the Yaqui's aboriginal relation to the world," and the Yoeme, who stayed behind on this world and combined the old ways with the new (18).[17] According to Evers and Molina, the old story of the "talking stick" or "talking tree" is an account of the Yaqui creation:

> The many versions of the story of the talking stick or talking tree . . . tell of a time before the coming of Europeans to the Yaqui world when a translator needed to be found to understand the future in a language of the past. Always the translator is a young woman . . . and sometimes she is a twin. . . . In the vibrations of the talking stick the young woman hears a message that marks a boundary between an ancient Yaqui way of living and a way of living that takes account of the new world created by the European presence, a boundary between myth and history, immortality and death, a boundary between the language of the wilderness and the language of the town. It marks . . . a re-creation, a time "when the earth was becoming new here." (37)

The pages of the Almanac of the Dead record the events predicted by the talking tree—the coming of "Christianity and baptism, wars, famine, floods, drought, new inventions, even drug problems" (Evers and Molina 38)—and prophesy another new beginning resulting from contact with new perspectives. Significantly, the first entry made in the English language in Silko's Almanac is Lecha's transcription of Yoeme's account of her seaside meeting with the "real" Geronimo, a man who "had certain work he must do" and who disappears before Yoeme's eyes, merging into the surrounding seascape. When Yoeme realizes this is the first English entry in the notebooks, she claims, "[T]his was the sign the keepers of the notebooks had always prayed for" (*Almanac* 130), a sign similar to the performance of the ancient Yaqui deer dances within the ceremonies of the Catholic Church, which Evers and Molina interpret as a reconnection of the old ways maintained by the Surem and the hybrid ways of the Yoeme, a reawakening of the old ways and other worlds within the new beginning prophesied by the speaking tree (Evers and Molina 40). The English account of the meeting between this mixed-blood Yaqui woman (once married to Guzman, namesake of Diego de Guzman, the historical Spanish slave trader who first encountered the Yaquis in 1533 [Evers and Molina 8]) with Geronimo, the great vanishing Apache medicine man and resistance leader, marks the appropriation of the English language itself by indigenous traditions and portends the coming end of Euro-American dominance in the Americas.

Silko's choice of the name Yoeme associates Yoeme's granddaughters Lecha and Zeta with the Yaqui twin girls, one or both of whom translate the prophecies of the talking tree/stick, and also gives mythic resonance to

Yoeme's role as grandmother, linking her with Grandmother Spider and her grandsons, the hero/trickster twins who figure in so many Native creation stories and are also embodied in the novel's twin brothers, Tacho and El Feo. Lecha and Zeta are visually and aurally identical (*Almanac* 99), but their ways of knowing and being in the world are very different, and Yoeme ensures that their differing talents will be complementary. She entrusts Lecha with the decoding of the written glyphs and notebooks, which speak like "mouths" and "tongues" (142). Lecha accumulates the words of her clients on tape, reads about her victims in the newspaper. She traces the patterns of their lives as "stories-in-progress" (143) and foretells the endings to their stories in order to exact revenge on old lovers, or locate the bodies of the dead for her clients. Zeta's "skills lie elsewhere" (132); it is she who can communicate with the snakes who hear the voices of the dead and can illuminate the drawings of snakes in the one bundle of pages that Yoeme gives her, which are the "key to understanding all the rest of the old almanac" (134). For Zeta this occurs beyond or outside words; she studies the beautiful colors and patterns in the skin of the old bull snake and receives its messages as imagery (131). Together the two women embody a kind of "double vision"—"an ear for the story, an eye for the pattern" (*Ceremony* 254)—which opens up a new/old way of seeing/reading based in oral traditions but complemented (not destroyed) by the written word.

The old/new world prophesied by the Almanac of the Dead comes to life in the text of the novel in the conjunction of word and image. Through Silko's use of imagery, it becomes clear that the old world emerging into the New World not only suffuses the present with timefullness and the written word with the dynamism of the spoken/aural, but also permeates the technologies of objectification that have rendered the world inanimate and consumable. The remapping and reclamation of the continent by the indigenous peoples of the Americas predicted and undertaken in *Almanac of the Dead* also recuperates Indian history and identity from appropriation by Euro-American scholarship and popular culture. To that end, Silko embraces the technologies of Western culture to enlist them in indigenous causes and recreate them as living instruments of justice and human survival.

Multiple Exposures

In her Preface to *Partial Recall*, a 1992 collection of essays on photographs of Native North Americans, Silko names as "voyeurs/vampires" photographers and anthropologists such as Curtis, Voth, and Vroman (10) whose images and texts freeze supposedly vanishing tribal peoples in an invented past, objectifying and commodifying them. A favorite subject of frontier photography (and of Silko's writing) was the Apache resistance leader called Geronimo, who evaded five thousand U.S. troops for more than fifteen years until his final surrender at Skeleton Canyon in 1886, documented in a famous photograph that attempts to fix his captivity once and for all (*Almanac* 129).[18] If photography can be voyeuristic and predatory, however, it is at the same time fundamentally reciprocal; as Silko puts it in *Partial Recall,* "[P]hotographs reveal more than a mere image of a subject. . . . The more I read about the behavior of sub-atomic particles of light, the more confident I am that photographs are capable of registering subtle electromagnetic changes in both the subject and the photographer" (8). Frederick W. Turner comments on Geronimo's use of this reciprocity—his reversal of the gaze—in his introduction to the 1970 edition of Geronimo's autobiography: "Out of the eyes of that incorruptible Chiricahua leader glares a challenge to our cherished notions of ourselves, of Western Civilization" (Barrett 46). Photographed often before his capture, Geronimo spent the last twenty-three years of his life as a prisoner of war, performing self-parodies as "the tiger of the human race" or "the worst Indian that ever lived" at exhibitions like Buffalo Bill Cody's Wild West Show and the 1904 St. Louis World's Fair (Roberts 309) and selling photographs of himself to tourists. In *Partial Recall,* Jimmie Durham elaborates:

> Geronimo, as an Indian "photographic subject," blew out the windows. On his own, he reinvented the concept of photographs of American Indians. . . . In every image, he looks through the camera at the viewer, seriously, intently, with a specific message. Geronimo uses the photograph to "get at" those people who imagine themselves as the "audience" of his struggles. . . . He is demanding to be seen, on his own terms. . . . This photo makes clear that no matter what had been taken from him, he had given up nothing. (56–58)

Drawing on the established resistance of Geronimo as photographic subject, Silko weaves a complex new trickster tale around his history, told in bits and pieces by several of *Almanac*'s characters. As Yoeme tells the story: "I have seen the photographs that are labeled 'Geronimo.' . . . But the Apache man identified in the photographs is not, of course, the man the U.S. army has been chasing. He is a man who always accompanied the one who performed certain feats" (129), feats of shapeshifting and invisibility that aid the

Apaches in eluding their pursuers. The smuggler Calabazas recalls another version, told by Yaqui elders: "In time there came to be at least four Apache raiders who were called by the name Geronimo. . . . The tribal people here were all very aware that the whites put great store in names. But once the whites had a name for a thing, they seemed unable ever again to recognize the thing itself" (224). The elders recount to Calabazas a meeting of three of the Geronimos to discuss the mystery of the photographs, taken of each of them, posed in fake warbonnets and disarmed rifles: "The puzzle had been to account for the Apache warrior whose broad, dark face, penetrating eyes, and powerful barrel-chested body had appeared in every photograph" (228). The theory advanced by the elders is that "the soul of an unidentified Apache warrior had been captured by the white man's polished crystal in the black box and was now attempting to somehow come back," and they speculate "over whether the crystal always stole the soul or only did so when white men harbored certain intentions toward the person in front of the camera" (228). In Silko's version, the "Geronimo" captured at Skeleton Canyon is none of the three "Geronimos," but "Old Pancakes," a drunken old warrior who claims to be Geronimo, gets himself captured, and uses "his skills as a liar and joker to seize the opportunity to save the others" (230). General Miles has the captive photographed, and when the face of the same mysterious warrior shows up that appeared in the other pictures, Miles accepts this as proof that he has captured the "real" Geronimo. According to the elders, the spirit of "one long dead who knew the plight of the 'Geronimos' . . . had cast its light, its power, in front of [their] faces" (232), moving easily in and out of the "crystal rock" in the camera (232).

The ancestor spirit "steals" the camera, claiming it as a site of resistance and its crystal lens as a doorway to power, reversing historical vectors of time and influence. The image of the ancestor manifested on the photographic plate is a presence of the past that is not mere trace nor suggestion of influence, but the past alive and visible, actively shaping the present and the future by altering the perceptions of viewers. The multiplication of Geronimo's identity shifts emphasis from the individual hero to communal patterns of resistance and ironically "disappears" Geronimo himself, preventing the appropriation of his identity by the dominant culture for its own purposes.[19] Identity thus asserts itself as a kind of narrative and visual mapping of intersecting fields of energy. What is reflected back to the viewer from the photographs is a defiance, not only of attempts to capture the objectified subject, but of the epistemological underpinnings of Western practices of representation and signification. Wide Ledge, one of the "Geronimos," had

> . . . done a lot of thinking and looking at these flat pieces of paper called photographs. From what he had seen, . . . the white people had little smudges and marks like animal tracks across snow or light brown dust; these "tracks" were supposed to "represent" certain persons, places or things. Wide Ledge explained how with a certain amount of training and time, he had been able to see the "tracks" representing a horse, a canyon, and white man. But invariably, Wide Ledge said, these traces of other beings and other places preserved on paper became confused even for the white people, who believed they understood these tracks so well. (227)

The photographs demand to be read as complex articulations of subject and object, of past, present, and future, of the worlds of the living and the dead, the fixed and the possible. Like names, like words, photographic images record not the subject/object thought to be "the thing itself" (224), but the tracks of complex fields of interconnectivity and interactivity. The "thing itself" recorded in these photographs is not any of the Geronimos, but rather the communal, transhistorical spirit and event of American Indian resistance and survivance.[20]

The new Geronimo story—like the story of the old Yupik woman who crashes oil exploration planes in Alaska by manipulating electromagnetic fields through the village television set, or Awa Gee, who uses his extraordinary computer skills to put the lights out on Enlightenment systems of thought and production—does more than turn "the destruction back on its senders" (156), however. These narratives and their embedded imagery map escape routes from the entrapments of essentialized identities, chart new connections among multiple cultural landscapes and systems of knowledge, and reconstitute Western technologies as living sources of power and transformation that can work to "re-indigenize" and heal a dismembered world. For example, pornographer Beaufrey and his very white cohorts, who market images of murder and dismemberment, on one level enact a reversal of the image of the "bloodthirsty savage" epitomized historically by Geronimo. Photographer David, Beaufrey's protégé, painstakingly shoots the bloody suicide of their mutual friend and lover Eric moments after Eric has shot himself. On the basis of his "clinical detachment and relentless exposure of what lies hidden in flesh" (108), David becomes a celebrity in an art world, exposing the voyeurism/vampirism of a culture that feeds on human suffering and violent death. Yet, even these horrific photographs, read like glyphs for "aspects of the divine world" written in them (*Yellow* 157), reveal multiple, complex, even contradictory, cross-cultural layers of meaning.

Eric's friend Seese describes her first reaction to the developing prints of Eric's suicide: "David had been playing with double exposures again. In the center of the field of peonies and poppies—cherry, ruby, deep purple, black—there was a human figure. Seese could make out feet and legs. She thought it was a great idea—the nude nearly buried in blossoms of bright reds and purples. The nude human body innocent and lovely as a field of flowers" (106). Eric's faceless white body lies on a white bed, against a backdrop of white paper originally intended for an "'all-white' series" (106), framed in its own blood. The invisibility of whiteness in a white-dominated world is made visible in the violation of the individual body's integrity and identity, simultaneously suggesting the tide of indigenous revolution rising to engulf the white world. Yet, in contrast to these white male artists' obsession with *sangre pura*—the pure blood of aristocracy which they hope to perpetuate by artificial reproductive techniques—the photographs also make a strikingly different comment on race: the "blood" that in its proportions supposedly marks racial purity or the contaminated other is revealed by the camera as a field of flowers enfolding the faceless/effaced body, a common ground linking body and world(s). What "lies hidden in the flesh" is the blood that connects human beings most intimately.

Similarly effaced and doubly displaced from the images of Eric's death, Seese "felt like a cartoon figure with a human body, but with a camera where her head should be. For a face she had a wide, glassy lens that brought all she saw into focus so cold and clear she could not stop the shiver" (105). Blond, blue-eyed Seese (whose name suggests "*sewa, sea, seya,* and *seye,*" Yaqui words that invoke the enchanted flower world of the Yaqui [Evers and Molina 52][21]) sees through this process of abstraction "double exposures"—the human body in both its isolated, objectified mortality and its transcendent immortality, simultaneously negated and merged with the Yaqui flower world *sea ania,* the mythic primeval world that "mirrors all the beauty of the natural world" and is associated with heaven among the Christian Yoemem (Evers and Molina 47). The intervention of the camera lens makes visible both Eric's and Seese's—two of the novel's more sympathetic non-Native characters—connection to a Yaqui universe that embraces and enfolds them. Eric's death is thus also linked to a "cherished story" of the Christianized Yoemem that "tells of the flowers which poured from the side of Christ when it was lanced on the cross" (Evers and Molina 54), translating his suicide into a sacrifice that has the potential to heal the violent rifts between cultures by opening viewers to different kinds of seeing. Even for one of the art critics who reviews the show, the photographs refuse fixity, revealing the "pictorial irony of a field of red shapes which might be peonies" (108)—a vision of an indigenous world emerging into and remaking the world the conquerors have made. The photos of Eric's death echo images of a "[w]hite on white" photographic series that an insurance agent shows Lecha of downed petroleum prospecting planes on snow-covered Alaskan tundra; the "scattered, mangled electronic equipment" reminds Lecha of "intestines. Engine oil appeared like black pools of what might have been blood" (159). The accumulation of such images in the novel—linking with "jungle snakes of electric cables" (162), Ferro's "black rubber body belt [that] uncoiled from the canister like a jungle snake" (186), the video of the six "spiderlike" eco-warriors (emissaries from Grandmother Spider) descending the face of Glen Canyon Dam to blow it up (727)—tell a phenomenological narrative of indigenous prophecy coming to life through technology.

Silko's representations of the photographic lens as means both to objectify/capture/dissect and to connect/reveal/transform link with similar images of crystals, glass, and lenses that pervade *Almanac of the Dead*. The image of the old Pueblo cacique futilely bumping his fingers against a glass museum case in an effort to reach the stolen stone figures of the "Little Grandparents" (31) contrasts with the later image of the old Yupik woman whose forefinger on the television screen downs airplanes: "The old woman had gathered great surges of energy out of the atmosphere, by summoning spirit beings through recitations of the stories that were also indictments of the greedy destroyers of the land" (156). The old woman's plane-crashing spell works through the television crystal to make compasses malfunction; she compares the television to the quartz crystals used by medicine people, which performed like "tiny television sets" (156) to reveal events at a distance. Silko consistently associates the power of spirit, the power of story and image, with the power of electricity and electromagnetism; "the energy or 'electricity' of a being's spirit was not extinguished by death; it was set free from the flesh . . . the energy had only been changing form, nothing had been lost or destroyed" (719). Revolutionary leader Angelita, bewitched by the "glint of the man's soul . . . captured . . . in the eyes of Marx's [photographic] image" (518), elaborates:

> Marx understood what tribal people had always known: the maker of a thing pressed part of herself or himself into each object made. Some spark of life or energy went from the maker into even the most ordinary objects. . . . Marx had understood stories are alive with the energy words generate. . . . He had sensed the great power these stories had—power

to move millions of people. Poor Marx did not understand the power of the stories belonged to the spirits of the dead. (521)

Almanac of the Dead layers multiply coded images and discourses to create a complex web of explanation, the same or similar events observed and interpreted through a variety of lenses and frames of reference. As Silko observes in *Yellow Woman and a Beauty of the Spirit,* "[T]he Laguna Pueblos go on producing their own rich and continuously developing body of oral and occasionally written stories that reject any decisive conclusion in favor of ever-increasing possibilities. This production of multiple meaning is in keeping with Pueblo cosmology in general" (133). A "communal truth" lives "somewhere in the web of differing versions" (32) and emerges through their interactions. By layering discourses from Native oral traditions and Western disciplines, Silko encompasses dualistic, objectivist paradigms within a cross-cultural vision of reality as a complex web of energy and interrelationship in which nothing is ever lost. Similarly, by requiring readers to negotiate multiple and competing frames of reference, Silko pushes us to incorporate a referential sense of language use within a sense of words and images and the material objects they refer to as living nodes in networks of flowing energy and space/time. As *Almanac of the Dead* demonstrates, words and codes only appear to be arbitrary signs when the connections that interlink signifiers to their referents, to each other, and to the world they construct and are constructed by have been lost or destroyed. Severed from context, text can literally dismember the world; recontextualized, with the power of their participation in the interconnected flow of life and death made visible, words can also bring the world back to life.

Notes

1. See Arnold, "'An Ear for the Story, an Eye for the Pattern': Rereading *Ceremony*."

2. Brewster Fitz argues, in contrast to many critics who approach Silko's writing as a continuation of the oral tradition, that Silko "belongs to a tradition in which the oral and the written are already linguistically and culturally interwoven" (18). Fitz sees tension and ambivalence in Silko's writing, a vacillation between "a literalist desire to reclaim orality, which is associated with truth and goodness, and to reject writing as a deplorable swerve from truth and life" on the one hand, and "a writerly wisdom in which orality and writing are interwoven in a syncretic . . . vision" on the other hand (28). What Fitz reads as an internal conflict within the author and her work, I will argue, is rather a deliberate shifting among perspectives

and modes of speaking, writing, reading, and interpreting. For Silko, destructiveness resides not in writing per se but in the removal of text from context, from the *intent* to objectify, control, and consume.

3. See also Silko's essay, "Language and Literature from a Pueblo Indian Perspective."

4. Toby Langen uses this phrase to describe *Storyteller* (7); Krupat similarly describes how *Storyteller*'s dialogism reflects the author's attempt to define herself in relation to the voices of many other storytellers, so that her "relation to every kind of story becomes the story of her life" (*Voice* 164). The reader must thus also negotiate multiple relationships with the stories in the text.

5. The term "paratextual" refers to the visual and spatial contexts of the printed text.

6. Lucy Lippard and the photographer/essayists in her collection of petroglyph photographs *Marks in Place* elaborate the way these ancient carvings tell stories in relationship to the land and to the position of both the maker's and the viewer's bodies in the landscape, in conjunction with the movements of the sun and other heavenly bodies.

7. In the unedited version of my interview with Silko, "Listening to the Spirits," she states that while she had little control over *Almanac*'s cover, she did have full control over the interior design of the novel: "On the inside the drawings are all mine" (Arnold, "Reworlding" 265).

8. Silko is ambiguous about the date; she reports in *Yellow Woman* that the stone snake first appeared in 1979 (138) or 1980 (126) and that she saw it in 1980 (132). She also uses a number of different spellings for the spirit snake Ma ah shra true ee, both within *Almanac* and in her essays. (I have chosen the one she uses most frequently.) These ambiguities and alterations illustrate Silko's insistence that written texts metamorphose over time like oral narratives (*Yellow* 200), implying that the written word also has a life of its own, and that efforts to fix the word permanently on the page are ultimately futile.

9. The mural has now been painted over; see Arnold, "Listening to the Spirits" (12–13).

10. In *Yellow Woman,* Silko refers to her Almanac as a fourth codex (158); many experts, however, include the Grolier fragments in Mexico City as a fourth Codex (Coe 44), making Silko's a fifth, as Silko herself did in an earlier interview (Barnes 104–05). Echoes of several other hieroglyphic texts, such as the *Popol Vuh* and *Chilam Balam,* which survived as transcriptions into phonetic Mayan, made by Guatemalan and Yucatec priests who learned alphabetic writing from their conquerors (see for example Bierhorst 192), can also be recognized in *Almanac*.

11. Bierhorst 269–72. Bierhorst and many other scholars refer to these names as the "gods" of the days, who have "dominion" over them and are "worshipped" by the Mayans; Silko interprets these as the names of the days themselves—the days

being living spirits—rather than as independent deities for which the days are named (*Almanac* 247; *Yellow* 136; Coltelli, "Leslie" 104). A count of days and months appears in the fragments of Silko's Almanac (570–78). Bierhorst states that the religious calendar of the almanacs is not related to celestial phenomena (269); others disagree. The recent (and controversial) work of David Freidel, Linda Schele, and Joy Parker (1993) suggests the mythology tied to the Mayan Long Count is in fact a precise literal account of astronomical events. William Sullivan makes a similar claim in *Secrets of the Incas: Myth, Astronomy, and the War Against Time.* Drawing on de Santillana and von Dechend's *Hamlet's Mill,* Sullivan observes that myth is a "technical language" that records and transmits astronomical observations of great complexity.

12. For instance, the 1987 Harmonic Convergence, an event which drew hundreds of thousands of people around the world to mountaintop celebrations of a predicted new age of peace and harmony to follow a period of upheaval, which was organized and publicized on the basis of José Arguelles's interpretations of Mayan and Hopi prophecies (and which may have inspired some of the events in *Almanac*).

13. Edith Swan and others have traced the similar movement of Tayo's initiation into the mythic world of Laguna oral tradition through the directions and their related colors and meanings. My intent here is not to provide such an analysis for *Almanac* but rather to suggest its multidimensional patternings and ways they might be read. One such exploration is Caren Irr's examination of the novel's structure in relationship to Navajo ceremonial cycles.

14. See for example, interviews with Silko by Arnold, Coltelli, and Gonzalez.

15. Since the almanacs used phonetic as well as pictographic representation, they might be conceived as bridges or mergers of oral and literate texts, just as they merge what from a modern Western perspective are termed myth and history, science and religion. Arnold Carlos Vento makes the point that all the pre-Columbian high cultures had no religion in any Western sense, but a cosmogony and metaphysics "based upon thousands of years of scientific observation and the hard sciences" of mathematics and astronomy (3).

16. See Gregory Salyer's discussion of the "timelessness" of Silko's poetry as "not . . . untouched by time, but so full of time that time appears to be endless" (26), and his discussion of the politicization of time in *Almanac of the Dead* (98–100).

17. Sharon Holland notes that Silko was on the editorial board of Sun Tracks Press when Evers and Molina's manuscript was submitted for publication, and thus is probably familiar with *Yaqui Deer Songs* (155). The text of *Almanac of the Dead* bears this out.

18. See, e.g., Barrett (137) for a reproduction of the actual photograph.

19. For excellent in-depth explorations of the Geronimo story and photographs as resistance see Eric Anderson and David L. Moore.

20. Here I borrow the term coined by Gerald Vizenor to convey a more deliberate, active, and powerful reality than the term "survival" suggests.

21. Seese also apparently has (like her Yaqui employer and mentor Lecha Cazador) *"seataaka"* or "flower body," a special power recognized among the Yaqui, characterized by the "ability to escape to safety in the nick of time" and "dreams of flying" (Evers and Molina 52–53).

Works Cited

Anderson, Eric Gary. "Photography as Resistance in *Almanac of the Dead.*" *American Indian Literature and the Southwest: Contexts and Dispositions*. Austin: U Texas P, 1999. 63–76.

Arguelles, José. "The Great Return, August 16–17." *Meditation Magazine* Summer 1987: 7–19, 50–51.

Arnold, Ellen L. "An Ear for the Story, an Eye for the Pattern: Rereading *Ceremony*." *Modern Fiction Studies* 45.1 (1999): 69–92.

———. "Listening to the Spirits: An Interview with Leslie Marmon Silko." *Studies in American Indian Literatures* 10.3 (1998): 1–33.

———. "Reworlding the Word: Contemporary Native American Novelists Map the Third Space." Diss. Emory U, 1999.

Barnes, Kim. "A Leslie Marmon Silko Interview." *Journal of Ethnic Studies* 13.4 (1986): 83–105.

Barrett, S. M., ed. *Geronimo: His Own Story*. New York: E. P. Dutton, 1970.

Bevis, William. "American Indian Novels: Homing In." *Recovering the Word: Essays on Native American Literature*. Ed. Brian Swann and Arnold Krupat. Berkeley: U of California P, 1987.

Bierhorst, John. *Four Masterworks of American Indian Literature: Quetzalcoatl/The Ritual of Condolence/Cuceb/The Night Chant*. New York: Farrar, Straus and Giroux, 1974.

Brotherston, Gordon. *Book of the Fourth World: Reading the Native Americas through Their Literature*. Cambridge: Cambridge UP, 1992.

Coe, Michael D. *Breaking the Maya Code*. New York: Thames and Hudson, 1992.

Coltelli, Laura. "*Almanac of the Dead*: An Interview with Leslie Marmon Silko." *Native American Literatures,* Forum 4–5 (1992–93): 65–80.

———. "Leslie Marmon Silko." *Winged Words: American Indian Writers Speak*. Lincoln: U of Nebraska P, 1990.

Cook-Lynn, Elizabeth. "American Indian Intellectualism and the New Indian Story." *American Indian Quarterly* 20.1 (1996): 57–76.

de Santillana, Giorgio, and Hertha von Dechend. *Hamlet's Mill: An Essay on Myth and the Frame of Time*. Ipswich, MA: Gambit, 1969.

Durham, Jimmie. "Geronimo!" *Partial Recall*. Ed. Lucy R. Lippard. New York: New Press, 1992. 55–58.

Evers, Larry, and Felipe S. Molina. *Yaqui Deer Songs, Maso Bwikam: A Native American Poetry*. Tucson: Sun Tracks/U of Arizona P, 1987.

Fitz, Brewster. *Silko: Writing Storyteller and Medicine Woman*. Norman: U Oklahoma P, 2004.

Freidel, David, Linda Schele, and Joy Parker. *Maya Cosmos: Three Thousand Years on the Shaman's Path*. New York: William Morrow, 1993.

Gonzalez, Ray. "The Past Is Right Here & Now: An Interview with Leslie Marmon Silko." *Bloomsbury Review* Apr/May 1992: 5+.

Hicks, D. Emily. *Border Writing: The Multidimensional Text*. Theory and History of Literature 80. Minneapolis: U of Minnesota P, 1991.

Hogan, Linda. *Dwellings: A Spiritual History of the Living World*. New York: W. W. Norton, 1995.

Holland, Sharon. "Qualifying Margins: The Discourse of Death in Native American Women's Fiction." Diss. U of Michigan, 1992.

Irr, Caren. "The Timeliness of *Almanac of the Dead*." *Leslie Marmon Silko: A Collection of Critical Essays*. Ed. Louise K. Barnett and James L. Thorson. Albuquerque: U New Mexico P, 2001. 223–43.

Jardine, Murray. "Sight, Sound, and Epistemology: The Experiential Sources of Ethical Concepts." *Journal of the American Academy of Religion* 64.1 (1996): 1–25.

Krumholz, Linda. "To Understand This World Differently: Reading and Subversion in Leslie Marmon Silko's 'Storyteller.'" *ARIEL* 25.1 (1994): 89–113.

Krupat, Arnold. "The Dialogic of Silko's *Storyteller*." *Narrative Chance: Postmodern Discourse on Native American Indian Literature*. Ed. Gerald Vizenor. Albuquerque: U of New Mexico P, 1989. 55–68.

———. *The Turn to the Native: Studies in Criticism and Culture*. Lincoln: U Nebraska P, 1996.

———. *The Voice in the Margin: Native American Literature and the Canon*. Berkeley: U of California P, 1989.

Langen, Toby C. S. "Storyteller as Hopi Basket." *Studies in American Indian Literatures* 5.1 (1993): 7–24.

Lippard, Lucy R., ed. *Marks in Place: Contemporary Responses to Rock Art*. Albuquerque: U New Mexico P, 1988.

———, ed. *Partial Recall*. New York: New Press, 1992.

Moore, David L. "Silko's Blood Sacrifice: The Circulating Witness in *Almanac of the Dead*." *Leslie Marmon Silko: A Collection of Critical Essays*. Ed. Louise K. Barnett and James L. Thorson. Albuquerque: U New Mexico P, 2001. 149–83.

Ong, Walter J. *Orality and Literacy: The Technologizing of the Word*. London: Routledge, 1982.

Owens, Louis. *Other Destinies: Understanding the American Indian Novel*. Norman: U of Oklahoma P, 1992.

Roberts, David. *Once They Moved Like the Wind: Cochise, Geronimo, and the Apache Wars*. New York: Simon and Schuster, 1993.

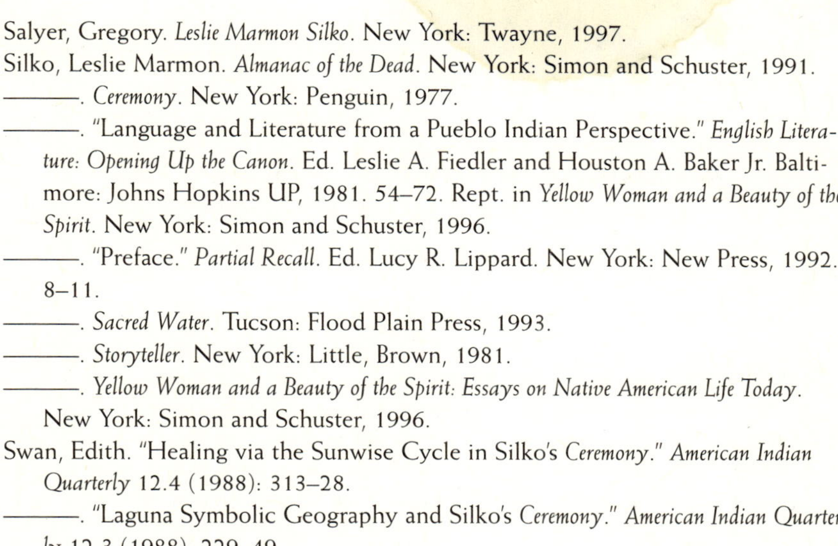

Salyer, Gregory. *Leslie Marmon Silko*. New York: Twayne, 1997.

Silko, Leslie Marmon. *Almanac of the Dead*. New York: Simon and Schuster, 1991.

———. *Ceremony*. New York: Penguin, 1977.

———. "Language and Literature from a Pueblo Indian Perspective." *English Literature: Opening Up the Canon*. Ed. Leslie A. Fiedler and Houston A. Baker Jr. Baltimore: Johns Hopkins UP, 1981. 54–72. Rept. in *Yellow Woman and a Beauty of the Spirit*. New York: Simon and Schuster, 1996.

———. "Preface." *Partial Recall*. Ed. Lucy R. Lippard. New York: New Press, 1992. 8–11.

———. *Sacred Water*. Tucson: Flood Plain Press, 1993.

———. *Storyteller*. New York: Little, Brown, 1981.

———. *Yellow Woman and a Beauty of the Spirit: Essays on Native American Life Today*. New York: Simon and Schuster, 1996.

Swan, Edith. "Healing via the Sunwise Cycle in Silko's *Ceremony*." *American Indian Quarterly* 12.4 (1988): 313–28.

———. "Laguna Symbolic Geography and Silko's *Ceremony*." *American Indian Quarterly* 12.3 (1988): 229–49.

Tedlock, Dennis, trans. *Popol Vuh: The Mayan Book of the Dawn of Life*. New York: Touchstone, 1985.

Vento, Arnold Carlos. "Aztec Myths and Cosmology: Historical Religious Misinterpretation." *Wicazo Sa Review* 11.1 (Spring 1995): 1–23.

Vizenor, Gerald. *Manifest Manners: PostIndian Warriors of Survivance*. Hanover, NH: Wesleyan UP/UP of New England, 1994.

Williamson, Ray A. *Living the Sky: The Cosmos of the American Indian*. Norman: U of Oklahoma P, 1984.

AMERICAN INDIAN SOVEREIGNTY

NOW YOU SEE IT, NOW YOU DON'T

✦

Peter d'Errico

Sovereignty is an especially odd phenomenon. Everyone seems to want it. Those who claim to know it all tell us that sovereignty is just what we have, although some may have more of it than others. It seems to have been around for as long as anyone can remember. Even so, for such an established fact of life, and for such a cherished ambition, there is a disconcerting uncertainty as to what it is exactly, or where it is to be found, or who has it and who does not, or where it came from in the first place, let alone what is happening to it now.

R. B. J. Walker, "Space/Time/Sovereignty"

ANOTHER Columbus Day has come and gone. Another year, now more than five hundred since the pope divided the world between Spain and Portugal, laying down the doctrine of discovery and conquest:

Inter Caetera, May 3, 1493—Among other works well pleasing to the Divine Majesty and cherished of our heart, this assuredly ranks highest, that in our times especially the Catholic faith and the Christian religion be exalted and everywhere increased and spread, that the health of souls be cared for and that barbarous nations be overthrown and brought to the faith itself. . . .Our beloved son Christopher Columbus, . . . sailing . . . toward the Indians, discovered certain very remote islands and even mainlands. . . . We, . . . by the authority of Almighty God . . . do . . . give, grant, and assign forever to you and your heirs and successors, kings of Castille and Leon, all and singular the aforesaid countries and islands. (Davenport 75–78)

An earlier papal bull had declared the legitimacy of Christian domination over "pagans," sanctifying enslavement and expropriation of property:

> Romanus Pontifex, January 8, 1455— . . . We bestow suitable favors and special graces on those Catholic kings and princes, . . . athletes and intrepid champions of the Christian faith . . . to invade, search out, capture, vanquish, and subdue all Saracens and pagans whatsoever, and other enemies of Christ wheresoever placed, and . . . to reduce their persons to perpetual slavery, and to apply and appropriate . . . possessions, and goods, and to convert them to . . . their use and profit. (Davenport 20–26)

We might look at these ancient documents with amusement or condescension, confident in the modern view that church and state are separate. This would be a mistake. These papal bulls are part of the fabric of United States and international law.

The fact that papal authority is the basis for United States power over indigenous peoples is not generally understood, even by lawyers who work with federal Indian law. This is due in large part to the sophistry of John Marshall, one of the greatest figures in the pantheon of the US Supreme Court. Marshall borrowed from papal bulls the essential legalisms needed for state power over indigenous peoples. He encased Christian religious premises within the rhetoric of European expansion:

> On the discovery of this immense continent, the great nations of Europe were eager to appropriate to themselves so much of it as they could respectively acquire. Its vast extent offered an ample field to the ambition and enterprise of all; and the character and religion of its inhabitants afforded an apology for considering them as a people over whom the superior genius of Europe might claim an ascendancy. The potentates of the old world found no difficulty in convincing themselves that they made ample compensation to the inhabitants of the new, by bestowing on them civilization and Christianity. (*Johnson v. McIntosh*, 21 U.S. (8 Wheat.) 543, 572–573 (1823))

Newcomb said it succinctly: "Indian nations have been denied their most basic rights . . . simply because, at the time of Christendom's arrival in the Americas, they did not believe in the God of the Bible, and did not believe that Jesus Christ was the true Messiah. This basis for the denial of Indian rights in federal Indian law remains as true today as it was in 1823" (309).

Johnson v. McIntosh has never been overruled. "Christian discovery" remains the legal foundation for United States sovereignty over indigenous peoples' lands. But it is concealed, as most foundations are, because *Johnson v. McIntosh* acts as a whitewash for religious concepts. After Marshall's opinion, no lawyer or court would need to acknowledge that land title claims in United States law are based on a doctrine of Christian supremacy. From that time on, in law and history books, "European" would be substituted for "Christian," so that schoolchild and lawyer alike could speak of the "age of discovery" as the age of "European expansion."

Marshall knew what he was doing. After writing that "Christian princes" could take lands "unknown to all Christian peoples," he admitted that the doctrine was an "extravagant . . . pretension" that "may be opposed to natural right" and may only "perhaps, be supported by reason." Nonetheless, he concluded that it "cannot be rejected by courts of justice."

The discovery doctrine was not self-effectuating. It required force. As Marshall wrote, "These claims have been maintained and established . . . by the sword." The (in)famous "Spanish Requirement" of 1513 is perhaps the most straightforward example. It was called the "requirement" because royal law required it to be read before hostilities could be undertaken against a native people. In Latin and/or Spanish, witnessed by a notary, the conquistadors read:

> On the part of the king, Don Fernando, and of Doña Juana, his daughter, queen of Castile and Leon, subduers of the barbarous nations, we their servants notify and make known to you, as best we can, that the Lord our God, living and eternal, created the heaven and the earth, and one man and one woman, of whom you and we, and all the men of the world, were and are descendants, and all those who come after us. . . .
>
> Of all these nations God our Lord gave charge to one man, called St. Peter, that he should be lord and superior of all the men in the world, that all should obey him, and that he should be the head of the whole human race, wherever men should live, and under whatever law, sect, or belief they should be; and he gave him the world for his kingdom and jurisdiction. . . .
>
> One of these pontiffs, who succeeded that St. Peter as lord of the world in the dignity and seat which I have before mentioned, made do-

> nation of these isles and Terra-firma to the aforesaid king and queen and to their successors, our lords, with all that there are in these territories. . . .
>
> Wherefore, as best we can, we ask and require you that you consider what we have said to you, and that you take the time that shall be necessary to understand and deliberate upon it, and that you acknowledge the Church as the ruler and superior of the whole world. . . .
>
> But if you do not do this, and maliciously make delay in it, I certify to you that, with the help of God, we shall powerfully enter into your country, and shall make war against you in all ways and manners that we can, and shall subject you to the yoke and obedience of the Church and of their highnesses; we shall take you, and your wives, and your children, and shall make slaves of them, and as such shall sell and dispose of them as their highnesses may command; and we shall take away your goods, and shall do you all the mischief and damage that we can, as to vassals who do not obey, and refuse to receive their lord, and resist and contradict him: and we protest that the deaths and losses which shall accrue from this are your fault, and not that of their highnesses, or ours, nor of these cavaliers who come with us. (Washburn 306–09)

It is fashionable, especially around Columbus Day, to speak about the "encounter" of the "old" and "new" worlds, as a way of trying to forget exactly how bloody this event was. But, as Shapiro wrote, "National societies that . . . have thought of themselves as a fulfillment of a historical destiny, could not be open to encounters" (56).

Michael Dorris wrote: "The pre-existent variety of Native American societies . . . has been consistently obscured and disallowed. Every effort has been made to almost existentially enclose the non-Western world into a European schema, and then to blame unwilling elements for being backward, ignorant, or without vision. . . . Federal Indian policy was . . . shaped from the beginning at least as much toward deculturation as acculturation" (75, 76).

Contemporary Nonrecognition of Indigenous Peoples

Over 300 million people on earth today can be said to be truly indigenous—living on lands which they have inhabited since time immemorial. In every instance, indigenous communities are legally circumscribed by one or more nation-states, within territorial boundaries drawn by government geography. These 300 million constitute an increasingly self-aware force for global rethinking of the nature of power. Their challenge is increasingly overt and serious to the world's political structure.

The United Nations' designation of the International Decade of Indigenous People (1995–2004) is a symptom of this challenge. The nature of the challenge becomes clearer when we consider the revision of the original designation, which referred to indigenous peoples. The plural form—"peoples"—triggered immense anxiety and successful resistance by member states of the UN, on the grounds that these 300 million people are individual citizens of states claiming jurisdiction over them, and not members of independent peoples.

"Peoples" in international law implies rights of self-determination; the United States took the lead to challenge this principle as not applicable to indigenous peoples. The United States argues that collective self-determination exists only through states, and that indigenous people are groups of individuals with shared cultural, linguistic, and social features, but without any internal coherence as "peoples." This argument contradicts the US claim that it deals with indigenous peoples on a "government-to-government" basis. Here is one example of "now you see it, now you don't."

In light of the history of treaty making and with an eye toward restoring the sense of equality between nations that justified the treaty process to begin with, American Indians are—in concert with indigenous peoples worldwide—asserting a sense of their own sovereignty. The United Nations Draft Declaration of the Rights of Indigenous Peoples is at the center of this global struggle for self-determination. The declaration is the product of twenty years of negotiating among indigenous peoples and UN bodies. Its very title draws the line of battle—rights of indigenous peoples (plural).

Federal Indian Law

When we enter into the realm of "federal Indian law," we need to keep in mind that we are traveling in a semantic world created by one group to rule another. The terminology of law is a powerful naming process. In working with this law, we will use the names that it uses, but we will always want to keep in mind that the reality behind the names is what we are struggling over.

According to the theory of sovereignty in federal Indian law, "tribal" peoples have a lesser form of "sovereignty," which is not really sovereignty at all, but dependence. In the words of Chief Justice John Marshall, American Indian societies, though they are "nations" in the general sense of the word, are not fully sovereign, but are "domestic, dependent nations" (*Cherokee Nation v. Georgia,* 30 U.S. (5 Pet.) 1, 17 (1831)). The shell game of American Indian sovereignty—its quality of "now you see it, now you don't"—started right at the beginning of federal Indian law. The foundation of federal Indian law is the assertion by the United States of a special kind of false sovereignty.

In 1973, the federal district court for the district of Montana stated the underlying principle in the case of *United States v. Blackfeet Tribe,* 364 F.Supp. 192. The facts were simple: The Blackfeet Business Council passed a resolution authorizing gambling on the reservation and the licensing of slot machines. An FBI agent seized four machines. The Blackfeet Tribal Court issued an order restraining all persons from removing the seized articles from the reservation. The FBI agent, after consultation with the United States Attorney, removed the machines from the reservation. A tribal judge then ordered the US attorney to show cause why he should not be cited for contempt of the tribal court. The US attorney applied to federal court for an injunction to block the contempt citations. The Blackfeet Tribe argued that it is sovereign and that the jurisdiction of the tribal court flows directly from this sovereignty. The federal court said: "No doubt the Indian tribes were at one time sovereign and even now the tribes are sometimes described as being sovereign. The blunt fact, however, is that an Indian tribe is sovereign to the extent that the United States permits it to be sovereign—neither more nor less" (194).

The court explained:

> While for many years the United States recognized some elements of sovereignty in the Indian tribes and dealt with them by treaty, Congress by Act of March 3, 1871 (16 Stat. 566, 25 U.S.C. s 71), prohibited the further recognition of Indian tribes as independent nations. Thereafter the Indians and the Indian tribes were regulated by acts of Congress. The power of Congress to govern by statute rather than treaty has been sustained. *United States v. Kagama,* 118 U.S. 375, 6 S.Ct. 1109, 30 L.Ed. 228 (1886). That power is a plenary power (*Matter of Heff,* 197 U.S. 488, 25 S.Ct. 506, 49 L.Ed. 848 (1905)) and in its exercise Congress is supreme. *United States v. Nice,* 241 U.S. 591, 36 S.Ct. 696, 60 L.Ed. 1192 (1916). It follows that any tribal ordinance permitting or purporting to permit what Congress forbids is void. . . . It is beyond the power of the tribe to in any way regulate, limit, or restrict a federal law officer in the performance of his duties, and the tribe having no such power the tribal court can have none. (364 F.Supp. at 194)

The fundamental premise of "American Indian sovereignty" as defined in federal Indian law is that it is not sovereignty. Federal power truncates "tribal sovereignty" in myriad ways too numerous to list here. Federal Indian law is perhaps the most complex area of United States law (including tax laws). In civil and criminal law both, the range and scope of "tribal sovereignty" is fragmented into overlapping and contradictory rules premised on one foundation: the "plenary power" of the United States. That such "plenary power" is nowhere stated in the US Constitution is no more than a small nuisance to the judges who have declared its existence. Administrative agencies and Congress alike cling firmly to their judicially created prerogatives of total power over their wards, in whose trust they act as they see fit.

Federal Indian law is the continuation of colonialism. On the basis of a deceptive "tribal sovereignty," the United States has built an entire apparatus for dispossessing indigenous peoples of their lands, their social organizations, and their original powers of self-determination. The concept of American Indian sovereignty is useful to the United States because it denies indigenous power in the name of indigenous sovereignty.

In 1831, the Cherokee Nation sued the state of Georgia in the Supreme Court to protect Cherokee lands. The Court denied the Cherokee suit on the ground that an Indian nation is not a "foreign nation" entitled to sue a state in the Supreme Court. That decision has never been overruled and is cited frequently today. In June of 1997, the Supreme Court decided that the Coeur d'Alene Tribe could litigate its land claims against the state of Idaho only in Idaho's courts. The Coeur d'Alene were claiming "aboriginal title," a subsidiary title subject to the trusteeship of the United States. They were trying to work within the limited concept of American Indian sovereignty. In throwing the Coeur d'Alene suit out of federal court, the Supreme Court stated that the basis of its decision is that "Indian tribes . . . should be accorded the same status as foreign sovereigns, against whom States enjoy Eleventh Amendment immunity [citing *Blatchford v. Native Village of Noatak,* 501 US 775 (1991)]" (*Idaho v. Coeur d'Alene Tribe,* 521 U.S. 261, 268–69 (1997)). The Cherokee were barred from suing in the Supreme Court because an Indian nation is *not* a foreign nation. The Coeur d'Alene were barred from suing in district court because an Indian nation *is* a foreign nation. Now you see it, now you don't.

Like every other colonial power, the United States found early that it did not have sufficient resources to maintain martial rule over territories it wanted to control. It resorted to indirect rule by puppet governments through the mechanism of appointed (and bribed) "chiefs." But it found that despite every attempt to make indigenous peoples disappear—including "allotment" of their lands and prohibition of their spiritual practices—indigenous peoples survived. By the twentieth century, the condition of their survival was an embarrassment to the government. In 1934, the United States set out to reorganize indigenous peoples into elected corporate political structures—a formalized system of "tribal councils." The concept of American Indian sovereignty was used to justify sufficient authority in the tribal councils to maintain order within the tribe, while denying these councils any authority beyond the territory which was reserved for them.

If we are honest about the legal history of the 1934 Indian Reorganization Act (IRA), we have to say that the tribal council system was intended as a puppet government. The system was not the result of the treaty process, but rather the distortion of treaties according to how the United States wanted to interpret and apply them. The IRA was passed in part to stabilize the land base and social conditions of American Indians, which had been devastated by the 1886 General Allotment Act. The fact that some of the worst abuses of indigenous peoples were stopped by the IRA provided some justification for the act. But the act was also passed—as its title states—to "reorganize" the Indians, overthrowing traditional organizations and promoting a "democratic" tribal council system structured as a corporate business. The fact that some tribal councils still raise sovereignty issues is evidence of the resilience and continued existence of indigenous peoples.

Let me illustrate so-called sovereignty under the IRA with the case of the Western Shoshone. In 1863, the Western Shoshone and the United States signed a *Treaty of Peace and Friendship* at Ruby Valley in the heart of Western Shoshone country. The treaty acknowledged Western Shoshone control over their homelands and provided for easements across their land and some mining and related activities. Today, massive strip mines ravage Western Shoshone lands and pollute and destroy the waters. The United States adds to this destruction by disposing radioactive waste in Yucca Mountain. Although Western Shoshone land title has never been proven to have been ceded or lost, the Supreme Court has ruled that they are precluded from litigating their title. Western Shoshone people who oppose the destruction of their lands as violations of their title are depicted as outlaws.

How did this come about? Was it through a denial of Western Shoshone sovereignty? No, it was through the affirmation of the kind of sovereignty that the Western Shoshone have under federal Indian law. As we have seen, this kind of sovereignty is not real self-determination. This sovereignty is the nonsovereignty of councils created by the United States government in the name of the Western Shoshone people under the Indian Reorganization Act.

In accordance with IRA principles, the federal government recognized various Western Shoshone tribal councils as the agents of Western Shoshone sovereignty. The Temoak Band, one of the councils empowered to govern the Western Shoshone people and to represent them in dealing with the outside world, filed a claim under the Indian Claims Commission Act of 1946. This act was intended to wipe out all Indian title for nonreservation lands by providing monetary compensation for such lands. The act did not require that a claim represent all or even a majority of the Indians in whose name it was filed. As a result of the Temoak claim—which the traditional, "non-recognized" Western Shoshone opposed and the Temoak council subsequently tried to withdraw—the commission told the Western Shoshone that their lands had been "taken" and that they would receive compensation.

The Western Shoshone refused to accept the compensation and one family (the Danns) went to court to defend title against the United States. The Ninth Circuit Court of Appeals ruled that Western Shoshone title had never actually been litigated, that none of the claims made against it were sufficient to take it away, and that since the Western Shoshone had refused the Claims Commission compensation they still held title. The United States Supreme Court reversed the Ninth Circuit, stating that the Western Shoshone could not argue about their title because the compensation had been accepted on their behalf by the United States, acting as their "trustee"!

The Western Shoshone case is not atypical. Similar events have unfolded for many other indigenous peoples under United States law. The point is that American Indian sovereignty in federal Indian law is a tool for limiting the powers of indigenous self-determination and for allowing the United States to determine the structure of indigenous government. We need to remember always that sovereignty in federal Indian law operates in conjunction with so-called trust and wardship doctrines—two other concepts proclaimed unilaterally by the United States to assert power over indigenous peoples. American Indian sovereignty can only be understood in context of the whole complex of federal court decisions over the last 174 years of colonial and neocolonial law.

Recurring proposals in the United States Congress to eliminate American Indian sovereignty as a condition for receipt of federal funds shows several important things. First, the struggle over Indian sovereignty—whatever it is—is far from over and is indeed a hot topic. Second, even the congressional defenders of this sovereignty say that the United States could eliminate it if it wishes. Third, the notion that federal funding is rooted in treaty obligations, not in discretionary programs, is almost wholly forgotten. Fourth, the attack on Indian sovereignty can be packaged rhetorically as "helping the poor Indians." Indians have been the victims of help since the first missionary efforts.

Sovereignty in International Law

Sovereignty in international law is a power system originated in the sixteenth century by Christian European states in their dealings with each other and the Catholic Church. By the nineteenth century, "The European outlook upon the extra-European areas . . . became one which instinctively applied the concept of the sovereign state and the notion of international sovereignty to conditions in which these ideas remained alien" (Hinsley 206). Sovereignty became "the dominant concept in the field of . . . political assumptions . . . [and] the essential qualification for full membership [in] the international community" (Hinsley 214–15). The concept of sovereignty provided state power with an "inside" and an "outside" (Bartelson 53–54). States claimed supreme power inside what they called their "domestic" realms and defined other states' realms as "outside."

Now, as the twenty-first century begins, "It is fashionable to argue that sovereignty is changing and that states are losing their validity and meaning" (Bartelson 9). "It has become virtually a cliché to discuss the decline of sovereignty" (Lombardi 153). "[S]overeignty cannot be an accepted dogma either in terms of its theoretical utility or political sufficiency. The . . . elevation of sovereignty and statehood to universal supremacy is not just being called into question, but is being eclipsed by the press of events and ideas" (Denham and Lombardi 3).

It is an irony of history that "the expansion/imposition of the European state system during decolonialization" of Africa and the so-called Third World brought into question "the very idea of sovereignty" (Denham and Lombardi 3). Decolonized peoples did not fit into the structure of the sovereign state. The result was (and is) extreme social dysfunction, as new states and their patrons tried to coerce peoples and fragments of peoples into sovereign allegiance. "Economic development, an explicit goal of a sovereign state," brought on repeated episodes of violence with "highly politicized elites grasping for non-African models of governance that ultimately failed to fit African traditions and cultures" (Denham and Lombardi 7). Today it is clear that the failure of postcolonial states to be a vehicle for indigenous self-determination is not a momentary problem of adjustment to "liberation."

Other events and ideas are eclipsing the notion of sovereignty. Multinational corporations—entities dependent on and yet more powerful than states—dominate the world economy. The overall ecological failure of the system of state sovereignty—the destruction of the biosphere in the name of sovereign interests—is also becoming frighteningly obvious.

"State sovereignty offers only a misleading map of where we are and an even less useful guide to where we might be going" (Walker and Mendlovitz 1–2). Such terms as "internationalization," "globalization," and "interdependence" "slip easily off the tongue, . . . but . . . [defer] all the hard questions. . . ." "What, for example, is it that is supposedly interdependent . . .?" (2–3). "We . . . need to think about how we think about sovereignty, and about how it . . . constructs the non-options available to us" (23).

The classical attributes of sovereignty already foreshadow the problem of applying this concept to American Indians and other nonstate peoples: absolute, unlimited power held permanently in a single person or source, inalienable, indivisible, and original (not derivative or dependent). These are characteristics of power associated with divine right monarchy and the papacy of the Christian Church. They are the core concepts of state power that arose around monarchs and church. They were the ideas of Western political theorists of the sixteenth and seventeenth centuries (especially Jean Bodin and Thomas Hobbes), proposed as a solution to the problem of violent religious struggle. They are not the characteristics of power in nonstate societies.

Camilleri wrote: "The emergence of the sovereign state was . . . the necessary instrument of Europe's colonial expansion" (14). With this remark we see the need for an inquiry into the question whether sovereignty can become the instrument of liberation from colonialism. If "state" and "sovereignty" refer to a framework of "supreme coercive power," and such power is absent in "tribes," is this a justification for "domestic dependent nation" or *terra nullius,* or is it rather a challenge to state sovereignty as the organizing principle of the world? Are we at the threshold of a new way of organizing politics that will—like the state before it—rearrange everything from villages to the world?

Camilleri pointed to "an increasingly powerful . . . desire to cultivate indigenous values, traditions, and resources that are often antithetical to conventional notions of state sovereignty" (35). In a long passage, he described the potential for a new era of social organization:

> The resistance to the present political and economic organization of society, expressed by the peace/antinuclear, ecological, communalist, consumer, feminist, gay liberation, human potential/self-awareness and other movements, cannot be overestimated. They represent a multidimensional response to the "colonization of the life-world." Their praxis may not yet pose a decisive challenge to the status quo, but it has already generated . . . a readiness to resist existing institutions and their life-eroding consequences. The point about these antisystemic movements is that they . . . are reaffirming the priority of . . . popular sovereignty over state sovereignty. For them the state retains a positive function only to the extent that it can be used as a vehicle for the realization of popular sovereignty. . . . Whether or not, and in what way, the state can be effectively integrated into the praxis of critical movements remains, however, a largely unanswered question. (35–36)

The conventional response to a suggestion that local politics might be the center of global organization is to dismiss it with the assertion that states are necessary because the functions they provide cannot be performed by smaller organizations. In a typical lecture "the mere assertion of the state's necessity is enough to set the audience nodding in approval" (Magnusson 47). But, "Why are we satisfied with such banalities? Why do we accept claims about the inevitability of the state, which, if posed in relation to capitalism or patriarchy, would be set aside in embarrassed silence?" (Magnusson 47). One might expect local politics to be the most celebrated arena of democracy. Why is it that the conventional view denies the possibility of local autonomy, and instead offers suggestions for "citizen participation" in state institutions? In conventional discourse, the idea of local democracy—of popular sovereignty—"fades as an object of political theory" and along with it fade "the . . . communities that could sustain . . . it" (50). State sovereignty "encloses" local and popular sovereignty in "parties" and "interest groups," in "domestic, dependent nations," "wardship," and "trust relationships."

The concept of sovereignty was a response to civil war in the Christian world at the close of the Middle Ages. It spawned an era of centralizing, territorial power that in our times—half a millennium later—is coming into question. Sovereignty—the notion of "absolute, unlimited power held permanently in a single person or source, inalienable, indivisible, and original"—is today a theory under siege. Indigenous peoples are not the only besiegers, but their presence is felt worldwide. Who would have thought even a generation ago that such an "old" state as Canada would be threatened by indigenous peoples within its borders, or that the Australian high court would find it necessary to abandon the concept of *terra nullius*?

The Way to Self-Determination

Indigenous peoples around the world are attacking the supremacy of state governments. From an indigenous perspective, state sovereignty is a claim that violates their pre-existing self-determination. Western jurisprudence has done a great deal to exclude "nonstate societies" from the domain of law because they lack hierarchical authority structures. If indigenous peoples imitate the model of state sovereignty—which they are being told they cannot do because they are not states—they may find that when they attain this model they have sacrificed the underlying goal of self-defined self-determination.

The critique of sovereignty jurisprudence is not just an academic matter. It is necessary to clear a space for nonstate peoples to exist in the world. Can there be space—in the world and in discourse—for nonstate societies, defined in their own terms? Is there a way to talk about indigenous self-determination without using "sovereignty"?

Tony Hillerman commented on the anti-Indian legislative strategy of those in the US Senate who want to strip "sovereignty" from American Indian tribes. He wrote that his friend Navajo elder Hastiin Alexander Etcitty "would say that the notion that any human, or group thereof, has sovereignty over any part of Mother Earth is a myth based upon the white man's Origin Story" (18). Hillerman concluded that the problem of Indian sovereignty "involves more than how to save what they have from the whites who yearn for it. It can become an internal fight over values."

We are talking about the clarification of the path toward self-determination. What can we say about "American Indian sovereignty" that might help us imagine a way out of the political confusion of this postmodern age? For starters, we could be clear that there is a problem in working with a concept of "absolute, unlimited power held permanently in a single person or source, inalienable, indivisible, and original." Why should indigenous peoples choose a model of thinking, organization, and development that was used to destroy nonstate societies?

Ahmad, in his discussion of the conception of sovereignty in Islam, suggested that a "realistic analysis" of sovereignty would discover "[t]hat the ultimate moving force which inspires and controls political action is a spiritual force—a common conviction that makes for righteousness, a common conscience" (67). This suggestion is startling because we are used to the Western notion of separation of church and state. Westerners can speak of "common will," but get nervous with the thought that this phrase only acquires meaning in spiritual terms. As we have seen, however, Western political thinking itself is grounded in theological concepts of "Christian nationalism." The notion of "absolute, unlimited power held permanently in a single person or source, inalienable, indivisible, and original" is a definition of the Judeo-Christian-Islamic God. This "God died around the time of Machiavelli. . . . Sovereignty was . . . His earthly replacement" (Walker 22). "All significant concepts of the modern theory of the state are secularized theological concepts, not only because of their historical development . . . but also because of their systematic structure" (Bartelson 88).

State sovereignty "is a 'religion' and a faith. . . . The skillfully drawn borders that cartographers have provided for us are . . . spiritual and philosophical abstractions representative of a form of quasi-belief. They are . . . not detached maps of reality as proponents would have us believe. These geographies reflect an ardent desire to make (or impose) sovereignty a physical reality as natural as the mountains, rivers and lakes" (Lombardi 154).

What does this mean for indigenous peoples, with a multitude of nonsovereign creators and an entire creation of sovereign beings? We are in need of a reassessment of political discourse, a terminology that will link postmodern politics and premodern roots of nonstate societies. "Indigenous is nearly synonymous with diversity" (Barrerio 2). The diversity of peoples' experiences and practices must be our focus, rather than the imposed "unity" of European experience and practice.

The sixteenth century "discovery of *non-Christian* forms of life in the Americas posed [a] . . . threat to the stability of Christian values."

> The discovery of the American Indians . . . the confrontation with something radically different from the Christian way of life raised the question of what kind of relations it is possible to entertain with this Other. First, to what extent is it possible to know the Indian except as something inferior . . . ? Second, . . . to what extent is it possible to bring him into the framework of universal law by giving him the status of a legal subject? (Bartelson 128, 131)

The Western response to this "discovery" was "an effort to . . . [make] everything speak . . . with one voice" (108). In this effort, nonstate societies were given a choice: to assimilate to the state system and give up their independent self-definition, or to maintain their self-definition and be denied a place in the world's legal and political order. The underlying assumption was that there is only one reality, and it is Western.

The problem of figuring out how to talk about indigenous self-determination without sovereignty is partially solved by learning how to talk about states and sovereignty accurately. Far from being an inherent and necessary aspect of self-determination, it appears that state sovereignty is but one form of self-determination.

Sovereignty is not an immutable fact, but a political choice made under certain circumstances which may no longer be relevant. The eclipsing of sovereignty in today's world threatens the international order of states and raises the possibility of new ways of understanding what it means to be a people. Half a millennium of sovereignty theory has not fully eradicated the "other" against whom sovereignty theory was constructed.

The task before us is to understand the immense differences between states and stateless societies. We must not fall for the line that all societies naturally lead to state formation or that state formation is even a social desire.

> The . . . emergence of the state reflects not the desire of a society for its kind of rule, but an urge in men to possess its kind of power. . . .
>
> The concept of sovereignty arises in the wake of the rise of the state . . . as an explanation of the basis of [its] rule. (Hinsley 10, 17)

Walker and Mendlovitz challenge us to reexamine the questions that sovereignty was meant to answer:

> The principle of state sovereignty formalizes a specific answer to questions about who we are as political beings that were posed in early-modern Europe. . . .
>
> Yet while there has been considerable interest in the questions posed by the principle of state sovereignty, there has been much less reflection on the questions to which state sovereignty is itself an answer. Who are "we"? What is the political community within which we ought to be thinking about principles of freedom and obligation, justice and democracy? How ought we to understand the relationship between specific communities and other communities, and between specific communities and humanity in general?

It is often tempting to minimize the significance of these questions. (Walker and Mendlovitz 5, 6)

These are spiritual questions. "What does it mean to be people?" is a spiritual question. The Western, Christian, rationalist answer to this question is not the only possible answer. This is not the place to catalog the ways in which indigenous peoples answer this question. Suffice it to say that the myriad versions do not require a concept of "state sovereignty." "Sovereignty," if it exists at all, is a quality of each Being in Creation. Beings join and part in myriad ways, none of them requiring state sovereignty.

Indigenous answers to these questions are not some kind of creed or dogma. They are alive, "borne by . . . people[s]" (Ruiz 85) in the life of a community. The question "what does it mean to be people" is answered in "the giving and receiving of confidence and commitment between persons who recognize and affirm a common community." When a community has been fractured, the possibility of self-determination is undermined.

The most pressing problem for indigenous self-determination is to determine what is meant by "the people." Indigenous peoples who have been subjected to centuries of state violence in the name of state sovereignty face "a profound crisis of the meaning of community, a crisis of political identity" (86).

In this crisis it is tempting for a people to take on the ways of the state. These ways can be taught. They are in fact the most basic part of the curriculum of the modern state education system. It is not accidental that education has been a primary vehicle for destruction of indigenous peoples. "Education" defined by colonizing states has aimed at eradication of indigenous traditions, at destruction of what Ruiz calls "confidence and commitment between persons who recognize and affirm" indigenous communities. When such education is complete, it is safe for the state to allow recognition of traditions, because traditions have become static relics of the past, no longer part of everyday relations. Ethnic diversity then becomes window dressing, decoration, new clothes for the emperor. The American state can tolerate and even promote the diversity of Irish Americans, Italian Americans, African Americans, and, yes, Native Americans. It would be possible for the American state to exist even if there were no "Americans" at all and everyone was an ethnic-group American.

Ultimately, it is land—and a people's relationship to land—that is at issue in indigenous sovereignty struggles. To know that sovereignty is a legal-theological concept allows us to understand these struggles as spiritual projects, involving questions about who "we" are as beings among beings, peoples among peoples. Sovereignty arises from within a people as their unique expression of themselves as a people. It is not produced by court decrees or government grants, but by the actual ability of a people to sustain themselves in a place. This is self-determination.

Self-determination of indigenous peoples will be attained "through means other than those provided by a conqueror's rule of law and its discourses of conquest" (Williams 327). The "anachronistic premises" (327) of the current system of international law—"discovery" and "state sovereignty"—must be discarded in order to understand self-determination clearly and see a way to manifest it. This is the real struggle of indigenous peoples: "to redefine radically the conceptions of their rights and status . . . [and] to articulat[e] and defin[e] [their] own vision within the global community" (328). On the plus side for all of us, this struggle has the "potential for broadening perspectives on our human condition" (328). As Phillip Deere said, "It is a mistake to talk about an American Indian way of life. We are talking about a human being way of life."

Works Cited

Ahmad, Ilyas. *Sovereignty: Islamic and Modern*. Karachi and Hyderabad: The Allies Book Corporation, 1965.

Barrerio, Jose. "First Words." *Native Americas* (Akwe:kon Press, Cornell University) 14.2 (Summer 1997): 2.

Bartelson, Jens. *A Genealogy of Sovereignty*. Cambridge: Cambridge UP, 1995.

Camilleri, Joseph A. "Rethinking Sovereignty in a Shrinking, Fragmented World." *Contending Sovereignties*. Ed. R. B. J. Walker and Saul H. Mendlovitz. Boulder: Lynne Rienner, 1990.

Davenport, Frances Gardiner, ed. *European Treaties bearing on the History of the United States and its Dependencies to 1648*. Washington, DC: Carnegie Institution of Washington, 1917.

Deere, Phillip. "A Conversation with Phillip Deere." Video recording. University of Massachusetts: Union Video Project, 1979. [Available at University of Massachusetts Amherst, W. E. B. Dubois Library, Audio-Visual Department.]

Denham, Mark E., and Mark Owen Lombardi. "Perspectives on Third-World Sovereignty: Problems with(out) Borders." *Perspectives on Third-World Sovereignty*. Ed. Mark E. Denham and Mark Owen Lombardi. London: Macmillan, 1996.

Dorris, Michael. "Twentieth Century Indians: The Return of the Natives." *Ethnic Autonomy–Comparative Dynamics*. Ed. Raymond L. Hall. New York: Pergamon, 1979. 66–84.

Hillerman, Tony. "Who Has Sovereignty over Mother Earth?" *New York Times*, September 18, 1997.

Hinsley, F. H. *Sovereignty*. New York: Basic Books, 1966.

Lombardi, Mark Owen. "Third-World Problem-Solving and the 'Religion' of Sovereignty: Trends and Prospects." *Perspectives on Third-World Sovereignty*. Ed. Mark E. Denham and Mark Owen Lombardi. London: Macmillan, 1996.

Magnusson, Warren. "The Reification of Political Community." *Contending Sovereignties*. Ed. R. B. J. Walker and Saul H. Mendlovitz. Boulder: Lynne Rienner, 1990.

Newcomb, Steve. "The Evidence of Christian Nationalism in Federal Indian Law: The Doctrine of Discovery, Johnson v. McIntosh, and Plenary Power." *Review of Law and Social Change* (NYU) 20.2 (1993).

Ruiz, Lester Edwin J. "Sovereignty as Transformative Practice." *Contending Sovereignties*. Ed. R. B. J. Walker and Saul H. Mendlovitz. Boulder: Lynne Rienner, 1990. 79–96.

Shapiro, Michael. "Moral Geographies and the Ethics of Post-Sovereignty." *Perspectives on Third-World Sovereignty*. Ed. Mark E. Denham and Mark Owen Lombardi. London: Macmillan, 1996.

Walker, R. B. J. "Space/Time/Sovereignty." *Perspectives on Third-World Sovereignty*. Ed. Mark E. Denham and Mark Owen Lombardi. London: Macmillan, 1996.

Walker, R. B. J., and Saul H. Mendlovitz. "Interrogating State Sovereignty." *Contending Sovereignties*. Ed. R. B. J. Walker and Saul H. Mendlovitz. Colorado: Lynne Rienner, 1990.

Washburn Wilcomb E., ed. *The Indian and the White Man*. New York: New York UP, 1964.

Williams, Robert A., Jr. *The American Indian in Western Legal Thought*. New York: Oxford UP, 1990.

WENNEBOJO MEETS A "REAL INDIAN"

✦

Richard Clark Eckert

WHO symbolizes a "real Indian"? thought the trickster known to the Anishinaabeg as Wennebojo. The biology of who their parents are? Nope. Well, that is part of it, of course, but that isn't all of it. Maybe culture makes a person Indian? Hmmm, thought Wennebojo, that would mean some distinction between an upper and lower case *c* at the beginning of the word. I don't think I want to get caught in that debate, thought Wennebojo with a grin. Politics? Well, that might identify a person as Indian for administrative purposes, but it doesn't make them "real." I don't think I want to go in that direction either, thought Wennebojo, with grin still in place.

Maybe a "real Indian" is a triad or a relational nexus of the biology, culture, and politics which makes a person a real Indian, Wennebojo thought out loud. He laughed louder as he thought of the conceptual density. The nexus idea tautologically returned Wennebojo to the original question about who symbolizes a real Indian. Maybe there is a place where the nexus of biology, culture, and politics unfolds as a drama on a stage. Perhaps if I go to a powwow I can meet a real Indian, Wennebojo said to himself. Perhaps I can discover what symbolizes a real Indian, he repeated in his thoughts.

✦

I found a good campsite this year—right next to the showers, Wennebojo thought. Actually it wasn't "his" campsite, as there were four other tents there already. As for the convenience of the showers, Wennebojo had a water faucet in his campsite that people from neighboring sites did not hesitate to use both late at night and early in the morning. The pavilion area adjacent to the campsite meant that lots of people would be walking through at all hours of the day.

Wennebojo looked around and took a deep breath of fresh air. Oh, this is a beautiful day for a powwow, thought Wennebojo. Looking at the tall trees, too big to wrap his arms around, Wennebojo was amazed at how good it felt to be back in Michigan. The other campers in his site included two medicine men, their trainees, and a guy who claimed to be a clan chief, but whom most people laughed at. Too many people recalled the chief's drunken days. Some thought the chief, now sober, had appointed himself to be a cultural watchdog. Was the chief a moral police officer or a moral entrepreneur? Wennebojo didn't care. Wennebojo just wanted to be where he could get a hot shower early in the morning before the other thousand campers.

Makwa stopped by and said, "*Boozhoo* [hello], I haven't seen you at a powwow in quite a while."

"*Aaniin* [hello]," replied Wennebojo. "I've been busy doing some ceremonies. Sure had a lot of fun in the sugar bush this year," Wennebojo added.

"Did you do any spearing?" asked Makwa.

"Oh," said Wennebojo, "those folks are crazy. I just went by myself down to the falls and took what I needed. Why should I get a permit from the Tribal Council? Catholics and Protestants don't need to get a permit to go to church. When I am spear fishing it is like I am in church."

"Did you have a trap line this past winter?" asked Makwa.

"Well, I did, but there was only one that I wanted to catch."

"Which one was that?" asked Makwa.

"An otter," answered Wennebojo. "Oh, that otter was smart."

"Oh, too bad you didn't get him," said Makwa.

"Oh, that reminds me," said Wennebojo, "I had a really good dream last night."

Makwa understood Wennebojo's cue that it was now time for a change of topic to things more serious.

Makwa then gave Wennebojo a soft, brain-tanned leather pouch filled with the inner bark of red willow. "*Megwitch* [thank you]," said Wennebojo. Makwa handed Wennebojo an eagle feather and said, "I found that by the mouth of the river when the ice first broke. I'm always in awe when I watch an eagle hit the water and come up with a fish. They must lose feathers then. But I don't think that feather fell out while fishing. The shaft is too smooth, unbroken. The feather tip looks like it has been pecked at a bit. Maybe that bird used its beak to pull out that feather."

"Oh, that is a beautiful feather," replied Wennebojo. "It is a steering feather. Only a steering feather on the eagle has such a long straight shaft with a symmetrical shape so perfect. *Megwitch*," Wennebojo added and then shook the hand of Makwa.

Wennebojo unrolled a bundle and pulled out a beautifully decorated otter skin. The otter bag had a shoulder strap sewn onto it and the otter tail was tucked back and sewn to the rest of the bag. The inside was lined with a designer-print satin. On the outside of the otter bag seven "stacks" of satin ribbons of different lengths and colors extended from the edge like a flag. Each stack consisted of blue, green, red, and black ribbons. On the other side there were seven tassels of yarn with colors mixed, blue, green, red, and black. There was a beaded six-pointed star that had a *migis* shell in the center and a shell at each point. Seven *migis* shells in all. Hanging from the bottom of the bag were seven copper tubes which dangled in an elegant rhythm. There were also seven beaded outlines of the old Mide symbols for otters and an old style of floral designs usually reserved for museum pieces.

Makwa's eyes widened. Wennebojo grinned and then took out the pipe from the otter bag. The pipe bowl was black and had four rings of silver inlaid so fine that the observer could see no lines separating the stone from the silver. The pipe stem was made of sumac. Wennebojo carved the stem in a way that created an illusion of pipe stem twisting from end to end. The stem was approximately 18 inches long and 2 inches in diameter. The mouthpiece of the pipe stem was carved to resemble the mouth of an otter. Two black beads created the illusion of otter eyes. There was a small piece of leather and some fine beadwork decorating it as well, but the seven eagle feathers drew most of the attention of any onlooker. More than anything else, the pipe stem and bowl appeared alive and ancient at the same time.

Wennebojo filled the pipe bowl with *kinnikinnick*. Then, in the ways customary to the Anishinaabeg, Wennebojo lit the pipe and began to smoke it. He handed the pipe to Makwa, who took four big puffs from the long pipe stem. Yet, in the midst of more than a thousand campers stuffed into less than a hundred sites, no one stared. Few looked at all.

There were a couple of children looking on. Unlike the adults, the children were not afraid of Wennebojo. The children, about five of them, came up to where Wennebojo was sitting. Wennebojo puffed four times and placed the pipe stem on each shoulder of each child. The children went away laughing and smiling. Everyone smiled when meeting Wennebojo, but adults always seemed to forget that later. Children, on the other hand, would come again and again to listen to his stories. When the children went back to the campsites, the adults—too proud and too scared to sit in on the stories—asked the children to tell them what Wennebojo said. Yet, hearing the knowledge without the teachings to go along with that knowledge only made the adults all the more ignorant. The adults loved Wennebojo when he was elsewhere but hated him when they saw him, as they almost always grew jealous and wanted to steal his dreams.

Wennebojo asked the children, "What symbolizes a real Indian?"

"My father is a real Indian," answered one.

"My uncle," said another.

Yet another quietly pointed to one of the medicine men in the campsite and said, "I think Jack is."

"Why?" asked Wennebojo.

"Because Jack does Indian things," said one child.

"Like what?" asked Wennebojo.

"He makes good fry bread and tells good stories," said one.

"Oh, he is a good dancer," said another. "He doesn't drink and he sings traditional songs," said yet another child.

"Jack speaks the language," called out another.

One child said, "The tribal chairman is a real Indian."

"Why?" asked Wennebojo.

"He is the Chief," said the child. "He makes sure the door is open for me; he paddles the canoe for me." This was all interesting to Wennebojo, but the children grew tired and wanted to play.

After smoking the pipe and asking the children questions, Wennebojo went to his new "casino-sponsored" royal blue pickup truck (no rust) and pulled out his hand drum. It was a two-sided hand drum, but not typical. The drum looked like it was hundreds of years old. The rim was made of an ash wood, maybe yellow ash, though I guess one could use black ash or white ash if they had to. The hide on each side was wrapped around a red willow branch that circled the drum frame. From the higher tone an experienced singer understood that the hides on this drum were deer hides. Tied to the drum were four ermine with legs that danced whenever the drum was used. There were also four eagle feathers hanging. The drum stick was made from hazel wood, cut at a length that was custom-made for Wennebojo. Buckskin so thin it resembled chamois cloth was wrapped around it, spiraling up the shaft like a tornado. It almost resembled a medical bandage wrap. "My light saber," Wennebojo joked.

Makwa started to look at the drum and was startled to see that Wennebojo used wrapping twine to tie or lace the two rims together. Wennebojo said, "Hey, it works," not bothering to tell Makwa that it was not packing twine. Wennebojo had made it from the inner bark of a particular kind of tree. Problem was that if Wennebojo told everyone, they'd go cut them down until they were extinct. Happened with the hazelnut bushes. Wennebojo reminded himself how difficult it had been to find a branch for the drumstick.

Makwa saw that the paint on the drum was not red and blue or red and black, as often seen. This drum was painted mostly green and orange. Not wanting to be intrusive, Makwa didn't ask. Wennebojo saw the question on Makwa's face and said, "The drum was painted that way because those are the colors which identify the home of the drum maker to those who understood the teachings that accompany the knowledge of the colors." Makwa asked, "What about the colors of the four directions, red, yellow, black, and white, and representing the four races?" Wennebojo replied, "I don't know what others do elsewhere, but where I come from the colors symbolize things a little differently."

"Huh?" replied Makwa.

"What color is the water in the ocean?" asked Wennebojo.

"Blue," replied Makwa.

"Then why isn't the color for east blue?" asked Wennebojo.

"What color is found in the south during spring?" asked Wennebojo.

"Green," said Makwa.

"Then why isn't the color for the south green? What color is the sky when the sun sets in the west?" asked Wennebojo.

"Red," said Makwa.

"Then why isn't red the color symbolizing the west?" asked Wennebojo. "And the north—what happens in the cold of winter?" asked Wennebojo.

"Well," said Makwa, suspecting a trap, "in the winter the days are shorter. There is less daylight."

"Further north means less daylight. So what color is that?" asked Wennebojo.

"Why, that is black," said Makwa—pointing to his hat at the same time.

"So why do people use white to symbolize the north?" asked Wennebojo.

"Why, because everyone does that and has been told to do that," answered Makwa.

Wennebojo then asked, "Do you think it is possible that the Anishinaabeg forgot who they were and in the call for inventing culture came up with new symbols that have nothing to do with being Anishinaabeg?"

"Well, I suppose," said Makwa, "—but no one thinks like you do. Culture isn't static. Where did you come up with those colors for the different directions anyway?"

"Well," said Wennebojo, "I did my research. I read the *Jesuit Relations*."

"What!" screamed Makwa.

"Oh, they were a bunch of lying thieves for sure," said Wennebojo, "but they did keep a record. It is decoding that record that takes time."

Makwa thought he was about to be tricked. He took out a pinch of *kinnikinnick* and put it in the fire.

Growing sarcastic, Makwa asked, "What do you hope to find in that record?"

"Well," said Wennebojo, "I want to see if I am right about a few things."

"Like what?" asked Makwa.

"I want to see if one has to be able to understand Immanuel Kant in order to reconstruct the Anishinaabeg state of mind to what it was five hundred years ago. I want to meet the symbolic mind of a real Indian."

"Well, how would anyone know the symbolic mind of a real Indian?" laughed Makwa.

"That is a good question," responded Wennebojo. "First thing is not to read the way you were taught to read. They taught you that way to make you stay peasant-minded."

"Huh?" said Makwa, scratching his head.

Wennebojo added, "Well, for example the Jesuits mentioned a medicine man who made them float in the air and stood them on their heads."

"Wow," said Makwa, "that medicine man must have really known his stuff."

Wennebojo continued, "If you know how to read, you know that the medicine man changed the way the Jesuits, a sixteenth-century version of the CIA, viewed the world and made them feel good at the same time. Sort of like what is happening to you today." Wennebojo grinned as Makwa digested the thoughts.

Wennebojo pulled out his hand drum and started singing another song. The medicine men, their trainees, and the self-appointed clan chief all started dancing. A few older women joined in the dance, as did the children. It was spontaneous. Everyone was laughing and enjoying themselves except Makwa. He sat speechless and astonished.

Wennebojo asked Makwa if the song made his mind wander to think back to when the Anishinaabeg were free. "Sure did," answered Makwa.

"Did I do my research or what?" proclaimed Wennebojo.

Makwa, feeling trapped, not wanting to disagree, but not wanting to think of blue for the east, frowned. Makwa knew his view of the world was now different. He knew he felt like he was floating in air. So why did he feel uncomfortable?

Wennebojo asked Makwa to close his eyes and imagine himself far out in the stars. "Are you there?" asked Wennebojo.

"Yes," replied Makwa.

Wennebojo told Makwa to turn around. Makwa started to turn his body around. "No, no, no," said Wennebojo. "Close your eyes and go back out into the stars. Way out there just as far as your mind can reach and then a little bit more. Are you there now?" asked Wennebojo.

"Yes," replied Makwa, wondering what was in store for him.

"OK, now in your mind turn around and face back toward earth," Wennebojo instructed Makwa. "Now, tell me what you see in your mind's eye," said Wennebojo.

"I don't know," said Makwa.

"OK, then keep that picture in your mind," said Wennebojo. "Now open your eyes." Makwa followed Wennebojo's instructions and discovered Wennebojo was pointing at the symbol painted on the face of the hand drum. It was the same image that Makwa had experienced in his mind's eye. Wennebojo continued, "If you want to understand the ancient symbols of the Mide, you have to take your mind way, way out into the stars, as far as your mind will go and then some more BEFORE you look back." Makwa was getting real uncomfortable with this thought as it implied he could acquire the mind of a Mide. With a big grin, Wennebojo asked, "Did I turn you on your head and have you floating in air?"

"Damn you," responded Makwa. "Well, I suppose you are going to tell me the translation of 'Anishinaabeg' is wrong now, too," chuckled Makwa.

"Which translation is that?" asked Wennebojo.

"From whence man descends," answered Makwa.

"Wow, that is a strange one—who thinks it means that?" asked Wennebojo.

"Everyone!" cried out Makwa, clearly agitated. Why was Wennebojo challenging everything?

Makwa hadn't seen Wennebojo in almost a year and was now remembering why. Wennebojo was always making him think things and then making Makwa figure out if it was true or not. Once Wennebojo even told Makwa the world was really flat and Makwa almost believed him before Wennebojo gave out a loud laugh.

"Well," said Wennebojo, "'Anishinaabeg' means 'spontaneous people' or 'original people' in the sense of being creative. Sort of like when I sang that song a few minutes ago and everyone started to dance. It was totally spontaneous. Nobody planned it, but it was beautiful," said Wennebojo.

"Never mind," said Makwa, "let's get ready for Grand Entry."

"Well, I hope you don't mind if I have a cup of black medicine water first," said Wennebojo.

"I need to go dress up as a symbolic Indian," Makwa said with a snicker.

"Dressing up as an Indian makes you feel real?" asked Wennebojo.

"Never mind," said Makwa as he paced away from the campsite. He was disturbed by the journey Wennebojo had taken him on and wondered if he had been tricked.

So Wennebojo picked up his hand drum and started to sing a woman's song. Two women came to the campsite. He was using medicine to attract women, said a neighbor. He was not, said another.

The song was beautiful. Sally was a tall, slender, blond-haired, blue-eyed New Ager and was accompanied by her friend Evonne. Wennebojo stopped and then started another song. It took the two women a moment before they realized that Wennebojo was singing a Frank Sinatra tune.

Still laughing, Sally gave Wennebojo some sage and some braided sweetgrass.

"*Megwitch*," said Wennebojo. "How can I help you?"

"Well, I think I was married to you in a past life," said Sally.

"Oh," said Wennebojo.

"But I was a man and you were a woman," said Sally.

"Hmmm—so let me see if I understand this—you are saying you are now the woman 'cause you didn't treat me right and that if I don't treat you right I will come back as a woman. Well then, who was Evonne?" asked Wennebojo.

"Oh, she was our son," said Sally.

Amik walked through the campsite. Wennebojo asked Amik if he'd like some black medicine water. "Sure," said Amik. "Who are those beautiful women?" "Well, one was my husband in a past life and the other was my son," Wennebojo said, grinning. Almost laughing out loud, Amik asked, "Who then was I?" "Oh, you were the wife that replaced me," said Wennebojo. Not sure what was going to happen, Amik pulled out a little *kinnikinnick* and put the pinch of it on the fire.

Still curious, Wennebojo asked Sally if her new age crystals can determine what symbolizes a real Indian.

"Oh," Sally said, "a real Indian is in touch with Mother Earth, lives in a lodge in the woods, lives completely off the land, buys nothing, is an artisan, sings well, knows the weather in advance, tells entertaining stories, writes beautiful poems, plays the guitar, gives great massages, and knows all the herbs to keep people healthy."

"Whoa," said Wennebojo. "What does he look like? Can you describe him?"

"Well," said Sally, "he is tall, long thick black hair down to his butt and wears only a breechcloth." Amik elbowed Wennebojo and said he wondered if a woman, tall, having hair down to her butt and wearing something real skimpy could be symbolic of a real Indian. Wennebojo whispered that Amik was incorrigible.

Wennebojo asked, "Evonne, what do you think symbolizes a real Indian?"

"Oh, I think a real Indian comes from another planet, isn't that part of the translation for 'Anishinaabeg'?" she asked.

"That is a long story, ladies, but I do need to get ready for Grand Entry," said Wennebojo.

"Can I braid your hair?" Evonne pleaded.

"Hmmmm," thought Wennebojo. "Sure, go ahead," said Wennebojo with a wink especially intended for Sally to also see.

"Evonne, we have to go," said a very jealous Sally. They left. Amik was laughing loudly. Wennebojo said, "Oh, that was close, Amik. I wasn't sure if Sally would get jealous." They sure had a strange sense of what symbolizes a real Indian, thought Wennebojo.

Wennebojo started to put on his Indian attire. The blue velvet leggings with six-pointed stars beaded on the outer seams and the beaded breechcloth were put on slowly, but not too slow. Wennebojo pulled his ribbon shirt over his head. It was black, with red, blue, and green ribbons. He put on a vest made of velvet and beautifully beaded floral designs. Wennebojo saw people going by with breastplates, chokers, and eagle feather bustles that spanned wide, as well as elaborate porcupine roaches. Again, he chuckled, wondering why Anishinaabeg would dress up as Sioux. Finally, he put on an otter turban. Wennebojo held an otter bag with his pipe in it. He carried a stick that had an eagle claw on the end. The stick with the eagle claw on it was different from most others because much of the feathered calf of the leg was mounted as well. The stick had an ermine sewn on to give a border to the eagle leg. It had some bells made of copper and four satin ribbons—blue, green, red, and black. In his other hand, Wennebojo held a large eagle feather fan. On the feather tips of the fan there were dots with horse hair extending from them. The dots were blue, green, red, and black.

The moccasins Wennebojo wore had cost him $100. Some people argued that he should not pay for them, but right after buying them he bought a lottery ticket and won $100. So they really weren't bought. Wennebojo wore a hand-woven sash of high honor that he received as a gift when he went to some ceremonies down south. Only a few people understand the meaning.

Wennebojo walked toward the arena where the Grand Entry would start in fifteen minutes. At the arena Wennebojo saw an arbor that was covered with cedar and had big speakers hanging from the posts holding up the frame of the roof. In the arbor some of the drum groups were starting to warm up and sing songs. Wennebojo listened and wondered where those Sioux singers came from. He asked and was politely told they were Ojibwe, not Sioux. But why were they singing using a Sioux beat? asked Wennebojo. Oh, that is the powwow beat—everyone does that. Hmmm thought Wennebojo, these people are singing like they are from the Plains and they are dressed like they are from the Plains—what is going on?

Wennebojo noticed a person wearing a canvas vest with rolls of film tucked away, a shoulder-strap bag that was also canvas, an expensive camera bag, and a microcassette recorder in a pocket. Wennebojo asked him, "Where do you teach? You walk like Harvard."

"I teach at Harvard," said the man, wondering how Wennebojo knew he taught there.

"Are you an anthropologist or a sociologist?" asked Wennebojo.

"Sociologist," answered the man.

"What are you doing here?" asked Wennebojo.

"Oh, I am looking for a real Indian," said the sociologist.

Hmmm, thought Wennebojo. Then he asked, "What if I show you a real Indian?" The professor gave Wennebojo a cigar.

"*Megwitch,*" said Wennebojo. "You got a light?"

"No, I don't smoke," said the professor. Wennebojo giggled, wondering why a professor would carry cigars if he didn't smoke. More important, why would a person go camping without matches?

Wennebojo decided to ask a few questions. "Tell me, Professor, what do you think symbolizes a real Indian?"

"Well," said the professor, "an Indian is full-blooded, is enrolled in a federally recognized tribe, can identify their clan, knows the language fluently, and has an Indian name."

"Anything else?" asked Wennebojo.

"Yeah, if they are a woman they make good fry bread, do the most beautiful beadwork, and are fun to party with too," said the professor. Wennebojo wondered where white men get such strange ideas about Native women, but decided that pursuit of that question should be left for a different adventure.

"What else do you think symbolizes a real Indian?" asked Wennebojo.

"Well, a real Indian is primitive and doesn't accumulate capital. They were the first real Marxists in America," said the professor.

"Huh?" asked Wennebojo, scratching his head. Indians were independent of the political economy driven by capitalism, said the professor. They had no personal property. The industrial revolution brought about a change in the means of production and Natives lagged behind the changes.

"Let me sing you a song," said Wennebojo. He tapped on the handrail that encircled the dance arena and sang a song.

"What was that about?" asked the professor.

"Well, you see that guy on the other side of the arena dressed like you?"

"Yeah," said the professor.

"Well, he is an ethnobotanist from Yale. He was trying to determine if wild rice had been altered from freezing and thawing of the bog in the Medicine River sloughs."

"Really," said the professor, "how interesting."

"Last year I sang him a song and he asked what it meant."

"What did it mean?" asked the professor.

"Oh, it was a song about wild rice that was sung when they were planting an inland lake type of rice in the sloughs back in the 1930s."

"Why is that important?" asked the professor.

"Well," said Wennebojo, "that guy claims in his book that there is no wild rice song. Where they planted the rice is exactly where he is finding the alleged mutations. He didn't believe it. The ethnobotanist decided to go scuba diving to prove to everyone that he was right," said Wennebojo.

"What happened?" asked the professor.

"He was attacked by giant turtles," answered Wennebojo with a big grin.

"Oh, glad you didn't do that to me," said the professor, chuckling and looking at Wennebojo for a clue that he hadn't.

"Well," said Wennebojo, "you know that song I just sang to you."

"Yeah," said the professor.

"Well," said Wennebojo, "it was one of the songs that sociologist Max Weber studied when describing the rational and social foundations of music."

"Oh my," said the professor, "can you sing that again?"

"Nope," said Wennebojo.

"Why not?" asked the professor.

"Because the song is my personal property, something you think I don't believe in."

"Yeah, but the music belongs to everyone," argued the professor.

Agitated, Wennebojo said, "Suppose I have a dream and in that dream I learn a song. Who does that song belong to if I choose to keep it to myself and not share it with others?"

"Why, it belongs to you," answered the professor.

"Well?" responded Wennebojo.

The professor's face blushed and he tried to write down as much as he could remember. He gave up and started speaking into his microcassette recorder.

Wennebojo continued, "Professor, are you familiar with that French sociologist named Émile Durkheim?"

"Oh yes," said the professor.

"Remember where Durkheim described the Anishinaabeg view of the sacred and the profane?" With great pride the professor noted that the Durkheim reading was part of his preparation for this fieldwork.

"Durkheim got it all wrong," replied Wennebojo. "'Sacred' just means so smart nobody can argue with it and 'profane' just means so stupid that no one wants to be affiliated with it."

"Huh?" said the professor.

"Been nice chatting with you, professor, but I need to get to Grand Entry. Besides, I want to see what the vendors have for sale," said Wennebojo as he walked to a vendor selling artworks.

Wennebojo waited until there were no customers. "What do you think symbolizes a real Indian?" asked Wennebojo. The vendor responded by saying he was Odawa and that the Odawa are traders by tradition. If he could support his family by getting people to buy his goods then he was doing something Indian and therefore he was symbolic of a real Indian.

"That is an interesting claim," said Wennebojo, "but what about the emcee, the drummers and dancers—are they symbolic of being a real Indian?"

"If they buy their supplies from me or bring me more customers," laughed the vendor.

"Everyone please rise," announced the emcee. A person holding an eagle staff entered the arena first, followed by those carrying the US, MI, POW, Marine, Canada, and Mohawk flags and a few others that Wennebojo was not able to recognize. Hundreds of dancers entered the arena one by one and started dancing. There was a flag song and then a veteran song. Wennebojo had gone out in the dance arena and saw many faces he knew from other powwows he had been to. He noticed that there were more skin drums this year. More than a few jingle dress dancers got his attention and he theirs.

When the veteran song ended he exited the arena and was standing next to the emcee table when the person who carried the American flag stood next to him. "Why was the American flag dipped?" Wennebojo asked the veteran.

"What do you mean?" the veteran asked. "United States flag protocol requires that the flag never be dipped."

"You dipped it. I am asking you why. You just symbolically had the US surrender to the flag of the Anishinaabeg. A nice thought, but I wondered if you intended to sneak that in so only those who understood the flag protocol would see your act of defiance."

The veteran blushed and said, "I hadn't thought about that. It is the same everywhere at all the powwows. I am not going to try to change it. Besides, at ceremonies there is no US flag so I don't have to worry about it there. This is a dog and pony show for the convenience of the audience." Wennebojo then asked, "But why is the US flag in the powwow?"

"Are you a Marxist?" asked the veteran. "Indian people respect the flag of the United States."

"Hey, you are the one that dipped the US flag," said Wennebojo.

"Well," said the veteran, "I think it might have come to the powwow during the times of Buffalo Bill."

"Is that when the Sioux rhythms and dance infected the Anishinaabeg powwow?" asked Wennebojo.

"I wouldn't use the word 'infected.' The Sioux are good people," said the veteran.

"So after more than five hundred years of kicking the Sioux butts and their kicking ours a few times we are conquered by their rhythms?" grimaced Wennebojo.

The veteran responded by asking Wennebojo if he was being critical of the Sioux.

"No, no, not at all," said Wennebojo. "What was given to them is theirs. What was given to us is ours. I'm just trying to figure out why we've forgotten ours and did a bad job at trying to imitate theirs!"

Just then a person from the powwow committee came up and gave the veteran an envelope. The veteran pulled out a $20 bill and said, "Twenty green eagles!"

"They pay you to carry the flag?" asked Wennebojo.

"No," said the vet, "they give me a small honorarium to help cover the costs of my travel. They can never pay me to carry the flag."

"Yeah, but it was dipped," said Wennebojo. "Why did you do that?"

"No one noticed," said the veteran, who then stormed away. Wennebojo thought, could the dipped flag mean surrender if no one understood the protocol? He wondered if he would be able to find what symbolized a real Indian at a powwow if no one paid close attention to the symbols.

A real old song started. Wennebojo recognized the song as being about spring eagles and wondered how long it would be before the drum broke into the stride of a Sioux rhythm. Then he heard a yelplike sound. That sounded like an otter, he thought. More yelping. That otter call is in high C, thought Wennebojo. No one can do an otter call with a high C except an otter. More yelping.

Standing next to the drum was a man with hair cropped short—like an otter. He wore sunglasses, a green Wimbledon lacrosse shirt, ocean blue designer shorts, and sandals. He wore a diamond gold ring. The man was short and barrel-chested, but his legs were skinny and he looked healthier than anyone there. He had his hands on each hip with elbows extending like wings. He had a Hudson blanket tied around his neck and let it fall behind him like a robe of royalty. Every part of his body was in motion, yet no single part dominated. It was hard to watch him for long as his eyes would play tricks. For a moment, Wennebojo thought he saw a bear, then an eagle, then a wolf, and even a crane.

Wennebojo found himself walking through the dancers and over to the arbor. Standing next to the guy yelping out, Wennebojo looked into his eyes and saw a man thousands of years old in the body of a twenty-year-old. Wennebojo saw the face turn into the face of a wolf. Wennebojo rubbed his eyes wondering what deception had brought him to hallucinate. Maybe Sally and Evonne were witches, he thought. No, no, no. Something was happening and Wennebojo wasn't sure if it was good or bad. This sure is an odd position for a trickster to be in, he thought. A trickster being tricked?

After the song ended people were whispering about the otter wolf singer and dancer wearing a Rolex watch and a diamond gold ring. Wennebojo went into shock. He had heard a real Anishinaabeg song at a powwow without it getting changed to a Sioux beat. What happened? People were laughing and smiling. Everyone except the emcee. The emcee couldn't stop talking for some reason. Boy, did he sound stupid. Wennebojo considered the possibility that he had seen a person who symbolized a real Indian.

Waboose was standing next to Wennebojo. "Who was that guy?" asked Wennebojo.

"Oh, he is a crazy man. Fell out of the sky and hurt his head."

"What?" said Wennebojo.

"He fell out of a helicopter, lived to talk about, but he was never the same. Took him seven years just to learn how to get out of bed again. But he sure can sing and dance."

"Where does he work?"

"Nowhere," said Waboose. "He gets social security each month because he is permanently crazy."

"Wait a minute," said Wennebojo. "I saw a Rolex and a diamond gold ring, not to mention I know that Wimbledon sweatshirt costs more than my suits and his shoes cost more than a house payment. His presidential fountain pen was not cheap either."

"Oh, those are all gifts the women give him when he sings like Frank Sinatra." laughed Waboose. Wennebojo was troubled, as he thought his earlier attempt to imitate Sinatra when using a hand drum was unique.

Finally, Wennebojo decided to approach this guy and see what was going on. Wennebojo found himself about to give the guy some *kinnikinnick* in much the same way as his friends had given it to him. The reversal in roles was not a familiar spot for Wennebojo. Yet, as he reached to get the *kinnikinnick*, Otter-Wolf asked him for two dollars. Wennebojo was disappointed, having thought he had finally met a person who might have symbolized a real Indian only to discover the guy was crazy, a woman chaser, and obsessed with money and fame. Wennebojo pulled out a two-dollar bill. Otter-Wolf asked, "Do you want cream in your coffee or do you drink yours black?" Wennebojo answered, "Black."

With the two dollars Otter-Wolf went and bought two coffees, both black, and handed one to Wennebojo. "Why would you think something so real could be bought for just two dollars?" asked Otter-Wolf. Was he talking about himself or about the coffee, thought Wennebojo. Otter-Wolf continued, "Those who sell it can't do what I just did. That was a million dollar performance there." "What do you mean?" asked Wennebojo. "Did you like the face of the wolf I put on?" asked Otter-Wolf. "That is always fun to feel the teeth of a wolf when it growls," said Otter-Wolf. Wennebojo gasped. "Yeah, I do that for play, just like the otter that plays. Besides, how many people do you know who can put the sounds of all the clans into one song and not one person in the audience understands what hit them. Can't let the common folk know I am raising their thinking. They would riot. The elite would put a bullet in my brain for being so stupid as to appeal to the masses. So instead I pretend that I am just a crazy fool—but hey, everyone there saw that wolf. Ha ha ha," laughed Otter-Wolf.

For the first time since childhood Wennebojo was speechless. Otter-Wolf said, "These people can't figure out what symbolizes a real Indian because they haven't read about Prometheus. Nor do they understand why Ulysses had to hear what none of his men could hear. If they understand Immanuel Kant, they can figure out what the sacred birch bark scrolls mean. Figure out Immanuel Kant and they can figure out what they symbolize in *a priori*. By the way, tell me, Wennebojo, did I turn your mind upside down and make you feel good about it?"

"Yes," answered Wennebojo.

"That is what symbolizes a 'real Indian,'" said Otter-Wolf. "The real Indian isn't a myth from the old days or what a person wears. A person symbolizes a real Indian by being a real Indian."

CONTRIBUTORS

Ellen L. Arnold is associate professor of English, ethnic studies, and women's studies at East Carolina University. She has published *Conversations with Leslie Marmon Silko* and numerous essays on Silko, Linda Hogan, Carter Revard, and other contemporary American Indian writers.

Holly L. Baumgartner is associate professor of English at Mercy College of Northwest Ohio. She completed her PhD in rhetoric and writing at Bowling Green University. She holds an MA in American culture studies with a thesis on Native American writing. Her research interest within rhetoric is in ethics, especially the work of Emmanuel Levinas, and in the ethics of film. Recent publications include "Levinas: Existence and Existents through *Memento, Mulholland Drive,* and *Vanilla Sky*."

Patricia Bizzell is professor of English at the College of the Holy Cross, where she has chaired the department and directed College Honors, English Honors, Writing across the Curriculum, and the Writers Workshop. Among her publications are a rhetoric reader co-authored with Bruce Herzberg, *Negotiating Difference,* which includes a unit on Puritan-Indian relations; a collection of her essays on composition theory, *Academic Discourse and Critical Consciousness*; and *ALT DIS: Alternative Discourses and the Academy,* a collection of essays co-edited with Christopher Schroeder and Helen Fox. She is president of the Rhetoric Society of America, 2004–2006.

Matthew Dennis is professor of history at the University of Oregon and the author of *Cultivating a Landscape of Peace: Iroquois-European Encounters in Seventeenth-Century America* (1993) and *Red, White, and Blue Letter Days: An American Calendar* (2002). He is currently at work on a book entitled *Seneca Possessed: Gender, Power, and Witchcraft on the Frontiers of the Early American Republic*.

Robin DeRosa received her doctorate from Tufts University and is now assistant professor of English at Plymouth State University. Her work has appeared in several journals—most recently an article on parody in Equiano's slave narrative which appeared in the *Connecticut Review*—and in the anthology *Women as Sites of Culture*. Her main research interest is in the relationship between performance and memory in texts relating to early America.

Peter d'Errico graduated from Yale Law School in 1968 and immediately went to work with Dinebeiina Nahiilna Be Agaditahe (DNA), the Navajo Nation legal services program. He has been active since then in American Indian legal issues, including hunting, fishing, and land rights and American Indian spiritual freedom in prison. He is an emeritus professor of legal studies at the University of Massachusetts Amherst. He is a webmaster for NativeWeb at http://www.nativeweb.org/, an Internet resource site for and about indigenous peoples worldwide.

Richard Clark Eckert received his PhD in sociology from the University of Michigan. He is the author of "Wennebojo Meets the Mascot: A Trickster's View of the Central Michigan University Mascot/Logo" in *Team Spirits: The Native American Mascots Controversy*.

Janna Knittel is an assistant professor in the Department of English at St. Cloud State University. Her essays have appeared in *Indigenous Nations Studies Journal, Middle-Atlantic Writers Association Review, Popular Culture Review,* and *Victorian Review*. While working for Grand Portage National Monument, she wrote a booklet entitled *Moccasins and Red Sashes* about the history of the monument and the different cultures that came into contact in Northeastern Minnesota during the fur trade; the manuscript was approved by the Grand Portage Band of Chippewa. Her poems have appeared in *The Jabberwock Review, Apostrophe: UCSB Journal of the Arts,* and *Parnassus Literary Review*.

Anthony G. Murphy is currently completing a PhD at McMaster University in Hamilton, Ontario, while teaching at the University of Saskatchewan. While his dissertation deals with African American Literature and jazz, he also specializes in American Indian literatures as well as American popular music, particularly culture, politics, and the folk music phenomenon of the singer-songwriter.

Malea D. Powell is a mixed-blood of Indiana Miami, Eastern Shawnee, and Euro-American ancestry. She is an associate professor of writing, rhetoric, and American culture at Michigan State University, where she is a faculty member of both the Writing and Rhetoric and the American Indian Studies programs. Her research focuses on examining the rhetorics of survivance used by nineteenth-century American Indian intellectuals and has appeared in *CCCC; Paradoxa; Race, Rhetoric & Composition; ALT DIS*, and other essay collections. She is currently editor of *SAIL: Studies in American Indian Literatures,* a quarterly journal devoted to the study of American Indian writing, and is editor of *Of Color: Native American Literatures* (forthcoming 2005).

Angela Pulley Hudson is a PhD candidate in American studies at Yale University. Her research, writing, and teaching interests include Native American studies, ethnic autobiographies, and cultural studies of the US South. She is particularly committed to the investigation of Southeastern Native American intellectual production and to the development of Native American studies as an academic field of inquiry.

Karen A. Redfield is lead instructor in the Department of English of Madison Area Technical College in Madison, Wisconsin. She is completing her dissertation at the University of Wisconsin-Madison in composition and rhetoric with a focus on American Indian studies. She is the author of "Opening the Composition Classroom to Storytelling: Respecting Native American Students' Use of Rhetorical Strategies" in *Perspectives on Written Argument.*

Ernest Stromberg is associate professor in the Department of English, Communication, and Journalism at California State University Monterey Bay, where he teaches courses in communication, literature, and composition and rhetoric. He has published articles on American Indian writers James Welch, Janet Campbell Hale, and Linda Hogan.

INDEX